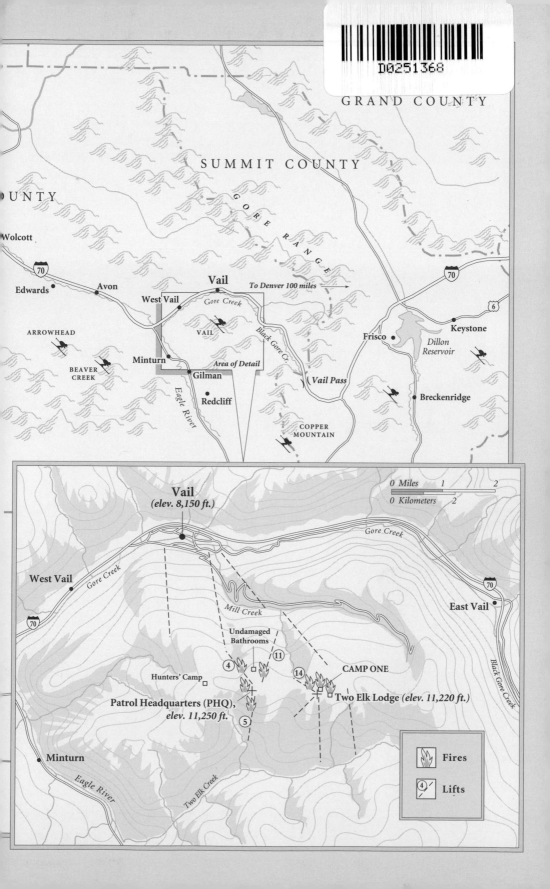

POWDER BURN

POWDER
BURN

● ■ ◆

Arson, Money, and Mystery

on Vail Mountain

DANIEL GLICK

PublicAffairs   New York

Book design by Mark McGarry.
Set in Minion.

Library of Congress Cataloging-in-Publication Data
Glick, Daniel.
Powder Burn: arson, money, and mystery on Vail Mountain/Daniel Glick.
p. cm.
ISBN 1-58648-003-0
1. Arson investigation—Colorado—Vail.
2. Ski resorts—Colorado—Vail—Corrupt practices.
3. Environmentalism—Colorado—Vail.
4. Deep ecology—Colorado—Vail.
5. Tourism—Economic aspects—Colorado—Vail.
6. Vail (Colo.)—Economic conditions.
7. Vail (Colo.)—Environmental conditions.
I. Title: Powder Burn. II. Title.
HV8079.A7 G48 2001
364.16'4—dc21
00—045875

9 8 7 6 5 4 3 2

To my big brother, Bob
Go long

And, for your information, you Lorax, I'm figgering

On biggering

and BIGGERING

and BIGGERING

and BIGGERING ...

—Dr. Seuss, *The Lorax*

Table of Contents

Acknowledgments

I'd like to thank my parents, not just for the obvious reason, but also for so graciously enduring my many years of wandering. Thanks for trusting me.

Thanks to my brothers, for many of the same reasons. And many more.

Books don't get written by one person, and it would be impossible to acknowledge everyone who helped me along the way. To single out a few of my mentors would be inadequate; to list them all would take too much space. Thank you all.

I want to thank the myriad sources, journalism colleagues, book authors, and librarians who have helped bring this book from concept to reality. Vail Resorts was very courteous in granting me access to their executives and workers and the ski area's backstage. To the people of Vail and the Eagle Valley, who were so generous with their time and their stories, I owe a deep debt—even if they wouldn't all want their names listed here.

To my friends and Nyland neighbors who supported me throughout, thanks. To Tory, for sticking with it, and Alex for generosity above and beyond. To Scotty, Marcelo, and the ostriches for inspiration in the final stretch.

My agent, Scott Waxman, deserves enormous credit for seeing a book where I had seen only a story. Thanks, Marty, for hooking us up.

To my editor, Geoff Shandler: YDFM.

I want to thank the Scripps Howard Foundation and the University of Colorado for the fellowship—and a chance to breathe while completing the manuscript.

And to my kids, Kolya and Zoe. You are my raisons d'être. Thanks for putting up with Dad spending way too much time in front of his stupid computer.

Prologue: Quaking Aspens

I first came to Vail, Colorado, in September 1994, from Washington, D.C., where I was based as a correspondent for *Newsweek*, to write about the World Mountain Bike Championships. Mountain bike racing was about to become an Olympic event, and the country's biggest ski area was hosting the fledgling sport's national coming-out party. I had talked the magazine into sending me to cover the event, amidst accusations from my colleagues that I had pulled off a Class One boondoggle. And maybe they were right: Boarding a Denver-bound plane, I was practically giddy. Vail. Autumn in the Rockies. Mountain biking. It sure beat covering another dreary subcommittee hearing on Capitol Hill or interviewing another federal bureaucrat about health-care reform.

When I arrived in Vail after a two-hour drive from the airport in Denver, the fall foliage was at its peak, with mountainsides of quaking aspens shimmering golden on either side of a stunning high alpine valley. I was smitten by the mountains, as many first-time visitors are. I inhaled the thin, crisp, clear air, gaped at the crystalline blue sky. If this wasn't heaven, I thought, it was awfully close.

But, as so often is the case in journalism, my plans changed. The day before the mountain bike downhill finals, when my story would also be due, *Newsweek* called with orders to catch the next plane home. My bureau chief told me it looked as if the U.S. military was going to invade Haiti, and I was on call as a pool reporter that would accompany the Pentagon's initial assault. I dashed down to Denver and caught the first plane east.

The next day, before daybreak, I was on a C-130 transport en route to Guantanamo Bay, Cuba. From there, I transferred to a Navy ship headed for Port au Prince, Haiti, commanded by General Henry Shelton, who went on to become the chairman of the Joint Chiefs of Staff. En route, the Haiti invasion was canceled and a friendly "intervasion" was hastily organized. We choppered from the command ship into Port au Prince amid great uncertainty about what the U.S. military would be doing there.

A couple days later, I went up-country in a Blackhawk helicopter with some Army Rangers to the town of Gonaives, the birthplace of the Aristide revolution. In Gonaives, certainly one of the poorest places on the planet, I tried to shake the now-discomfiting images of ski chalets, mock-Tyrolean clock towers, and restaurants featuring elk medallions au jus that I had just left behind. Here, open sewers ran through the town; the villagers lived in cardboard shanties and cinderblock shacks. From Vail, Colorado, to Gonaives, Haiti. I don't believe there has been a week of more intense contrasts in my reporting career.

After I moved to Colorado to cover the Rocky Mountain West for *Newsweek* in late 1994, the region's own internal contrasts began to strike me: the Mexican immigrants who work in the service sector and live in trailer parks out of sight of the tourists, and the part-time resident corporate titans who pull in *bonuses* that exceed $100 million in a good year; the worker bees who cram themselves ten to a double-wide and hold down three jobs, and the home owners who pay millions of dollars for monstrous second houses, only to tear them down and rebuild even bigger "starter castles" that they visit two weeks a year.

Vail, like many places across the American West, is home to a jarring juxtaposition of the people who have eked a rough-hewn living off the land for generations and the *nouveaux arrivés*—the wealthy elite who come to recreate and to show off their wealth in the most ostentatious ways possible. Since Vail's birth in 1962, the Eagle Valley has been transformed from a high-altitude lettuce patch and sheep pasture to the hub of a publicly held corporation controlled by a New York investment firm. That corporation is banking on expanding its already profitable business by finding ever more elaborate means to service the recreational needs of those who have reeled in unfathomable wealth during the years since 1980. The cultural and social dislocation in the Vail region has been considerable.

While in Washington, I had covered a fair number of national environmental stories, including the ongoing debates about how millions of acres of public land should best serve Americans. It seemed likely that while in Colorado I would be covering tense standoffs between grizzly-bear advocates and ranchers; loggers and fierce green protestors; miners and Environmental Protection Agency regulators. Instead, I was treated to a rash of bizarre and unsettling stories, including militia standoffs in Montana, the untimely and senseless death of Michael Kennedy after a ski accident at Aspen, the tragic murder of JonBenet Ramsey, and the searing Columbine massacre.

It's ironic that I would choose to write a book, then, about an arson and a ski resort town; but of all the stories I mention, it struck me that Vail best embodies the key issues that define what has been dubbed "the New West," and, for that matter, the "new economy." In Vail's tale lies a parable for our times: how global-dot.com capitalism stretches its tendrils into the most unlikely places—like this bucolic alpine valley in the Rocky Mountains; how the post–Drexel Burnham Lambert junk-bond mentality has shifted insidiously toward vulture investors, even in the unlikely environs of the ski and recreation industry; how environmental conflicts over recreation have shifted the western debate from cowboys, miners, and loggers to the impacts of mountain bikers wearing Lycra and skiers wearing Gore-Tex; and how, after forty years, the unintended consequences of creating a faux-Austrian ski resort, then building a community as an afterthought, have come to haunt Vail—ultimately making it the target of an arson that was dubbed the costliest "ecoterrorism" act in history.

Although Vail is peculiar, even unique in the West, in many other ways it is indistinguishable from a number of places around the country. Jackson Hole, Sun Valley, and Aspen are perhaps the best-known first cousins of Vail. Like Vail, they all boast an international cachet and a plethora of similar problems ranging from a lack of affordable housing for service sector workers to the bizarre politics of running a seasonal ghost town predominantly owned by wealthy people who rarely visit but exercise enormous power nonetheless. But increasingly, Vail's problems are fast becoming the problems of Taos, New Mexico; Telluride, Colorado; Park City, Utah; Big

Sky, Montana; Lake Tahoe, California; the Florida Keys; and the Hamptons of New York.

Vail at the time of the October 1998 arson that destroyed or damaged $12 million in ski lifts and on-mountain buildings, was a town in the throes of intense transition. Four years before the arson, the ski area's previous owner, George Gillett, had declared bankruptcy after overextending himself in the junk bond market. Vail and its neighboring ski area, Beaver Creek, had been acquired soon after by Apollo Partners, LLP, a Wall Street investment firm with a reputation of feeding on corporate carcasses and reorganizing, refinancing, and reselling business assets with ruthless efficiency.

Just two years before the fires, Apollo doubled its Colorado ski holdings when it acquired two of the largest ski resorts in the country's biggest skiing state, Breckenridge and Keystone, a move that required approval from the U.S. Department of Justice antitrust regulators. Soon after, Apollo had an initial public offering for the newly created Vail Resorts, Inc., trading on Wall Street as MTN. The IPO revealed the enormously high stakes at play in this high-altitude town as dozens of Vail Associates executives either reaped windfall profits from their stock options or, to their immense frustration, lost out. After Vail Resorts went public, the exigencies of quarterly reporting placed enormous strains on the new resort company's public persona. The resulting fear and loathing created an atmosphere of distrust, fear, anger, and frustration among a wide band of the social spectrum. The conflict boiled down to a simple and abrupt clash of cultures and paradigms. On Wall Street, it's grow or die. In small-town America, growth often murders traditional ways of life. In this small town in the Rockies, already reeling from in-migration, rapid real estate development, and rising property values, the new corporate arrivals from New York and their fast-paced changes added a burning ember to a growing fuel load of social and economic dislocation. In many ways, Vail was almost ready to combust spontaneously before somebody literally poured gasoline on the place and lit a match in the early hours of another beautiful fall day.

PART 1

FLASHPOINT

Lynx to the Past

Communiqué claiming credit for the arson fires of October 19, 1998, atop Vail Mountain:

From Joseph "Anonymous" Howe, 10/21/98 5:55 P.M. –0300, Vail fires communiqué
Date: Wed, 21 Oct 1998 17:55:57 –0300
From "Joseph 'Anonymous' Howe" [nobody@privacy.nb.ca]
Comments: This message did not originate from the Sender address above.
It was remailed automatically by anonymizing remailer software.
Please report problems or inappropriate use to the
Remailer administrator at [remailer-admin@privacy.nb.ca].
Subject: Vail fires communiqué
To: vtrail@vail.net
Earth Liberation Front Communiqué
ATTN: News Director
On behalf of the lynx, five buildings and four ski lifts at Vail were reduced to ashes on the night of Sunday, October 18th. Vail, Inc. is already the largest ski operation in North America and now wants to expand it even further. The 12 miles of roads and 885 acres of clearcuts will ruin the last, best lynx habitat in the state. Putting profits ahead of Colorado's wildlife will not be tolerated. This action is just a warning. We will be back if this greedy corporation continues to trespass into wild and unroaded areas. For your safety and convenience, we strongly advise skiers to choose other destinations until Vail cancels its inexcusable plans for expansion.

—Earth Liberation Front (E.L.F.)

•

The solitary lynx, supremely adapted to its ecological niche after millions of years of evolutionary trial and error, paused in the snowdrift behind a stand of aspen and trained its pointy ears like tufted radar dishes toward the upper reaches of the frozen Eagle River. With the ethereal glow of the Milky Way reflecting off the snow cover, the wildcat tilted its head and sensed the faint padding of a snowshoe hare's paws in the willows below. The lynx's muscles tensed; the tawny creature sprang through the crystalline powder that blanketed the forest and reflected starlight like a dusting of stage glitter. As the cat's enormous hind feet—formed, as if by a mold, in the shape of oversized, furry snowshoes—skimmed the deep snow, the lynx appeared to float in fast motion. With breath like tiny puffs of smoke in the frozen, cloudless midnight, the predator sped toward its prey.

The snowshoe hare, equally well adapted to winters in the harsh, high alpine environment of the Colorado Rockies, took a millisecond to sense the lynx's pounce before setting its own enormous snowshoe paws into desperate, instinctual motion. But it was too late. The lynx, no bigger than a large housecat, had found enough food to survive a few more days.

■

Snow can tell a story, and Kim Langmaid, walking near her home in Redcliff, Colorado, in February 1998, knew how to read it. Langmaid, a high-cheekboned thirty-three-year-old naturalist with a complexion permanently bronzed by the high-altitude sun, crouched along the east side of the riverbed's floodplain. In the snow, she could see where the lynx had hidden, and where the hare was when it had realized it was about to become cat food.

Langmaid was puzzled. She knew that lynx were almost extinct in the area, but these tracks were distinct: too big for marten, definitely not coyote, certainly not an ungulate such as a deer or an elk. Just to make sure, Langmaid went home and consulted her field guides for a match to what she had seen. Out came Olaus Murie's definitive oeuvre on the subject; it confirmed that the imprint Langmaid saw on the page was identical to what she had seen in the snow. From the direction of the tracks, Langmaid figured, the lynx must have come down Iron Mountain toward the Eagle River drainage; that would be just three miles from where Vail, already the biggest ski area in the country, was planning to open an adjoining ski area the size of Aspen Mountain—a plan that many residents of the valley opposed.

Vail Resorts, the name of the corporate entity that managed Vail and three other ski resorts in Colorado, maintained that a lynx hadn't been sighted in the area since 1973, when a trapper killed the last known lynx near Vail (and was fined about $100) after he had spotted the cat during a ride on one of Vail's lifts. Since that time, occasional sightings of possible lynx tracks had kept alive the hope that the missing lynx was still in the state. The lynx was once found in twenty-one states; these stretched from the Northwest down the spine of the Rockies as far as northern New Mexico; and throughout the Great Lakes area and into northern New England. In the lower forty-eight today, only small lynx populations remain; these are scattered around Washington, Montana, Colorado, and Maine. As the cat's Colorado habitat was lost to second homes and strip malls, the U.S. Fish and Wildlife Service, using the legislative wallop of the Endangered Species Act, was considering whether to list the lynx (*felis Canadensis*) as threatened or endangered. The absence of lynx was critical to Vail's expansion plans.

Langmaid was aware that the story she had read in the snow might make a difference to somebody. A band of ragtag but determined environmentalists asserted that the expansion, ironically known as Cat III (short for "Category III"), was one of the last refuges for the elusive lynx in rapidly developing Colorado. Cat III lay smack in the middle of an unroaded area that was, in biological principle, perfect for a cat who required a huge home range; the area also had an elevation high enough to be out of the way of bobcats and other lower-elevation competitors not as well adapted as the lynx to deep snows.

Langmaid also knew she'd be taking on some powerful interests if she came forward. "VA," as the ski resort company is known in the area from its longtime corporate moniker of Vail Associates, Inc., proclaimed in court and to the press that the greenies were making much ado about not much. Porter Wharton III, a VA spokesman, argued that environmentalists, in an effort to raise money for their organizations, had manufactured the lynx issue as a desperate ploy to harass the ski company and to exploit Vail's notoriety. He grumbled that "the environmentalists came up with an animal only slightly less mythical than the unicorn" in their efforts to stop the new ski lifts from going into the Cat III area.

It was an odd exaggeration for Wharton to make. The lynx's ephemeral presence, Langmaid remarked, was noted by the ski company at the boundaries of all its ski trail maps: "Please stay out of this potential lynx habitat." VA had even put out a press release in 1989 that was conveniently forgotten during the controversy concerning Cat III: "Canada Lynx Found on Vail Mountain." The lynx, crowed the press release, existed in "developed areas as well as in potential expansion areas of Vail Mountain." Wharton knew the cat in question was no mythical creature; indeed, he proudly displayed a stuffed lynx inside his sunny office at Vail Resorts' corporate headquarters, a huge blocky concrete structure known locally as "the Death Star."

In some ways, though, Wharton was right: The lynx *is* an animal almost as poetic as a unicorn. The elusive cat is what Langmaid calls an "indicator species"; it confirms that all the parts of a natural system are accounted for, from the tiniest bacteria to the top predator. The lynx is one of nature's most solitary creatures; it forms temporary unions for the sole and fleeting purpose of mating. After the mother lynx gives birth, usually in the spring, the kits stay with her for less than half a year. By winter, the young lynx are on their own. The animals' home ranges are enormous, one lynx often claiming some fifty square miles or more. In isolated country, and where snow falls regularly during the winter, finding lynx tracks is no easy feat.

With an average elevation of 6,800 feet, Colorado had plenty of high-altitude alpine spaces for the lynx to roam. During the twentieth century, widespread trapping, development, and a concerted effort to wipe out other predators may have spelled the lynx's doom. In a successful program to make the West safe for cows and sheep by exterminating wolves, grizzlies, coyotes, and other large predators, government agents often left poisoned meat in the wild. Although lynx were never targeted as varmints, they still died, victims of strychnine and steel traps and human encroachment.

Langmaid's grandparents moved to Colorado from Massachusetts in 1961; they opened the first ski rental shop at Vail when it opened the following year. Her parents came out in 1969 when Langmaid was three, and her dad built the Eagle River Inn in nearby Minturn. She had grown up in the valley, before the McDonald's and the Subway sandwich shops and the rude drivers and the modem cowboys in a hurry at the checkout line at City Market. Back then, Vail Village, the site of the first development on private land at the base of the ski mountain, really was a village. "I used to go down to Bridge Street in my pajamas to get milk, without money," she recalls. Vail in those early days was the kind of place where everybody knew everybody else and everybody else's kids. She even knew the names of everybody else's dogs.

Langmaid spent her childhood exploring the forests, the creeks, and the beaver ponds around her home; she paid regular visits to a spruce tree that seemed sickly but is still there today. She moved away for part of high school, and each time she came back to visit, she became more disturbed. "I started getting pissed off in high school," she recalls. "I would go away and come back and every time there would be a new subdivision." She took off to Colorado State University in Fort Collins to study biology, subsequently attended the Teton Science School in Jackson, Wyoming, and later received a master's in environmental studies from Prescott College in Arizona. Then she decided to do something radical: She would start a school for environmental education in her own backyard.

Langmaid knew how distrustful many of the locals were about all things environmental, and that her plan to raise environmental consciousness in the valley where she grew up depended on her appealing to a mainstream audience with well-lined pockets—including VA's well-lined pockets. Yet she was fearful about, and often depressed to witness, every drainage in the forty-five-mile-long valley where she was raised filling up with high-end housing developments and their accouterments of Eddie Bauer Edition Ford Explorers and Hummers and Audi Quattros. The valley, scoured by the relentless flow of ancient rivers, lies between the massive upthrusts of granite that formed the Gore Range and is no more than a half-mile wide on average. Lately, though, the place was becoming a Disneyland, she thought, where the ski area's owners had created "Adventure Ridge" on the top of the mountain, then carted visitors up there by gondola to sell them rides on snowmobiles and let their kids play laser tag at 11,000 feet. Langmaid was no radical environmentalist, but she could sense something was wrong here if the lynx was being sacrificed so that spoiled twelve-year-olds could shoot electronic beams at each other on a ridge top while their parents dropped a hundred bucks a head for dinner in the town below. "If playing laser tag ever becomes more important than that incredible creature, we're doomed," Langmaid says.

For the moment, Langmaid decided, she would say nothing. Instead, she would go back the next day to take photographs of the lynx tracks in the hope of bolstering her options in case she decided to report the sighting. But that evening it snowed. The lynx tracks vanished overnight, as chimerical as if they had come from the hooves of a unicorn.

2

Pete 'n Earl Went up the Hill

Vail, Colo.–It took a small group of gusty men, along with a healthy dose of luck, and a hand from Mother Nature to give birth to the success story that is Vail.

–VAIL ASSOCIATES' PRESS RELEASE

The extent of our imagination was very limited. We thought we needed to have a page from European Tyrolean architecture because we'd all skied there and it was all we knew. We didn't pull it off.

–DICK HAUSERMAN, CREDITED WITH CREATING THE DOUBLE "V" VAIL LOGO,
INTERVIEWED IN 1992

Vail was founded by men who literally carved the slopes out of the wilderness and loved the mountain as much as the money it eventually attracted. Ski-history lore is rife with stories about the visionaries who saw opportunity for sport in the country's wild winter wonderlands, and who, for sheer joy, used Model-T engines and a few hundred feet of rope to rig rudimentary lifts. Although skiing had a long history in Europe, the Winter Olympics had started only after World War I, when Chamonix, France, hosted the inaugural games in 1924—before the first rope-tow lift had been invented. The first bona fide chairlift wasn't in use until 1936, in Sun Valley, Idaho; and skiing was still relatively nascent in the United States when World War II ended. A few places—Sun Valley, Aspen, and Lake Placid in New York—were up and running, but Americans' love affair with snow sliding had yet to catch on.

Vail's creation myth, as colorful as it is simplistic, centers on a reclusive miner named Earl Eaton, who was born and raised in the Eagle Valley, and a wounded World War II Army veteran named Peter Seibert, who had been a ski bum in Aspen before the war and always dreamed of creating a ski area in the European style. According to myth, "Pete 'n Earl," as they are known in their unofficial "founder emeritus" status, climbed Vail Mountain one day, shouted "Eureka," and proceeded to all but clear the ski runs by hand.

The reality is a bit more convoluted.

Eaton had grown up in the Eagle Valley where his family raised lettuce and loaded it into railroad side cars to be shipped to Denver and other far-flung destinations. Born in Edwards, about fifteen miles from where Vail is today, he recalls that the valley boasted little more than a few sawmills, some high-altitude lettuce patches, and great fishing and hunting. An acre of lettuce went for nine hundred dollars, and in the Roaring Twenties things were pretty good for the Eaton family. Then the Depression came, and it was a hunt-and-subsistence existence. "Nobody in Eagle County ever had much money," recalls Eaton, his seventy-seven-year-old face lined with something akin to annual rings on an ancient fir tree, a record of his years spent in the outdoors of his Rocky Mountain homeland. "They had milk cows, some sheep. Everybody had a cellar. We fished out of season, 'cause there wasn't nobody around to catch you." After the war, with the mines mostly shut down and the lettuce industry in shreds, the chances of finding employment in Eagle County were slim.

Eaton recalls that he and his siblings started "skiing" when they accompanied their father up to where Beaver Creek resort is today to work at the sawmills. They'd ride up in horse-drawn sleds and work all day, then ride down on steam-bent pine boards that their dad had made, strapped in by their toes with leather straps he had fashioned for them. Dad made all three brothers and two sisters their own skis, and the kids would go around stabbing the snow with one long pole, trying to get down the hill alive. "We never really learned how to turn, but it was a helluva lot of fun," Eaton recalls.

Eaton acquired his first store-bought pair of skis and boots in Leadville in 1947—some kind of aluminum/magnesium ski, he thinks, and leather lace-up boots. He headed for Aspen because he'd heard it had turned into something of a ski town—with some work to be done on the side. The idea of living in a ski resort was appealing after a childhood spent in the unglamorous Eagle Valley. But, shrugs Eaton, "there weren't too many places you could ski back then." In Aspen, skiing already cost four dollars a day, although every other place in Colorado was still a dollar. Eaton did some construction work for the Aspen Ski Corporation, and even joined the ski patrol for a while.

Eaton had a habit, from his old mining days, of disappearing into the mountains, just roaming by himself and looking for promising mining claims or anything else that caught his fancy. During much of the 1950s, he became an itinerant miner working the molybdenum mines near Leadville. He also did a stretch at American Smelting and Refining, working with lead, silver, zinc—and looking for gold on his own. He laid down a few mining claims for himself, hoping to sell out to one of the bigger companies, but never made the big find. "I went uranium prospecting in the summer," he says. "I was gonna get rich." He didn't.

While prospecting around, his eye kept gravitating to "that mountain on the west side of Vail Pass." He knew the front side of the mountain wasn't all that steep, but he figured that was about all the average skier could handle. The front side was only part of it, however; Eaton kept returning to the ridge top to gaze at the vast, open slopes on the south face of the ridge. "The back bowls is what really got me," he says.

Eaton eventually showed his spot to a few Aspen buddies, who agreed the mountain was impressive, even if the valley at the bottom wasn't wide enough to support a good-sized ski town. "Then they put a freeway through it and made it even narrower," says Eaton. Getting the idea matched to money was tough, though: Because he had finished only one year of high school, Eaton didn't know how to round up the necessary dough.

By this time, Eaton had already met Pete Seibert, another dreamer, while they were working trail crews cutting Ruthie's Run at Aspen a few years previously. Seibert had subsequently headed closer to Denver, where he worked at the Loveland ski area and harbored his dream of opening his own resort. Eaton paid Seibert a visit and told him about the mountain on the west side of Vail Pass. Would he like to see it?

•

Seibert's story was entirely different from that of the homegrown Eaton. Of stoic New England stock with a little family money, Seibert was already something of a ski bum before the war. He had moved to Aspen in the early 1940s and carved out a living teaching skiing in the winter and doing construction work in the summer. When President Roosevelt agreed to start the 10th Mountain Division, an elite force of skiing mountain men to fight in the European theater, Seibert signed up.

After Seibert was crippled by a mortar shell that ripped his body from foot to face in the Apennine Mountains of northern Italy during the Allied campaign, doctors told him he'd never walk again. But he healed, despite the prognosis, and when the war ended, the wounded veteran decided to kick around Europe for a few years. During this time, he learned something about the hospitality industry and skied a lot. In the early 1950s, he attended the *Ecole Hôtellière* in Lausanne, Switzerland, on the G.I. bill; there, he had a vision of the ski experience that was different from the athletic mentality he had seen in Aspen. "Americans count the number of times they go up and down the mountain," Seibert says. "Europeans count the sunshine and the wine they had for lunch."

Seibert returned to the Rockies armed with a Purple Heart and a Bronze Star; he wanted to start a resort that he would model on the genteel resort towns and villages of Austria and France. Postwar United States was going mobile, moving west in droves on President Eisenhower's new Interstate Highway System. The time, Seibert thought, was ripe. Howard Head had invented the first Head Standard in 1956, a metal-edged ski that allowed people to ski in powder and enjoy more control; and lace-up thong bindings were being replaced with the newfangled releasable kind.

Seibert found a job at the Loveland ski area, the closest resort to Denver. All the while, though, he had been searching in vain for the place to start his own resort. When Eaton, his old acquaintance, said he wanted to show Seibert something, he was game. In March 1957, Eaton and Seibert took a long day trip from Loveland. They drove to the base of Vail Mountain, where they strapped on skis with cable bindings and skins to grip the snow. After a seven-hour climb, they were at the top of the mountain; when they reached their destination, Seibert eyed the valley below with a grin. "Pete," Eaton recalls with a bit of understatement, "got real interested."

■

You might say the final impetus that got Vail started was a brawl in Aspen.

While Eaton and Seibert were prospecting for white gold in the peaks above the Eagle Valley, Bill Whiteford had found his way across the Continental Divide and up the Roaring Fork Valley to Aspen from his home in Oklahoma. Whiteford had married well, and had enjoyed himself immensely since he had climbed from humble Plains wildcatter to member of the slightly more high-society world in Colorado.

Although Aspen, which had opened in 1947, had designs on becoming a magnet for the young, the rich, and the beautiful, it couldn't shake its well-deserved reputation as a pretty rough town, born of its heritage as a miners' way station with a roughshod past. Despite the efforts of Chicago industrialist Walter Paepeke to make the town a Chautauqua for the cultured, gentility was not the mountain town's strong suit.

One night, Whiteford and a friend from Denver, George Caulkins Jr., witnessed a disastrous party. The host's son's eyes were gouged out with a highball glass during a nasty fight in the Blue Room of the Jerome Hotel, just as the first rock 'n roll band at Aspen, the Moonrakers, was shaking up the partygoers. Caulkins, disgusted, said it was time to do something different, and in a place that was more refined.

"This town's up for grabs," Caulkins told Whiteford. "C'mon, let's go back to the place Seibert told us about."

♦

After several unsuccessful attempts to pull together some investors for Seibert's dream resort, Caulkins teamed with Harley Higbie, member of the Grosse Point, Michigan, millionaire's club, to do some high-class panhandling. "Siebert will say he raised the money," says Whiteford. "He didn't raise a piss pot full of money." Instead, the first set of investors was found pretty much through word-of-mouth among Caulkins, Higbie, and the initial investors' friends, including Texas oilman John D. Murchison of Dallas. Soon, the partners started surreptitiously pecking around Vail for available land in the narrow valley below the place where Seibert and Eaton had discovered the back bowls—hundreds of acres of treeless, gently sloping terrain that was accessible from the highway. Because the mountain was public land, managed by the U.S. Forest Service, it was critical that the partners gain control of the ranchers' private land along the half-mile-wide valley floor. They didn't want to spook the natives, or worse, raise property values, with leaked word of their grand scheme.

So they lied.

One of the original investors, Jack Conway, was, according to Whiteford, "a typical oil lease hound" who concocted a scheme to purchase land in the name of the "Transmontane Rod and Gun Club." For the first purchase in 1957, they paid $55,000 for five hundred acres of the old Hansen ranch, the owner listed as the fictitious hunting and fishing club. "That was what we told the sheep ranchers," says Whiteford. "I thought it was kind of chickenshit," he adds, but nonetheless went along. The deceit, once discovered, caused a lot of resentment from the other landowners in the area. One of them was so angry that he took to shooting at anybody who rafted down Gore Creek near his home. "He hated their guts," says Whiteford. That same rancher sold five hundred more acres to the investors in 1960.

The original group quickly realized that if they were to build the lifts and resort infrastructure, they had to recruit more investors. Caulkins and Seibert took off on a road trip in a silver '56 Porsche and tried to scare up some money. ("Porsches still turned heads in most of the places we went in those days," Seibert recalls.) They were a good team. Seibert had earned himself an impressive name in the ski world by making the 1948 Olympic team, and he was a war hero to boot. Caulkins had entrée to where the money was. The pair cruised from country club to country club in Miami, Dallas, Houston, and Chicago, performing a Willy Loman act with their prospectus and their film. Caulkins and Seibert tried to convey the impression that "you had to have a pedigree to go to Vail," says Whiteford—an impression that began, soon after, to fuel anti-Vail sentiment in the Denver press.

At first, Seibert recalls, they had difficulty in enticing people to bite. The idea of investing money in remote Rocky Mountain real estate for a brand-new ski area struck most people as a venture about as appealing as buying Florida swampland to build an amusement park. "You couldn't find many people who want[ed] to build something in a sheep pasture," recalls Eaton.

After coming up empty in Tyler, Texas, Caulkins and Seibert headed south, and en route came up with a sublime brainchild: sell Vail as if they were selling membership to a bona fide club, with small premiums they could offer as gifts. Each member would receive an option on a lot, a lifetime family ski pass, shares in the corporation, and the chance to get in on a legitimate start-up company. It beat the hell out of offering a toaster to anyone who opened a savings account.

By borrowing techniques used in running a presidential campaign, where geographic diversity in the ticket can mean the difference between election and defeat, the salesmen recruited investors from key areas around the country. "We knew where the money was," says Seibert. "We knew where the market was for Aspen." Over time, the original owners from New York, or St. Louis, Cincinnati, Milwaukee, Chicago, Minneapolis, or San Antonio would tell their friends about Vail, who would tell their friends. Seibert and Caulkins eventually scrounged together "a bunch of enthusiastic investors who never expected to get their money back," says Seibert. One of those original investors was former President George H. Bush, who bought a partnership interest with two friends when he was still a mere Texas oil man.

For the ones who got in, it was a better investment than buying Xerox on the ground floor. Any purchaser, wrote Harley Higbie Jr. on March 1, 1962, to a prospective buyer, would have the right to a half-acre lot, appraised at $2,500 to $5,000 "and should appreciate in value as time goes by." It sure did. One of those early lots would easily fetch $5 million today.

Higbie also laid out the strategy that would haunt the enterprise decades later. After buying the private land at the base of the ski mountain, he wrote, "VA, Ltd., will lease its land to lodges, motels, restaurants, gas stations and any other business which may be established, so that Vail will receive a percentage of their gross. Thus, Vail will realize a profit on every activity in the Valley."

Eventually, the founders had wrapped up enough private land at the base of the mountain to build several lodges and restaurants. When they applied for a special use permit from the U.S. Forest Service for a ski area, however, they were initially turned down. At that time, the forest service was concerned that the other ski areas in the state weren't turning a profit, and they didn't want to clear-cut more mountainside for failed business ventures. Seibert and his lawyer friends reasoned that the forest service's position could become a potent legal attack point. "The forest service had no right to guarantee a net operating profit to anybody," he says. "Besides, a ski area owner could cook the books and figure to net operating profit for years." They reapplied, and in December 1961, they received their permit.

●

With $1.1 million in limited partnerships, a $500,000 loan from the First National Bank, and a Small Business Administration loan of $350,000, the newly minted Vail Corporation opened the Vail ski area to much fanfare in 1962.

It was a wide-open start-up. The town attracted hardworking frontier types, many of them newly divorced or on their second or third marriages, all trying to reinvent themselves in the fledgling enterprise. Fortunes were to be made selling lift tickets, real estate, gin, coffee, golf; renting skis and condos; hauling garbage, building houses, even selling gas.

Seibert had his vision of what Vail should look like: a sort of Bavarian knock-off on the banks of Gore Creek—and he didn't brook much dissent. Whiteford, with his ex-wife's money, built Casino Vail, a bar and restaurant with draft beer, strippers, and barbecue that became the central watering hole and party central for the construction workers who flocked to Vail in the early days. As would often be the case at Vail, surface impressions were all-important. "Pete told me to paint it white to make it look like the rest of the village," recalls Whiteford. "I told him I didn't want my bar to look like early Hansel and Gretel." Thus Casino Vail was the beginning of a rift between those who wanted Vail to appeal to the tourists as a perfect ersatz Alps village, and the people who had to put up with the visitors. Whiteford once lost his liquor license for six months for hanging a liquor inspector up on a meat hook. He was shut down several times for rowdy behavior, which included disagreements that often reached the point where darts were thrown with malicious intent around the bar. "Hell, at that point Vail was just a wide spot in the road," recalls Whiteford. "I didn't give a goddamn if the tourists came in or not," he says. "It made everybody mad as hell."

The early years were tough, but by almost every account there was a special feeling of community that the old-timers remember fondly. Vail was a jumble of dust, construction workers, dreamers, and loafers. "There was no money except for the people who had it already," recalls Whiteford. "Everybody was clawing for a way to exist."

■

As Vail opened, with a hotel, a bar, a gondola, three chairlifts, and a lot of muddy streets, the place was as rustic as it was isolated. However, skiing in America was about to take off. In 1964, three U.S. skiers won medals at the Winter Olympics in Innsbruck, Austria: A young man named Billy Kidd won the first U.S. men's Olympic medal in skiing, taking a silver in the slalom; Jimmy Huega took the bronze, and Jean Saubert took two silvers in the women's slalom and giant slalom. Kidd and Huega graced the cover of *Sports Illustrated* for their exploits in the race.

Vail would benefit from the sudden explosion of interest in skiing, but the ski area's visionaries would not. Unfortunately for Seibert, a number of bad business decisions left him, as they did Eaton, without a significant share in Vail's prosperity. VA respectfully trots out Pete 'n Earl for an occasional event, but it's hard to shake the sense that the current owners are simply tolerating the aging founders. "I doubt if Pete could even balance his own checkbook," says Paul Testwuide, a VA senior vice president who has been with the company almost as long as Seibert has. "Once the business got over the initial promotional stage and into the business of the business, he just didn't have it. Isn't it always that way with visionaries?"

Eaton doesn't disagree. He also recognizes that the changes he pioneered in his home valley became out of control. "I always thought that if I could get skiing going in Eagle County, it'd do something for the folks who lived there," says Eaton. Sometimes, Eaton says, old-timers seethe at him when they are in a particularly bitter mood about how the valley's transformation has completely destroyed their old way of life. "This is all your fault," they'd tell him. "You started all this."

"One guy blamed me for it, and then he thanked me," recalls Eaton. "He was a sheepherder who just sold his land for a million bucks." Eaton shakes his head at what his explorations to "the mountain west of Vail Pass" have wrought. "In my dreams," he says, "I never thought it would have the impact that it has had."

Eaton was not alone in his astonishment; but not everyone was as conciliatory as the suddenly rich sheepherder. Somebody, or a group of somebodies, was angry, and had an idea about how to send a message to VA.

"The Whole Mountain's on Fire"

Development associated with ski areas in the upper Eagle River Valley discourages some elk from using traditional summer and winter ranges. Colorado has become the Disneyland of the West, where demand for recreation has caused some humans to encroach on areas that used to be exclusively the home of wildlife. Wildlife simply cannot move to another area to avoid human contact. We're running out of room.

—COLORADO STATE UNIVERSITY BIOLOGIST BILL ALLDREDGE, WRITING IN 1989

Sometime during the predawn hours of Saturday morning, October 17, 1998, hunter Dave Alt heard a faint scratching outside his tent. Alt, then twenty-four, was sleeping in the tent with his father, Ken, just below a ridge of 11,200 feet on Vail Mountain, near a stand of pine trees about one hundred yards below the Ski Patrol Headquarters, known as PHQ. His friend Steve Gaal had pitched a tent with his brother nearby, and Dave wondered whether the two jokers were up to something, maybe making noises to scare him. Dave stuck his head outside the tent expecting to see the brothers playing a practical joke, and instead saw a coyote rummaging through his pack. He shooed the varmint away, saw that it was beginning to snow pretty hard, and went back to sleep.

Later that morning, the first day of hunting season, the snow kept coming. By noon, the mountain was coated with maybe eight inches of the season's first real snow blanket—good for hunting. The snow must have touched an instinctual chord in the elk; they were agitated and moved in good-sized herds. The dawn hunt was damp and cold, and didn't yield a sighting, much less a shot. In the late afternoon, Steve had the first luck, near a ski run known as Northwoods. In the fading light, after it had stopped snowing, he nailed a four-point bull with his thirty-ought-six from more than a hundred yards away. Then it was Dave Alt's turn. From his perch on a cliff he could survey the 14,005-foot Mount of the Holy Cross snowcapped by the storm. He quietly watched a herd move, then ran almost a mile to another ski run called Blue Ox, where he got his shot. Dead on, he stopped a 550-pound cow elk with his Winchester.

The pair of happy hunters field-dressed the animals, then slid them down the mountain like furry sleds. The next day, Sunday, Alt and Gaal drove the hundred miles to Denver to have their animals butchered, and returned up the mountain late that afternoon with fresh elk tenderloins.

During the day, Dave's dad, Ken, had bagged his own bull, and decided to drag it down the mountain and stay there. In the meantime, another friend, Neil Sebso, had joined the hunting party. Sebso wasn't prepared to spend the night out, but when Ken offered him his zero-degree sleeping bag, Sebso took him up on the offer.

Sebso hunted on Sunday, without luck. At dusk, the four men built a roaring bonfire, cooked Dave and Steve's elk tenderloins, and ate them with Ramen soup. Alt, who had moved to Vail three years previously from Brookville, Pennsylvania, and worked for a hotel that had just been purchased by VA, was disturbed about the effect that a proposed ski area expansion would have on the elk herds. They talked for a while about how they had heard that the elk migration had changed over the years; how golf courses and 12,000-square-foot trophy homes had taken the elks' wintering grounds. "Soon, there won't be any place for them to go," Dave said, looking down the hill toward Interstate 70, which bisected the Eagle Valley below and made north-south animal migration an exercise in high-speed road kill. "We take away their wintering grounds," he says. "Now we take away where they give birth. What the hell are we doing to them?"

From their vantage point on the mountain that moonless night, they could see the craggy, jagged Gore Range, its snowy outlines highlighted on the horizon. The range was named after a wealthy and loutish Irish tourist named Sir St. George Gore, who passed in the United States for royalty under the name Lord Gore. Gore arrived in the United States in 1854 for an elaborate hunt, and traveled in outrageous luxury. His entourage included a silk tent with carpeted floor, a bathtub, linens, a down mattress, and even a commode with a fur-lined seat. During his hunt, Gore laid waste to wildlife, plied Native Americans with 180-proof grain alcohol, and eased his way through the West by offering cheap trinkets and the nineteenth-century equivalent of Saturday night specials. Although he hired the famous mountain man Jim Bridger as a guide for part of his journey, Gore eventually ran afoul of the natives of North Dakota: A war party of Uncapapa Sioux stripped him and his party of everything they owned before turning them loose in the wilderness, naked, to grub for roots. Gore made it back to Ireland the next spring, poorer but not much humbler.

Directly below, hidden by trees, sat the town of Vail, snuggled against

I-70 at the far eastern reaches of the Eagle Valley. The town was quiet at this time of year; little stirred among the picturesque if contrived collection of Tyrolean-style buildings and quaint streets that housed high-end fur merchants, jewelry shops, real estate stores, bars, upscale restaurants, and expensive hotels. All was tastefully laid out on private land at the foot of the ski mountain and traversed by the babbling Gore Creek. With the highway that ran through it, they might well have named Vail "Innsbruck-on-the-Interstate."

Most ski towns in the West were named after an aspect of the natural world: Aspen, Sun Valley, Winter Park, Steamboat Springs. Vail was named for Colorado Department of Transportation engineer Charles Vail, who forged a highway over a 10,600-foot mountain pass in 1939. That road—the old Highway 6—brought mountain recreation to the masses gathering in the growing town of Denver when Vail was founded in 1962. The town of Vail incorporated in 1966 because the ski area owners recognized the benefits of a municipality's taking care of such mundane tasks as trash removal and police work. In 1967, construction began on Interstate 70, which would serve as an efficient artery (until it got so crowded that, on winter weekends in 2000, it looks like a parking lot) to carry millions of out-of-state visitors who flocked to Denver after the nation's airlines switched to a hub-and-spoke system. (Since 1990, increasing numbers of visitors have flown by commercial aircraft into the upgraded Eagle County Airport, a mere half-hour drive from waiting chairlifts.)

Aspenites liked to sniff that Vail is "half as far and half as good" as Aspen, but only the distance from Denver is indisputable. From Colorado's capital, it's a two-hour drive on I-70 to Vail's "Checkpoint Charley," the electronic gate that marks the entrance to Vail Village and sits between The Lodge at Vail and the ersatz Bavarian hotel called the Sitzmark. Checkpoint Charley, named after the crossover point between East and West Berlin, prevents all but the most essential (or privileged) drivers from entering the village's mostly pedestrian enclave. Once past the gate, visitors find themselves inside a carefully rigged Austrian fantasy façade. The effect is heightened on winter evenings when snow is falling lightly and horse-drawn carriages ply along the rows of twinkling lights that wrap the landscaped conifers; above all this, the monstrous ski mountain climbs like a great white beacon out of the valley floor.

The young hunters on the top of the mountain had seen how, over time, wealth begot wealth. Seibert, Eaton, and their partners had managed to secure financial backing to build the resort from a Who's Who list of U.S. industry, including Thomas Watson Jr. of IBM, Bob Galvin of Motorola, Charles Bell of General Mills, and many other corporate chieftains. What Aspen had become to Hollywood's celebrities, Vail became to Wall Street's tycoons. As the resort matured, a cadre of financial heavyweights, including Henry R. Kravis and former Shearson-Lehman chairman Peter Cohen, built lavish second (or third or fourth) homes there. Conservative politicians—former President Gerald R. Ford, H. Ross Perot, Jack Kemp, and Dan Quayle—also came and were greeted with gushing acceptance among Vail's industrial and Wall Street elite. The resort's owners were so enamoured of their cache of national politicians—and their potential marketing clout—that VA for years kept Ford on a $90,000 annual retainer, and his wife, Betty, on a $35,000 retainer, just for showing up at a few golf tournaments and social events every year.

Through successive owners that mirrored their times, Vail rode the country's postwar fortunes. After Seibert and Eaton came an oil-rich Texan, Harry Bass, who ran the show from the 1970s oil boom through the Carter-era malaise and the mid-1980s oil bust. As the United States climbed out of its last economic doldrums and moved toward the unrelenting prosperity of the 1990s, meatpacking and media magnate George Gillett bought the company in 1985, poising the resort for the go-go times of the investment banking boom during the *Bonfire of the Vanities* years. After Gillett lost the company in 1992 in his junk-bond-related bankruptcy, the present owners, led by "opportunistic investor" Leon Black's Apollo Management, picked up the prized Vail property for pennies on the dollar.

Through shrewdness, good timing, and demographic fact, Apollo was primed to capitalize not only on the latest dot.com creation of wealth but also on the pending intergenerational transfer of wealth—the largest in the world's history. According to the Social Welfare Research Institute at Boston College, baby boomers would inherit an estimated $11.6 to $17.5

trillion between 1998 and 2017 from their frugal Depression-era parents. Throngs of newly flush boomers were already descending upon the real estate agents of the northern Rockies with the enthusiasm their grandparents might have shown had they been given permission to spend a whole dollar in a penny candy store. Vail, with its name recognition, real estate sales, and high-end leisure market, was a gold seam waiting to be mined. And Apollo was standing by with high-powered pickaxes.

The hunters huddled around the fire as the temperature dropped. Steve Gaal and his buddy, Dave Alt, had been upset about VA's plans to clear-cut 885 acres to build new lifts in the Cat III area off the back side of the mountain, a couple miles from where they were hunting. Gaal wasn't an activist, but he wasn't pleased that the elk calving area back there would soon give way to ski runs. Despite his hunting success this season, Gaal knew that successive mild winters had given the elk an easy ride. Things were going to get tougher as the low-elevation terrain where the elk used to winter continued to sprout fancy homes with absentee home owners.

At about 10:30 or so, Sebso decided that he would be too cold if he slept out in the tent; he decided to take his sleeping bag into a bathroom structure at the top of the mountain. His friends joked that he was too much of a wuss to sleep outside, but Sebso preferred being a warm wuss to a shivering mountain man. Indeed, Sebso tried to convince the others that a heated bathroom was the better part of valor, especially in subfreezing temperatures at 11,000 feet, but the others scoffed that even a zero-degree bag wasn't good enough for Neil. At first, Sebso tried to sleep on the men's side, but the buzzing noise of the broken automatic flush toilets in the urinals kept him awake; at around 11:30, he took a bench from the men's room, moved it to the women's side, and fell asleep at about 12:15.

The three remaining campers stoked the bonfire; they had planned to spend a few days on the mountain and wanted to keep a good bed of coals going. They shot the breeze and talked about where they would hunt the next day, then crawled into their bags before midnight—Steve Gaal in a tent with his brother, Greg, and Dave Alt sleeping alone because his dad had gone down and Sebso had opted for the john.

At about 3:20, Dave recalls, he was awakened by a scratching sound, which he thought "was the same damn coyote again." Tired from the long day, he paid the sound no mind and went back to sleep.

A few minutes later, Greg Gaal, who lives on the East Coast and still hadn't set his watch to Mountain Standard Time, woke his brother up at what he thought was 5:30. "C'mon, Steve," he said as he shook his brother. "We gotta get up and start hunting." Steve looked at his watch and saw it was only 3:30, and told his brother to go back to sleep. Steve heard a sound he thought was plastic wrapped around an unfinished building and flapping in the wind, but thought nothing of it. About an hour later, he woke up to the same sound, now unmistakably that of fire. "Oh my God, what about Neil?" he thought, then shouted to the next tent: "Dave, get up! Man, get up, the mountain's on fire!" Steve threw on his boots and scrambled up the hill toward the flames, about a hundred yards away at the crest of the ridge.

Dave fretted as he pulled on his vest and boots. "The first thing through my mind is that Neil's probably a marshmallow up there," he recalls. He and Greg hurried after Dave, and stopped near PHQ at the top of the mountain. A nearby snack bar, Buffalo's, was already almost in cinders. PHQ, which had an apartment in which a patrolman usually lived year-round, appeared to have been empty, but Dave still wondered whether the caretaker might be inside. The building appeared to be burning "from the inside out," Dave recalls. He knew it would be suicide to go inside.

Meanwhile, Steve had reached the bathroom and awakened Neil. From where he stood, Dave could see Neil standing on the bathroom porch in his long underwear, gaping. The men tried to use a pay phone outside the bathrooms, but it was dead. Steve then grabbed Neil's cell phone and reached a 911 dispatcher in Vail, 3,000 feet below at the base of the mountain, at 4:26. The dispatcher apparently didn't believe them. "The whole fucking mountain's on fire!" he repeated. "Slow down," said the dispatcher. "What do you see?"

He saw not only Buffalo's and PHQ ablaze but the three chairlifts as well. The lift shack at Chair 5, also known as "High Noon," which connected to Vail's famous back bowls and was one of the busiest chairlifts on the mountain, was crackling. "It was like fireworks," Steve recalls. "There were big blue sparks popping out everywhere." Chair 4 was also engulfed, although Chair 11 was still relatively untouched. When Steve scrambled farther up the mountain in search of better reception for the cell phone, he was stunned to find another display of pyrotechnics: About a mile and a half away, along the ridge to the east, Two Elk, 33,000 square feet of upscale boutique restaurant, was burning like a gargantuan version of their own oversized bonfire the evening before.

Dave, who works for VA as a banquet captain at The Lodge at Vail, realized that they were probably in a lot of trouble. He knew their bonfire had been big, but surely they couldn't have caused all this fire. Still, he wondered whether an errant spark could have started the flames, which then jumped from building to building somehow. As he gaped in dismay, he heard an unusual sound: a diesel engine that was the backup motor for Chair 5 was chugging away. "It sounded like a helicopter coming," he recalls. Dave saw a thin blue line of flame, which he thought looked like gas, on the concrete floor of Chair 11's top structure. Could it be a leak? He peered along the ridgeline a mile and a half to the east and took in the dramatic sight that had already staggered Steve: Two Elk, enveloped in whipping flames. Holy shit.

Maybe it wasn't the sparks from the bonfire, after all.

After the 911 call, the young men backed off and waited. Sebso was dumbfounded. "It was the hardest thing for me to walk out of that building and see every structure around me on fire. I can't tell you how heavy that was," Sebso recalled later. After at least twenty minutes, at around 5:00, two snowmakers who worked for VA bounced up the hill in a company four-by-four. The hunters wondered what was going on. If the sounds they had each heard at 3:20 and 3:30 had been the fires taking off, why hadn't the alarm brought firefighters up there by now?

Dave grabbed one of the VA snowmakers and suggested that maybe they could put out the Chair 11 fire by throwing snow at it. The two headed over to it, fearful that the fireworks show at Chair 5 would be repeated; but the fire was easily tamed with a few snowballs. From just under the lift, Dave picked up a gas can that was still full and moved it away from the flames. Then, under the top of Chair 11, he saw another can. It resembled the kind of gallon metal can that was distinctively associated with fuel, similar to a Coleman camping gas container. This can was well charred.

More people arrived. A security man from VA. A couple of Eagle County sheriff's deputies, who surveyed the scene briefly, told the hunters to stay put, and drove over to Two Elk. By the time a water truck had groaned up the hill, it was too late to bother spraying the structures. Steve told the authorities that he had taken pictures and volunteered to get them developed right away. "They said, 'Thanks, but we'll do it for you,'" he recalls.

Once again, Steve was afraid that maybe somebody would think they had lit the fires. From everything he could tell, *somebody* sure had set them, and with a vengeance. One VA security guy, Jim Roberts, asked them a lot of aggressive questions, which made them uncomfortable. "Dude, we're only going to tell the sheriff," they told him. But hadn't the sheriff's deputy looked at them suspiciously, too? Dave made his way back to the tents as discreetly as possible and doused their bonfire. He began wishing that his dad, a minister, was still with them. Somehow, he thought, it would have looked better if one bona fide grown-up had been with them; tending a huge bonfire along with three other twenty-something snowboarder types with Winchesters—all holding grudges because VA's expansion plans would affect their sacred hunting grounds—made *them* targets for suspicion.

4

Exploding Peaches

THE HISTORY OF VAIL

Vail, Colo.–The craggy peaks of the Gore Range, the awe-inspiring backdrop for many a family photograph on Vail Mountain, were named after Lord Gore, the first white man known to have explored and hunted the area from 1854–56. He and famous mountain man Jim Bridger were also first to encounter some of the original residents of the Gore Valley, the Ute Indians.

Local legend has it that the Utes were angered in the late 19th century, when the gold rush brought scores of prospectors flooding into their mountain paradise around Leadville, Breckenridge, Redcliff, and what is now Vail Mountain. Leaving the mountains, they set fire to thousands of acres of timber. It may have been one of those "spite fires" that burned off the ridge and back bowls of Vail Mountain, creating the wide open terrain that would help set Vail's skiing apart from other resorts.

According to many locals, that was not the last Vail would see of the Utes.

—FROM A VAIL ASSOCIATES' PRESS RELEASE
CELEBRATING THE COMPANY'S TWENTY-FIFTH ANNIVERSARY

The Rev. Don Simonton, a local historian, wrote a letter on December 30, 1987, protesting VA's disinformation when they repeated the "spite fire" myth. The truth was that then Colorado Governor Frederick W. Pitkin blamed the devastating forest fires of 1879 on the Utes as an excuse to round up the tribe and send them to reservations:

> To state "legend has it" when there is no historical evidence to the contrary is certainly legitimate. But to continue to use that lead when there is reliable documentation to the contrary—as in the case of the "spite fires" in the Back Bowls—can only be described as something akin to deliberate falsehood.

At 3:30 A.M. Monday morning, October 19, 1998, an alarm from the smoke detector in the basement of the shabby Ski Patrol Headquarters sounded abruptly in the town of Vail's communications center. The alarm, linked to a building 3,000 feet above town, jarred the dispatcher from her night-shift doldrums. She knew that the alarms had a habit of going off for reasons other than fire, so she didn't panic. PHQ, after all, was one of the oldest buildings on the mountain, dating from Vail's beginning in the early 1960s. Sometimes, she had heard, pack rats chewed through the wiring; sometimes power fluctuations triggered the alarm; sometimes the snow gremlins set it off for no reason anybody could fathom. She called over to VA's nightshift security at 3:31 A.M. to ask them to check it out, but they weren't staffing twenty-four hours a day on the mountain yet and the security guard who answered the phone had to rouse some workers to see what was up.

Almost exactly a half-hour later, at 3:58 A.M., another alarm went off from the Two Elk restaurant, which was a mile and a half from PHQ along the same ridgeline. The structure, completed just seven years earlier, had a state-of-the-art fire sprinkler system, so the dispatcher reasoned that one of three things had occurred: The system had malfunctioned, had been disabled by uninvited visitors, or had been activated by heat or flames. She called the Vail Fire Department, and the captain on call immediately paged Assistant Fire Chief John Gulick, who was in charge because the chief was out of town on a hunting trip.

Gulick began worrying before he could answer the page. The forty-five-year-old had lived in the area since he had come out as a seasonal firefighter from San Diego more than twenty years previously; he knew the two structures were located more than a mile from each other on top of a distant ridge that separated the north and south sides of the mountain. The recent snowfall and steep, slippery climb would make for rough slogging in the tanker trucks. In good conditions, getting to the ridge by way of the winding switchback road meant a slow and treacherous trip for a truck loaded with five hundred gallons of water. Even if they made the ridge, there wouldn't be enough water to put out a big fire anyway.

Nevertheless, Gulick mobilized. He dispatched a crew with the five-hundred-gallon water truck to head up the hill; security teams from VA, the ski area's owner, accompanied them. One of Gulick's captains called back right away with news of more fires at lift shacks, and at a picnic area as well. "You'd better get up here," the captain yelled. Gulick hopped in his truck and sped the thirty miles from his down-valley home in Eagle to join a second crew that followed the first. As was the case with many of the worker bees in the town of Vail, Gulick couldn't afford to live in town because of skyrocketing real estate prices. Since 1978, Gulick and his family had steadily moved down the Eagle Valley into homes that were more affordable. Hell, with starting pay for firefighters at just $34,000 a year, he was having trouble hiring people who could afford to live *anywhere* in the valley. From nearly fifteen miles away, he could already see the flames from town painting the ridge in a surreal glow.

Despite Gulick's fast decision to send trucks, dawn was well advanced when the first water tanker arrived at the top of the mountain. When Gulick's vehicle had struggled to the top, a few minutes behind the trucks, the career firefighter was dumbfounded by what he saw. "There was stuff blowing up and going off," Gulick says. "It looked like a volcano was erupting."

Gulick drove over to Two Elk, which was even more impressive. The fire was consuming the 33,000-square-foot log structure as effortlessly as a bonfire would vaporize a box of wooden matches. The vaulted ceilings, old-growth cedar and Douglas fir posts and beams were engulfed, the flames burning a blue-green; these immediately told Gulick the fire might have been started with diesel fuel, perhaps mixed with gas. If a petrochemical accelerant was used, the fire had probably topped 2,000 degrees, and the copper from the plumbing and electrical systems would have melted. Inside Two Elk, more than one million dollars' worth of Native American buffalo- and elk-skin robes, blankets, murals, and Old West memorabilia were turning to ash. The blaze looked eerily like the northern lights, and close by was so bright that Gulick could write notes without a flashlight.

"Everybody's eyes were pretty wide," he recalls. Gulick wasn't accustomed to being so useless at a fire.

Gulick stood, listening to the percussive noises coming from Two Elk—what firefighters liked to call BLEVE: boiling liquid expanding vapor explosion; each cylinder of canned peaches, black beans, and tomato sauce was turning into a small grenade. As they helplessly watched Two Elk rage, the firefighters listened to a cacophony of explosions.

Thanks to a newly minted mutual-aid agreement, trucks from eleven western Colorado jurisdictions responded, some eventually making their way up the ridge. (The road up the mountain was so slick that VA had to help by winching the fire trucks up the final slope with the company's powerful snow cats.) All the firefighters could do was make sure the fire didn't jump to the lodgepole pines along the ridge and then spread into the surrounding forest. At one point, Vail Fire Department Captain Tim Lahey stood next to VA's main security guy, Bob Egizi, and the towering flames. "I've got five hundred gallons in that truck," Lahey said. "Where do you want it?"

Egizi just shrugged, dumbstruck.

Gulick was growing increasingly worried that firefighters might get hurt. He could not figure out why arsonists believe they're inflicting property damage only, and never seem to think about the dangers firefighters must face. The "Big Bird" six-wheel-drive, 1,000-gallon wildlands tanker truck from nearby Minturn had collided with another tanker from down valley in Gypsum, and it was only by sheer luck that one firefighter hadn't been crushed. Still, they kept coming. "Taxpayers don't like their pretty red fire trucks sitting around when something's on fire," says Sean Gallagher, Minturn's fire chief, who had sent Big Bird.

On top of the mud and smoke and confusion, the fires had destroyed the on-mountain radio system; all the fire fighting and law enforcement agencies were scrambling to figure out a common communication frequency for the 170 firefighters who had responded. Many of them resorted to using their private cell phones. Because so many skiers at Vail carried cell phones these days, cellular reception, at least, was pretty good.

Gulick, a dedicated firefighter who subscribed to and read every issue of the *National Fire Protection Association Journal*, knew that structures with adequate sprinkler systems usually don't burn as completely as had the charred ash heap that confronted him now. Two Elk had a well-designed "wet" sprinkler system that had been installed a few years previously. The six other fires that burned the lift shacks, the ski patrol headquarters, and a few outbuildings were suspiciously similar—and suspiciously self-contained. The National Weather Service hadn't reported any lightning strikes that night; and anyway it was unlikely that lightning strikes would start seven simultaneous fires spread out along the ridge.

Thank goodness, thought Gulick, for the recent snowfall that had dumped half a foot of snow on the top of the mountain. It made it a bitch to get the trucks up there, but the snow had probably prevented the fire from spreading into the adjacent forest—in the same vicinity where the ski area owners were planning that very day to begin new construction on a controversial expansion.

"I've never seen that much fire," thought Gulick. "How in the world did this come to be?"

Whatever the case, Gulick knew in his gut that not much was natural about what he was seeing. Surveying the mud and ash disaster in the cold dawn air, he picked up a handful of dirt and smelled it: gasoline.

5

Spreading Suspicion

At about 5:15 A.M. on October 19, 1998, James Van Beek got a call at his home in Gypsum, about forty miles down valley from where the fires had started. The Eagle County sheriff's investigator muddled through his morning fog and understood that some buildings were on fire up on Vail Mountain. He dressed and headed up I-70 toward the mountain, driving fast. On the way, Van Beek paged a fire investigator, Special Agent Al Blank, from the Bureau of Alcohol, Tobacco and Firearms (ATF) in Denver. The two of them had worked before on arsons; Van Beek suspected that something odd was going on that morning and that he might need help.

Blank called back quickly. "How many buildings?" "Five to ten, we think," said Van Beek. "All way up on the mountain."

Blank paused. "Holy cow," he blurted.

As Van Beek sped up the valley, the two brainstormed over the phone. One or two buildings, you could think maybe a lightning strike, they figured. But five to ten, stretched across a ridgeline at 11,000 feet after a snowfall, and you start thinking about assembling a couple of ATF's National Response Teams. There wasn't much doubt in their minds. "It was arson right off the bat," says Van Beek.

When Van Beek arrived at the makeshift incident command center at the main Vail Fire Department station, he met up with Gulick, the fire marshall, and a few others. It was tough getting reliable reports from the fire trucks Gulick had sent up the mountain because official communications were so spotty. By daybreak, Van Beek was assembling teams to cover possible escape routes from the ridge top. It would have been a bold move for the arsonists to come straight down the hill into Vail Village; but, given the delays in getting the fire trucks up to the ridge, it was possible that suspects could have left the mountain before the fire trucks even started up the hill. The area had any number of drainages with paths that led off the mountain to trailheads. With the hope of finding something unusual—or somebody who saw something unusual—Van Beek sent anyone who was available to the Game Creek trailhead; Mill Creek Road; Shrine Pass; the Turkey Creek road that led to the town of Redcliff; the bottom of the Vista Bahn and Forest Road at the base of the ski mountain; and the trailhead at Vail Pass on I-70.

Van Beek had received a report that a bunch of young environmental protestors had camped near the Two Elk trailhead, which was five miles away near the town of Minturn; he now sent two deputies over there to obtain names, license plate numbers, and reports from anybody who saw anything on the mountain that night. Another deputy had been dispatched to talk to the hunters who had phoned in the 911 call from the top of the mountain. Some guy apparently had been sleeping in the toilet, Van Beek was told.

With so many people on the mountain, Van Beek also had to think about supplying rest areas, food, shelter, and an incident command center. Because the press would be on to them soon, they had to arrange a place where the media could be kept away from them while they worked. Van Beek called the FAA (Federal Aviation Administration) in Denver at about 7:20 A.M. and closed the airspace from 14,500 feet down in a five-mile perimeter around the fires. "We don't need a midair collision between the news helicopters," he thought. He then wondered whether he could authorize a National Guard helicopter to do some reconnaissance, even if he couldn't really argue that lives were at stake. Then again, lives might be at stake. One report said that the fire had consumed the dynamite cache that ski patrolmen routinely use to set off avalanches before a wayward skier sets one off by accident. Fortunately, this was just an unfounded rumor; another was the report from Two Elk that burning chlorine was emitting toxic gas. The VA people were still worried about the natural gas lines that ran to the lodge, however; and the transformers were popping and blowing at PHQ, too. At around 5:30 A.M., workers heard more loud noises that sounded like ordnance exploding—probably the air cylinders and oxygen packs the patrol kept for emergency first aid, mixed with the sound of exploding propane tanks from Two Elk. Fires are always dangerous, and nobody could be sure that the bulk of the damage had already been done.

Van Beek met up with Bob Egizi, who had received some initial reports from the top of the mountain. Nobody had seen signs of unusual vehicle traffic—no ATVs, no mountain bikes, nothing but a few footprints—and those could have belonged to hunters or hikers on the mountain over the weekend. Tracks from snowmobiles also appeared in the fresh snow, but those were probably from VA employees working on the mountain over the weekend. Because there was no sign of burnt grass between the structure fires, it was unlikely that the fire had spread from one building to another naturally. Egizi was still in a state of shock. VA was so unused to vandalism that the company routinely left the bathrooms at the top of the mountain unlocked so that mountain bikers, hikers, and hunters could use the facilities and replenish their water. Still, Egizi knew there were plenty of disgruntled current and ex-VA worker bees who had it in for the company for one reason or another. He would not have been surprised if it turned out that a VA company employee, or a former employee, had wrought the destruction.

•

Ruddy-faced Paul Testwuide, an operations guy, had no doubt that he was in for a shitty day when the telephone jarred him awake in the predawn darkness. Testwuide's experience was that "calls at night send a chill up your spine." Usually it was an equipment breakdown, or lost or injured people; but those were mostly during the ski season. In the fall, like now, forest fires were never far from his mind. When the burly, round-faced man got the news, he lumbered to the window. He lived in Sandstone, across the valley, and he had a good view of the fires. "The dirty sonofabitches," he said out loud to himself. He immediately connected the flames to the protestors who wanted to stop Cat III.

Testwuide, or "Weed," as he was known, more for the pronunciation of his last name than his proclivities with mind-altering substances, was the local's local—a big man with a big appetite for drinking and carousing, his exploits known to anyone who has spent time in the town. Testwuide had gone to nearby Breckenridge in 1962 to "cut down trees, run bulldozers and raise hell in Leadville," and eventually came to check things out at Vail. He remembers sitting in the bar at the Red Lion Inn when the owner came up and asked whether Testwuide wanted a job as a bartender. He said, "Sure, when?" The owner replied, "Just as soon as I fire that sonofabitch behind the bar, you're hired." Testwuide grins, his eyes darting back decades. "And I've been here ever since."

Almost from the moment he arrived in Vail, Weed proceeded to build a reputation as the hardest-drinking, hardest-charging guy in town. He rode into the Cornuti bar one day on his horse "because I was thirsty and I was on a horse," and the owner told him not to because the horse would surely shit on the floor and make a mess. Testwuide promised the horse wouldn't make a mess. Sure enough, the horse lifted his tail, but Testwuide was quicker. He grabbed a customer's hat—a green Tyrol hat with an Innsbruck logo—and put it under the tail to catch the droppings. Then he returned the hat to its dumbfounded owner. "See, I told you he wouldn't shit on the floor," he told the barman.

Testwuide remembers those stories fondly, all the more so because of the contrast between then and now. Over the decades, Testwuide had himself ambled his way almost unwittingly up the corporate ladder at VA, and under the new régime, he had hit senior vice president. He was hardly the classic corporate type, though, and his friends say he had grown increasingly uncomfortable with the corporatization of the mountain. "Every single person I knew in the early sixties came because they loved the outdoors and loved to ski," he says. "There was no need to keep stores open during the day because everybody was up on the mountain. If people didn't have the five bucks or seven bucks it took to buy a ticket, they could sidestep and pack the slopes for half a day, then ski the rest." But the "New York boys" who bought the resort a few years back had changed the mountain forever. "The passion is out of it," he says. "It's not just because it's a corporation. Look at the houses—it's like a *Who's Who* of corporate America. People pay a lot of money to say Ross Perot's their neighbor."

The phone call announcing the fire, though sketchy, gave Testwuide enough clues to know this wasn't about a couple of wayward snowmakers sparking a joint and setting the mountain on fire by accident. Weed, who had arrived in Vail the same year PHQ had been built, started ticking off in his mind a couple of facts that made him think this was an organized

vendetta. The area at the top of the mountain provided a neatly concentrated target grouping. In close proximity, within a hundred yards or so
from one another, stood PHQ, Buffalo's restaurant, and the tops of Chairs 4,
5, and 11. It wasn't just the cluster of targets that made Weed wonder; the
general public never went in PHQ's basement, which was almost always
locked and filled with toboggans and junk. "Not everybody would know
that the guts of the communication system was in the basement at PHQ," he
says. "That is absolutely the heart and soul of the mountain," with phones,
radio systems, alarm systems, even the security system for dispensing gas to
employees from the on-mountain caches. Chair 4 was the lifeblood to the
front side of the mountain and connected with mid-Vail and the most popular route up the mountain via the Vista Bahn from the village. Chair 5 was
the route to the real icon of Vail, the treeless open slopes of the back bowls.
"If you wanted to close down Vail and hurt 'em financially with one shot,
that's where you hit," reasoned Testwuide. The other fire, at Two Elk, he figured, was more symbolic. It was the area's most magnificent structure and
obviously the gateway to the new Cat III development. Perhaps not coinci-
dentally, it was also one of the top on-mountain profit centers for Vail.

The strike was so strategic, Testwuide concluded, that "there were people in the community or who have been in the community that helped set
this up. Somebody from Vail was part of this conspiracy."

From years of working with the Secret Service with VIP protection for
national and international political figures, Testwuide had a few friends he
could call for advice and help. He phoned John Lipka, from the Denver FBI
office. He also called a buddy who was ex–Secret Service, but who now
owned a private security consulting business that counted Vail as a client.
The buddy, Dale Wonderlick, was in Moscow getting ready to fly to Siberia
for a consulting job on a Russian gold mine when Testwuide reached him.
Wonderlick told Testwuide that it would be a mistake to lay back and let the
feds run the investigation. For VA's own protection, especially with the
insurance claims, it would be a good idea to keep a private eye on things as
well. Somebody had to watch out for the corporate interests, and also to
start reassuring employees. They also had to beef up security in a big way;
who knew what the kooks would try next? Wonderlick caught the next

plane out of Russia, to Frankfurt, and continued west until he arrived in Vail. "When he heard there was more than one fire on the ridge, it was clear to him it was a conspiracy," says Testwuide.

Testwuide didn't have time to spend out on the grassy knoll contemplating who might have pulled this caper off, however. He had to arrange for bulldozers and snow cats to crawl up the mountain to help pull up the tanker trucks. Assign guards to secure other buildings. Sweep for unusual things on the mountain. Tell law enforcement agencies about possible escape routes. Establish traffic patterns and one-way routes up and down the mountain. Make sure there was an ambulance standing by. Check the availability of hose to tap into the snowmaking system. "These things just clicked off like neon signs," he says.

Figuring out who lit the match would have to wait.

■

Brian McCartney, VA's head of mountain operations, was strangely relieved when he received one of the early calls from security. "PHQ's on fire," he was told, and McCartney practically grinned. PHQ was the oldest building on the mountain and had problems with everything from bad plumbing to mice. "Great," he told the caller, sleepily. "Don't let it get into the trees." Then he hung up and thought, "If somebody set PHQ on fire, I wish I had their address to send them a thank-you note."

Then-chief of security Jimmy Roberts called him back. "No, you don't understand, Brian. There's more." McCartney was filled in about the burning lifts, about Two Elk. "If it had just been PHQ, it could have been a rat in the wiring," McCartney says. But when he heard about the location and number of fires, it dawned on him that the top of the mountain was strategically hit; after all, a company this size potentially has a lot of enemies.

McCartney also knew that he had probably made a few of those enemies himself in his role as VA's enforcer. He looked the part: McCartney is a gruff, burly man with close-cropped graying hair who cultivated the look of a not particularly friendly high school football coach of the Bear Bryant school. McCartney had plodded his way through the ranks since starting on the ski patrol in 1968, eventually rising to become manager of mountain operations in the Apollo régime. His office, near the Lionshead gondola, is a testimony to quick response: On his window sill a half dozen cell phones and radios are lined up. In the corner are piled blueprints of every aspect of the mountain's infrastructure. In his head is a roster of all the people, present and past, who have crossed ski poles with him. Before the fires, if somebody wasn't working out, McCartney had the heart-to-heart. If somebody was messing up major league, McCartney was the one who sent him packing. And there had been a few of those, over the years.

◆

Paul Witt, VA's spokesman, was more accustomed to hooking ski writers up with boondoggles than he was at crisis management. A classic nice-guy PR meister who had come to the public relations fold at Vail after working as a financial analyst at Disney in London, Witt got his wake-up call at 5:45 A.M. from a television station in Denver asking if he could comment on the fires going on Vail Mountain. "I'll get back to you," he said, and immediately called the risk management people. "Yeah, we had a couple small fires," Witt was told. Another media person trying to make a story out of smoke, he thought. "To me, it wasn't any big deal."

He got a call back from the same risk management guy with a different story. PHQ, Two Elk, and several lifts were all in flames. Fresh out of the shower, Witt immediately thought arson. They had just begun building the road into CAT III a couple days earlier, and the timing was just too coincidental for the fires to be an accident. More TV stations called, and Witt hightailed it the thirty miles up the valley from his home in Eagle to meet with a gathering crew of mountain operations folk and VA execs in the old gondola building in Lionshead in the west part of the mountain. As he came around the curve where the interstate opens to the mouth of a valley that gives a view of the mountain, "there was this tower of smoke that must've been a mile high," Witt recalls. "Up until then, I was thinking, 'No big deal.'" He now serially called every person in his department with an order: All hands on deck.

Witt met with Testwuide and Andy Daly, VA's president. "I know we talked about the connection to Cat III," he says. "We all thought that it looked like the environmentalists probably did this." Still, they had to be careful with their public statements. Witt argued for a quick release revealing the known damage: to the massive lodge, to the Patrol Headquarters, to the lifts. Just the facts. "We didn't want to come out and start pointing fingers."

•

Andy Daly had seen a lot of strange things in his thirty years in the ski industry. During the 1989 World Alpine Ski Championships, His Royal Highness Prince Alphonse de Borbon y Dampierre of Spain decapitated himself by skiing into a race banner cable, and VA had to settle with the royal family even though HRH had skied where he shouldn't have. Then there was the lawsuit filed by the family of a child who was killed by a skiing VA employee on the last day of the ski season with just under the legal limit of alcohol in his blood. Daly had worked himself up from ski patrol into the upper echelons of upper management, and had even owned a small ski basin called Eldora, a homespun resort in Boulder's backyard. He was named president of VA during the last years of the previous owner, George Gillett, in November 1989, and stayed on during the transition to Apollo's ownership and the IPO; he reaped at least $6 million in stock options in the deal. In 1996, Daly suffered a minor indignity when Apollo hired Adam Aron, an import from the cruise industry, as CEO over him when the company doubled in size with the acquisition of Breckenridge and Keystone; but Daly stayed on as the silver-haired public face of the company. In contrast to the new CEO, Aron, who was seen as effusive and "eastern" and from outside the ski industry, Daly was generally perceived as reserved and local—and a lifelong ski guy.

On the morning of the fires, Daly was up, as usual, at about 5:30, preparing to go to the club for his workout, when Testwuide called. Daly lives in Potato Patch, one of the more exclusive developments around Vail, on the north side of the valley across the highway from the ski area. "As he was talking, I could see the glow of PHQ and, farther to the east, the glow from

Two Elk," he recalls. Testwuide had only sketchy information, but it was clear that those two buildings were on fire and that some of the lifts were also burning. Security was already on the mountain, and Daly was already convinced it was arson. As to who was responsible, he says, "I didn't want to jump to conclusions."

Daly, all business, got dressed and set out to "do what we needed to do to contain the damage." Damage to the forest. Damage to the facilities. Damage to the company's image. He met Testwuide in Weed's office near the Lionshead gondola, and the two of them thought that the fires set simultaneously along the ridgeline at 11,000 feet "raised questions about a larger conspiracy." There was also the news that the sprinkler system at Two Elk had gone off, emptying a reservoir of 30,000 gallons of water without making a dent in the fires. "If it had been an internal fire, the sprinkler system would have knocked it out quickly," says Daly.

As the sketchy reports started filtering down the mountain, "it was a wait-and-see-morning," says Daly. First, he wanted to make sure they could limit the damage, especially to the surrounding forest. That seemed possible; Weed and Daly had sent up snow cats and bulldozers to help pull the fire trucks up the muddy slopes. An assessment of the damage was slow in coming, however, because some of the lifts appeared to have been hit with a splash-and-burn arson rather than the more effective method that burned Two Elk and PHQ to cinders. They needed to begin their media response, establish internal communications, secure the rest of the resort, and lay out the first elements of a recovery plan.

Already, Daly was moving on.

Daly knew that plenty of people were pissed off at VA, but had always thought the animosity was more in keeping with that of a teenager who rebels against his parents than with somebody who would take such malicious action. "I couldn't personally come up with a single name of anybody that would have been that angry," he says. Nonetheless, the names of recently disciplined employees, including those who had been busted in the company's drug-testing policy, were turned over to authorities.

Daly mentally went down his own list. He was used to periodic threats—bomb threats on chairlifts, an occasional bizarre interaction with local

environmentalists—but nothing this bold. He thought of the Minturn residents who were still smoldering because they had lost a legal fight over
water rights, then dismissed the idea. "The town of Minturn is just not
going to do something like that," he said. "It may be naivete on my part. But
I've been in this business for thirty years."

After making more calls, Daly and Testwuide headed up the mountain
in a company truck. When they arrived at the top, "I felt an extraordinary
sense of relief," Daly recalls. The top of Chair 5 was completely destroyed,
but hell, it was one of the oldest lifts on the mountain. Chairs 4 and 11,
among the most popular lifts, weren't a total loss. All in all, "the extent of
the damage was not insurmountable and could be fixed," Daly concluded.
"I was feeling we had been blessed."

He couldn't banish a nagging thought, however. "Whoever did this had
a pretty good idea of what they were doing," he says.

■

By late morning, the first feds—FBI and ATF—arrived and sat down with
sheriff's deputy Van Beek. The federal investigators asked him who he
thought might have a grudge against the ski area: an angry ex-employee,
perhaps? A competitor in the ski business? Anybody from the town?

The agents found Van Beek's response perplexing. Mentally, the longtime Eagle County resident ticked off potential suspect groups: the enviros,
of course, but also disgruntled ex-employees, merchants in town, current
employees from ski patrol to the night groomers, Minturn locals, maybe
one of the former VA management team; hell, maybe even the former
owner, George Gillett. "Who *couldn't* have done this?" Van Beek asked the
feds. "The list of people pissed off at VA is pretty long."

It also occurred to him that, as in any arson, the property owner's possible motive for setting the fires had to be examined as well.

6

Barbarians at the Slopes

The 1980s took many of the restraints off the accumulation of wealth, wealth which would then head off in search of novel and satisfying ways to exercise purchasing power. One target of that quest would be real estate in handsome Western settings. And that real estate would carry particular attractions precisely because of the conglomeration of factors that had reduced its attractions in earlier times—isolation, aridity, altitude, heavy snow, or general ruggedness, particularly if there was a good airport a short distance away.

—Patricia Nelson Limerick, in an essay titled "The Shadows of Heaven Itself," published in the Atlas of the New West by the Center of the American West, University of Colorado, Boulder: W. W. Norton & Company

As a hiker kicks over a rotting log to reveal colonies of termites living inside, the arson burned the bark that had hidden the region's significant divisions. With the flick of a match, someone had lit a $12 million flare that signaled open warfare on VA.

But who?

Everybody who lived anywhere near Vail knew that the timing of the fires was suspicious. Just two days before the fires, on a Friday, a federal appeals court had rejected a last-ditch appeal by a coalition of environmental groups. The coalition had sought to halt VA's plans to build four new ski lifts and clear-cut 885 acres of mostly old-growth forest on U.S. Forest Service land adjacent to the town of Vail. With the judge's ruling, the United States' biggest ski area had received the all-clear to grow even bigger. Construction crews were scheduled to begin first thing Monday morning. But first came the fires.

Within hours of the first alarm, as Eagle County Sheriff Department's investigator Van Beek told the FBI, it was obvious to anybody familiar with Vail that each person on the gondola, as it were, had motive and opportunity to torch the place. Townspeople imagined potential arsonists behind every Douglas fir. Besides the usual environmental suspects who had vociferously opposed the expansion, plenty of others didn't like VA. That list of people had grown substantially in the six years since a town favorite, former owner George Gillett, had declared bankruptcy and lost the resort to a group of investors headed by Leon Black, a reincarnated 1980s junk bond trader who had been a protégé of convicted insider trader Michael Milken at Drexel, Burnham and Lambert. Black had been part of a group responsible for selling Gillett billions in junk bonds; they went bad and forced the bankruptcy when the economy temporarily tanked around the time of the 1992 Gulf War. The new owners, Black's Apollo Partners, inspired fears that the valley was being toyed with by these new barbarians at the slopes.

Because of the bad blood that had boiled between the ski area's new owners and the community up and down the Eagle Valley, the list of *un*usual suspects turned out to be unusually long: Mom-and-pop business owners were scarred by the behemoth company's sharp competitive claws when VA began venturing into such local businesses as restaurants, equipment rentals, and real estate development; other Colorado ski area owners were still apoplectic about a 1996 Justice Department antitrust ruling that allowed Vail to gobble up two neighboring resorts and gain a firm grip on nearly half the skiers in the country's most alluring ski state; longtime ski area employees were furious with VA for benefit reductions instituted under the reign of Apollo-installed CEO Adam Aron, who hardly ingratiated himself with the locals by coming from the cruise ship industry and showing up at ski lifts wearing tasseled loafers. The elite cadre of ski instructors had just received a zero percent raise, which had them muttering about unionization. Ski patrolmen thought they were being treated like on-mountain concierges rather than revered saviors of the slopes. The suspect list had to include backcountry skiers, who feared the expansion would shut them out of their favorite terrain; and hunters, who were angry because the elk herd would be decimated to make way for more real estate development. Even the neighboring town of Minturn, whose nasty water rights litigation with Vail had ended badly for the town just months before the fires, had a reasonable motive.

Dark rumors surfaced that VA had set the fires as a twisted way of gaining sympathy and support for the company's controversial expansion. After all, people whispered, insurance covered the expenses, and the lifts that burnt down (and were rebuilt with insurance money) were among the oldest on the mountain. VA had been winning the court battles, people figured, but the company sure as hell had been losing the PR wars. At the outer fringes of the Area 51 crowd, some even suggested that the FBI did it as a way to crack down on radical environmental groups.

The suspect list was a crowded place.

●

Vail is a ski area and a town, with a gravitational pull that stretches westward all the way down the Eagle Valley and throughout Eagle County. To
the south and east, Vail's influence is felt across several mountain passes in
adjacent Summit County, where two of VA's sister resorts, Breckenridge
and Keystone, are located.

The entire valley has been transformed almost beyond recognition;
nary a sign remains of the bucolic sheep ranches and lettuce patches that
existed before Pete Seibert and Earl Eaton started cutting trail in 1962. Vail
at the beginning was a rough-hewn place, founded by hardworking self-
styled new-frontier types looking for the proverbial fresh start and trying
to reinvent themselves as grown-up ski bums, way before the words
"lifestyle refugee" became part of the popular lexicon. In the early days,
bartenders wore ski helmets for self-expression (or self-protection) and
doled out friendly-sized shots while drinking as much as their customers.
The only consequence of your actions back then was your own monstrous
hangover. And there were plenty of those.

Whether you were from Austria, New York, or Denver, if you came to
Vail in the early 1960s, you got in on the ground floor. A lot of people made
fortunes. But many others didn't figure out how to get in on the action—or
didn't care to.

As Vail grew, so did the fears for its future; almost from the beginning,
there were some who warned of the consequences of unchecked growth in
this high mountain valley. Vail residents rallied against bringing the
Olympics there in the 1970s, and public comments about the current ski
area expansion plan ran more than 90 percent in opposition. At the time of
the fires in 1998, those warnings were still going unheeded, as evidenced by
plans for several large-scale developments.

Although the area has come to be referred to as the Vail Valley in Colorado Public Radio's weather reports, its topographically correct name is
the Eagle Valley, named after the Eagle River, which joins Gore Creek just
below Vail. In those forty-five miles, the Eagle Valley drops from some 8,200
feet in Vail down to 6,100 feet, and its sentinel mountain walls are meticulously constructed of sedimentary rock bands that have been carved by
eons of wind and water into nature's inimitable erosion art. From the

higher-altitude aspens, which light up the hillsides in the September sunset like rows of bright yellow holiday lights, to the beginning of the red sandstone carvings, which reach their apogee in southern Utah, the Eagle Valley crouches, patiently, beneath the weight of the growing human habitation.

Long and narrow, the result of millions of years of geological shifting and glacial carving, the valley opens to human habitation at the confluence of Gore Creek and Black Gore Creek near the first tract of private land in East Vail. The valley closes down again some forty-five miles to the west, after the Eagle River joins the Colorado River in the town of Dotsero. Beyond Dotsero lies the formidable topographical boundary of Glenwood Canyon, a narrow, gorgeous sandstone gully impenetrable to real estate development (as is the federally owned land that rises out of either side of the Eagle Valley into the White River National Forest). On the other side of the canyon, the town of Glenwood Springs serves as the down-valley terminus for another ski area's sprawl along yet another mountain valley: Aspen and the Roaring Fork Valley.

Eagle County, about 83 percent federally owned, has a population of about 37,000, double that of just fifteen years ago. The town of Vail (permanent population less than 4,000) is defined by the interstate on the north, a championship eighteen-hole golf course to the east, and the ski area to the south. Westward, the village segues into the afterthought of Lionshead, a development of concrete structures that dates from an architectural time and place in the late 1960s that most city planners would like to forget. Vail also stretches a couple of miles to the east into a more thickly wooded area; varying degrees of expensive houses line the golf course into East Vail, where the valley narrows and the highway begins its 2,400-foot climb up to Vail Pass and the headwaters of Black Gore Creek. Along the north side of the valley, the trophyest of trophy homes in a gated development called Spraddle Creek rise along the barren rocky slope; they command huge vistas of the entire ski area on the other side of the valley—and price tags that have surpassed double digits: in millions. Farther west, Vail's more mundane architecture of 1970s-era condos, fast-food restaurants, gas stations, and chain markets hug the highway along a frontage road, until the valley pinches down to just little wider than the four-lane interstate about three miles west of the village.

As I-70 heads down valley, what used to be small pockets of human set-tlement are now inexorably becoming a nonstop mountain city-state. Just a few miles from Vail sits Minturn, a century-old railroad town locked in a struggle to maintain its own identity amidst a tsunami of new money that has drenched the rest of the region. Heading back down the Eagle Valley on I-70, between Vail and Eagle, the nearly consecutive towns of Avon and Edwards have sprung to life over the past forty years, now burgeoning with new home developments, new "old town" developments, commercial developments, retail developments, trailer park developments, and golf course developments. The names are prosaic: Mountain Star, Wildridge, Singletree, Bachelor Gulch, Cordillera—and the homes within them fetch enormous sums from droves of part-time residents who dream of retiring in their well-appointed mountain retreats. Another ten miles down valley, where highway 131 heads north toward Steamboat Springs, sits Wolcott, where county planners have approved two new eighteen-hole golf courses that will provide the calling-card amenity to drive yet more homesite devel-opment.

After Wolcott, the valley narrows again and opens up ten miles later in the town of Eagle, a place with a rich agrarian history and a daunting growth rate as the county seat of one of the fastest growing counties in a state overflowing with fast-growing counties. Below Eagle, the townships of Gypsum and Dotsero, once mere wide spots in the road, are the next targets for development and the last conceivable construction that can piggyback on Vail's name recognition.

Undeveloped private land has become more precious than the minerals that used to be dug out of it. On virtually every private parcel in the valley, somebody has a plan or a dream to build on it. Brad Udall, son of Stewart Udall, who was Secretary of the Interior under John F. Kennedy and who was instrumental in getting the landmark Wilderness Act passed in 1964, runs a land conservation group in Vail called the Eagle Valley Land Trust, which is trying to acquire private land to maintain some islands where development doesn't take over every view corridor and wildlife winter range and link every hamlet in a continuous throb of sprawl. "We're trying to prevent a fifty-mile-long strip city," Udall says.

Enter into these roiling forces that this small town's pride—its world-class ski resort—was purchased by a New York firm, and Wall Street really did come to Bridge Street (the name of the main pedestrian thoroughfare through Vail Village). Suddenly, Vail wasn't like the Sun Valleys or Aspens of the world; their more or less benevolent private owners, despite their quirks, had managed to allow a certain laissez-faire management to dictate slower growth. Earl Holding, who owns Sun Valley, has sat on thousands of developable private acres of land at the base of the mountain—just because, it seems, he can. The Aspen Ski Company, owned by the Lester Crown family of Chicago, operates in a town that has been progressive, some would say to the point of being socialist, in providing such workers' benefits as affordable housing (admittedly this is an odd concept in a town where the *average* home price exceeds $3 million). But unlike such flagship resort towns that started as mining communities and became retrofitted resorts as an afterthought, Vail was built from the ground up as a ski resort—so much so that they forgot to put in alleys, loading docks, and underground delivery areas, or to provide enough affordable housing to allow for an indigenous workforce.

Into this cauldron of change came the new owners of VA, who, in just five years, had made enough enemies to give Agatha Christie a potboilerful of plausible suspects. "VA," as the company is still known (even though Vail Associates has changed its name to Vail Resorts, Inc.), had gone public less than two years before the fires; a quarterly-reports Wall Street sensibility had invaded a town that prided itself on being run by grown-up ski bums, even if they were now lawyers, MBAs, and real estate developers. Led by reincarnated junk bond peddlers straight from the *Predator's Ball* crowd, VA had methodically, if unintentionally, begun alienating Eagle Valley locals. Nobody personified this more than the man who took over as Vail Resorts' chief executive officer in 1996, Adam Aron.

■

As all hell was breaking loose on the top of Vail Mountain on the morning of October 19, 1998, Adam Aron found himself in a sublimely ridiculous scene down in south Florida—the kind of predicament that the hyperbolic author Carl Hiassen might have invented. Here was Aron, in Disney World with his wife and twin nine-year-old sons, on what should have been the slowest month of the year for his recreation business, and a couple thousand miles away Vail was in flames.

At just after 9:00 A.M., Florida time, as he was leaving the hotel, he got the call. Not wanting to talk on his insecure cell phone, Aron continued on to the park, intending to call back on a land line to discuss strategies in responding to the fires. Aron found a pay phone right in front of the ice cream parlor on Disney World's Main Street—just about the least private spot in the park. While his twins did the rides with his concerned wife, Aron spoke alternately to Andy Daly, various investor relations folk in New York, the designated Vail liaisons at the corporate headquarters of Apollo Partners on the Avenue of the Americas in Manhattan, and various public relations crisis management consultants. He called the executive team, key members of the board of directors, and top shareholders. He called them all again whenever he had updates.

"Every forty-five minutes, Goofy would walk by," recalls Aron, still incredulous. "The media was descending on Vail, and I'm watching Mickey Mouse stroll by me at Disney World. It was surreal." Aron stood next to the Main Street phone for the next three or four hours, dazed.

The fires presented a massive challenge for Vail's relatively new CEO, who hadn't exactly begun a mutual love affair with the natives when he moved from Miami two years earlier. When Aron hired on with Vail Resorts in July 1996, he was forty-one and had the reputation of being something of a marketing wunderkind. He was also known as someone with the requisite amount of sangfroid to perform major cost-cutting surgery on corporate cellulite. When hired, Aron had been the president and chief executive officer of Norwegian Cruise Line Limited, the world's fourth largest cruise company with some $800 million in annual revenues. Before that, he had risen quickly and built his reputation in various travel-related fields. He had made vice president for marketing at Western Airlines at the age of thirty, then left there to become a senior vice president at Hyatt before being named a senior vice president at United Airlines. Crain's Chicago Business picked Aron as one of the Forty Under Forty, "the forty shakers and movers in Chicago under the age of forty."

Although Aron had been skiing since he was in college at Harvard and had taken many trips to Stowe, Vermont, he didn't fit Vail's golden boy image of the ski bum. Aron's unathletic, disheveled form and gruff, hurried, fast-talking manner was anathema to the old-school Austrian transplants, Vail's WASPy conservatives, and the local ski bums. Aron's luck was bad, too; he exacerbated an old hockey injury shortly after taking the reins at VA and was unable to ski the first year of his tenure. In Vail, where one's prowess on the slopes is still a gauge of worthiness, the injury cost Aron many points in the perception sweepstakes. The previous owner, George Gillett, people remarked repeatedly, could *ski*—and he was always on the mountain letting people know he was there. Aron earned a reputation as "the cell phone king," and people never knew where he was.

The skiing prowess issue notwithstanding, Aron was out of his urban element in Vail. He earned everlasting infamy in town by wearing tasseled loafers to tour the ski lift operations, a faux pas akin to showing up to a black tie dinner in shorts and a T-shirt. An effusive Jew in the WASP-infested world of Vail, Aron was scrutinized for his tipping habits at restaurants, his sartorial slovenliness, and his generic East Coast ways. People begrudged him his enormous home in Beaver Creek, and the millions in salary and stock options that CEO status brought him. Aron became the butt of mean-spirited jokes and comments about his energetic eating habits and his being a little portly: Who would you like to be stranded with on a desert island? Adam Aron, because you could always make soup out of the food left on his shirt.

The Harvard Business School grad had come to Vail at a time when the ski industry was going through a major transition. The industry as a whole had seen flat skier numbers for nearly twenty years, and despite a few exciting and hopeful years when snowboarding took off as the Next New Thing and reenergized younger "snow sliders," nobody was predicting that huge demographic shifts would bring hoards of new skiers into the fold. The baby boomers were aging, which was great for selling second homes, but not so hot for selling lift tickets. Competition for the leisure dollar was crowded with volcano expeditions in Costa Rica, snorkeling tours in Cozumel, and skiing in Canada's Whistler/Blackcomb, where the U.S. dollar went a lot further toward an elegant après-ski experience. In the United States, ski companies had begun a steady process of mergers and acquisitions, slowly losing the mom-and-pop affect they had cultivated ever since the ski areas' original owners, sometimes quite literally themselves, hacked the resorts out of the hillside.

During his tenure at United Airlines, Aron was credited as a driving force behind taking that airline from a so-so domestic carrier to a world-wide fleet with a top-drawer, instant-recognition marketing campaign involving George Gershwin's classic *Rhapsody in Blue.* However, although Aron was proclaimed as a marketing genius, he has never been able to sell himself successfully to the local press. Aron's thin skin, legendary in Vail, has not made things easier; the day after the fire, he publicly berated a local reporter for calling him "chunky" in an article published months before. After having had glowing profiles written about him in everything from the Chicago *Sun-Times* to *Travel Agent* magazine, getting his chops busted by a third-rate local scribe baffled him. He remembers every slight: "On my third day in Vail, I was eviscerated by the *Vail Valley Times,*" he comments, his voice still full of disbelief.

The *Vail Valley Times* profile was less than flattering. The reporter had, in Aron's words, "found the one person, in twenty-plus years in the business world, who hates me more than any human being alive: the president of Carnival Cruise Lines."

Norwegian Cruise Line had been faltering when it hired Aron, and Carnival Cruise Lines was the undisputed industry leader. Aron came up with a sexy ad campaign that said, "There's no law that says you can't make love at 4:00 P.M. on a Tuesday." The awards, and the customers, started cruising in. Then came the Great Debate. Bob Dickinson, the dean of the cruise industry and CEO of Carnival, had agreed to debate Aron about the future of cruising in front of the cruise industry cognoscenti at a conference in Florida. To hear Aron talk about it, the one-hour dialogue was the equivalent of a World Wrestling Federation championship—no holds barred, winner-takes-all. The subject: Should the industry pursue first-time cruisers, or target repeat cruisers? Aron prepared for the debate by studying the courtroom scene from *A Few Good Men,* in which Kevin Bacon tore apart the much flashier Tom Cruise with his straightforward speech to the jurors.

Aron recalls the movie scene verbatim. Aron's Bacon-esque strategy worked perfectly, and the CEO beamingly retells the debate story with the pride of a boy who hit a grand slam during the Little League all-star game. When the audience voted after the debate, Aron won by a margin of nine-to-one. His position? Go after everybody.

When a student at Harvard B School, Aron would ski at Waterville Valley. But it wasn't until he was a senior vice president at Hyatt that he heard about Vail. In the mid-1980s, Hyatt planned to put a property in a new ski area built by VA called Beaver Creek. The Hyatt, says Aron, "put Beaver Creek on the map," and also brought Colorado to the consciousness of Vail's future CEO. "Ironically, before that, I was a Utah skier and a New England skier," he says.

When Aron took over at Vail Resorts in July 1996, he almost immediately stepped in it. At a chamber of commerce dinner a few months after being named the CEO, Aron told the community business leaders that VA would begin expanding some of its on-mountain businesses into the off-mountain retail arena. At the same time, he tried to assuage their fears. "We don't want to compete with the local businesses," he said. "That's what gives Vail its character." But to the locals, Aron's message was clear: The new kid on the slopes was going to be fierce competition for the small-time business owner.

The Harvard B School concept of "vertical integration" was a logical business strategy for Vail Resorts: If you own a ski area that sells lift tickets, why not own a hotel, a ski rental store, a restaurant or two, and a reservation system that funnels every visitor into your own businesses in one bow-wrapped package on the Internet? VA was poised to do what had become natural in much of the corporate world but had been a relative rarity in the ski business: mergers and acquisitions on a major scale. VA, which already owned Vail and Beaver Creek ski areas, made a bid in 1996 to take over Breckenridge, Keystone, and Arapahoe Basin ski areas. The new company, renamed Vail Resorts, would own more than 40 percent of the Colorado ski business. An antitrust suit followed, the U.S. Department of Justice telling Vail that they had to give up one of the three acquisitions, and one of them couldn't be Arapahoe Basin, known locally as "A-Basin." (A-Basin was the smallest of the three, and the only one that had no appreciable developable private land near the resort to fill up with condos, hotels, and golf courses.) "The Justice Department told us we could have any two resorts, as long as one of them wasn't A-Basin," Aron says. "We told them we would take any two resorts, as long as one of them *wasn't* A-Basin."

Chutzpah, sure. But that's what happened. Vail won the suit, and for $310 million, it acquired Ralston Corp.'s Keystone and Breckenridge ski resorts. A-Basin, meanwhile, was sold to what one ski industry analyst called a "kissing cousin" of Vail's owners—and the company continues to do joint marketing with Vail on many fronts.

The next step was the $266 million IPO of the new company, Vail Resorts. Aron oversaw the public listing of VRI's shares on the New York Stock Exchange, which resulted in the third largest IPO in history for a Colorado company; it also doubled the corporation's size, and extended its reach into another county, Summit County.

In the Keystone/Breckenridge deal, Aron also acquired thousands of new employees, and different cultures, corporate and civic. "Breck" was an old mining town with a skiing provenance as old as Vail's and an identity already firmly entrenched. Keystone had less of a historic character, but had a corporate persona that was far more laid back than that of its new owners.

Aron, as advertised, set about growing the cash flow. From his years in the hotel, airline, and cruise businesses, Aron had studied baby boomers intently, that demographic bulge whose stock portfolios had fattened along with their waistlines. "There's 75 million of them," says Aron. "A lot of them grew up skiing, and they want to grow old golfing." Soon, there was the purchase of smaller Arrowhead, just down valley from Beaver Creek; and a small ski hill that had been popular with budget-conscious families gave way to slope-side homes that topped out at more than $2 million. Keystone got a new, $10 million golf course, and home*sites* were listed at a cool half million—and more.

With VA's acquisitions, competition for the day skier from the Front Range, which included a growing megalopolis from Fort Collins down to Boulder, Denver, and south to Colorado Springs, was tilted in favor of Vail. VRI now owned the first, second, and third largest ski resorts in the United

States, with $400 million in annual revenues, an enhanced ability to market and bundle, and a marketing budget that dwarfed the smaller, independently owned areas—Loveland, Winter Park, and Eldora—within reach of the Denver day skier.

But capturing more of the uphill transportation business was only one facet of the new régime's designs; they purchased the Jackson Hole Lodge in Wyoming in the hope of moving deeper into the four season, high-end resort business. In Vail, Beaver Creek, Keystone, Breckenridge, and all along the Eagle Valley, the company started an extensive real estate development business and managed restaurants, retail stores, hotels, golf courses, private membership clubs, and wholesale tour and travel businesses; and it acquired a stake in the largest ski rental and retail outdoor sports chain in Colorado when VA merged with Specialty Sports, owned by the Gart family of Colorado. The merger combined seventy stores, twenty-six of which are in the Vail Valley and enjoy total revenues of nearly $70 million. They were well on their way to creating what *High Country News*, Colorado's indigenous muckraking newspaper, called "a recreational empire."

In the eyes of many locals, Aron had taken over with all the grace of a Mafia don running a small-town mall's video arcade. He ostentatiously entertained the high rollers in the Democratic Party, and even had Vice President Al Gore fly in to his Beaver Creek home in a black Secret Service helicopter. Democratic politicians such as House Minority Leader Dick Gephardt and more than a dozen U.S. senators were also Aron's houseguests. He'd lunch with Peter Jennings one day and show Matt Lauer around the next. Over the course of a four-day summer seminar at Beaver Creek, Aron says with pride and amazement, he rubbed fleece elbows with Gerald Ford, former French President Valerie Giscard D'Estang, former South African President F. W. DeKlerk, Secretary of Defense William Cohen, Secretary of Health and Human Services Donna Shalala, Brent Scowcroft, Dick Cheney, Newt Gingrich, and the CEOs of Enron and Dow Chemical. Aron playing host, Vail his hostess.

After the acquisitions, he continued to increase the company's size by purchasing five hotels, including The Lodge at Vail and the Breckenridge Hilton. He boasted that a Ritz Carlton would open up in Beaver Creek, and when the auction for twenty-three Ritz penthouse condos ensued, they sold out in hours—for an all-time record $67.5 million—almost $1,000 a square foot. But as with all empire-building, there's the problem of forcing the conquering army's language and culture on a people who are resistant to it. Locals at Breckenridge were particularly mistrustful of the invading Goths, and even locals in Vail were uneasy with VA's aggressive marketing of four resorts, which might pull customers away from Vail. Rome got restless.

"They came in like gangbusters," says Josef Staufer, a founding businessman at Vail who has been vocal in criticizing VA. "Everybody felt threatened." Staufer pulls out VA's annual report to prove his point. Nonskier revenue went from 25 percent of VA's bottom line in 1997 to 49 percent in 1999. In sheer dollars, Staufer calculated that they made a 274 percent gain in their nonskiing retail business. "Where do you think that came from?" he asks, then answers himself. "It came from the community's pockets. They got it and the small business operator paid for it." As if defending himself from the inevitable charge that he's being unduly critical towards the company town's owners, he points again to the annual report. "These are their numbers, not mine," he says woefully. "Among ourselves we haven't been a ruthless business world. They are willing to destroy what we have built over four decades for this quarter's earnings."

Aron earnestly defends himself. "I think we've done nothing but good for the Colorado ski consumer," he argues. He says his adversaries exaggerate the number of competing businesses they've gotten into, and the effect on the locals' ability to make a living. He acknowledges that when they came in and separated the wheat from the chaff, "there was also a little housecleaning here," which probably alienated some longtime VA workers who lost their jobs.

Some of Aron's perception problems couldn't be avoided. Longtime Vailites felt a deep antipathy toward, as they perceived it, a New York invasion of their beautiful valley. Already, the entire town knew when New Yorkers flocked to Vail during spring break, and, like Paul Revere sounding the alarm, the cries would ring out the week before: "The 212's are coming, the 212's are coming." (The widespread perception was that Aron, Daly, and the rest of VA's management were marionettes whose strings were being pulled from mid-town Manhattan, where the area code is 212.) Indeed, after the IPO in 1997, "New York" exercised tight control over its new charge in the Rocky Mountains. "Let me be honest with you, at the beginning I didn't go to the bathroom without asking them," admits Aron. But as things eased, Apollo had bigger lifts to fry and the New York presence receded. Locally, however, mid- and even upper-level management types continued to use the "New-York-won't-let-me" line when they had to make unpopular decisions.

In 2000, Apollo owned only about 7 million shares, or less than a quarter of the resort. (The largest owner is a mutual fund investment firm, Barron Capital. Ralcorps Holdings, the company that previously owned Keystone, owns 7 million shares.) A full 4 percent of the stock is split, however unevenly, among 350 people in the Vail Resorts management team. Apollo still controls the board of directors, however, and many area residents pointed at Aron when they grew fearful of what they believed was a New York bogeyman stalking the town of Vail.

For his part, Aron is adamant in his defense of the ski area's expansion. "Cat III is the most environmentally sensitive expansion of a ski area in the history of the ski industry," he says, and he's probably right, at least technically. VA studied and restudied the lynx issue, he contends, "by scientists, not just emotional opponents," and cleared hurdle after regulatory hurdle at the local, state, and federal government level, as well as in federal and appellate courts. "The facts and the science support that this will be a highly environmentally conscious expansion," he says. "We're the best developer around."

To Staufer, a longtime local, that was beside the point. What bothered him was the ruthlessness and guile that seemed to accompany the development; they were just so cunning in the way they went about getting what they wanted. The idea that Vail was under the control of evil Machiavellian forces fueled the rumor that began almost before the flames were extinguished: VA, in a cynical attempt to gain public support, had set the fires themselves.

Those who believed that VA had been complicit in setting the fires could not forget a suspicious fire of the previous year, at the Red Tail Lodge in Beaver Creek. Vail had landed the 1999 World Alpine Ski Championships, second in prestige only to the Olympics, but when the town applied to expand the Red Tail Lodge, it was denied. Shortly afterward, some VA workers had been conducting a controlled burn of some slash piles near the restaurant. Because of a heavy downpour, the night watchman left the site unattended around midnight. When workmen returned in the morning, Red Tail was irretrievably burned. Insurance investigators ruled that the fire was probably the result of a lightning strike, but one U.S. Forest Service official says that their detectors didn't register a lightning strike within three miles of the building that night. The insurance company paid for a new Red Tail Lodge, which curiously was bigger than the original —just as VA had wanted.

The echoes of Red Tail floated through town. Hadn't VA executives wanted to expand Two Elk as well, and hadn't they been told to wait at least until the White River National Forest officials were finished with their new, fifteen-year forest plan? And hadn't Two Elk eventually been rebuilt with more insurance money—5,000 square feet bigger than the original?

The original lodge had been impressive in its own right. The Oregon cedar and Arizona lodgepole pine structure had started at 20,000 square feet when it opened in late 1991, and grew to 33,000 square feet the following summer. Two Elk exhibited a seventeen-foot-wide by thirteen-foot-high mural, a reproduction of a petroglyph found on the Ute Mountain Indian Reservation in Cortez, in southwestern Colorado. Two Indian robes, hand-peeled pine tables and chairs, and Southwestern-style rugs greeted skiers ducking in from the wind. The door handles were made of dropped elk horn racks, and each eighteen-inch-diameter pole holding up the structure came from a Douglas fir tree at least one hundred years old. Two Elk's restaurant was one of VA's top moneymakers, pulling in from $30,000 to $40,000 a day in eight-inch, twelve-dollars-a-pop venison sausage pizzas, apple-and-chili-glazed chicken breast, buffalo bratwurst, and cappuccinos.

But if Two Elk was a fancy profit center, PHQ was a dilapidated old thing that everybody knew ought to be replaced. Camp One, which burned down near Two Elk, was not making much money, and VA didn't even bother to rebuild it. It was widely known that VA had taken out business interruption insurance that paid off well into the millions. Two Elk was insured for $4,320,000 and its contents for nearly a million more.

Setting the fires was a risky strategy, but it would be hard to underestimate the rising tide of antipathy toward Aron and the new owners—or the heavy-handedness of Aron and his New York masters, especially vulture investor and business bottom feeder Leon Black. Even inside the company, eyebrows went up early. Paul Witt, head of Vail's public relations squadron, recalls calling Aron in Florida to tell him that the top of the mountain was on fire.

"He didn't seem all that perturbed by it," recalls Witt.

He stops, chooses his words, smiles. "Which I thought was interesting."

7

An Inside Job?

Growth must be prudent, varied and sustainable. It is unfair and unrealistic to "lock up" so much of nature as to prevent the spread of economic activity. But all growth must be calibrated to remain in balance with nature. Human beings must act as stewards of the earth, rather than conquerors and extractors; we must develop a fraternal relationship with the environment.... Reverence for creation, founded on self-restraint, stands in direct contrast to the past boom-and-bust cycles of Colorado's economy.

The dangers of a lopsidedly tourism-dependent commerce are its economic shallowness and the damage it will inflict by overusing the environment....

If the distinct beauty of Colorado—one might say its form or soul—resides anywhere, surely it must dwell, at least part of the year, in the character of this high country and its people. And just as it is possible for a person to lose his or her soul through a lifetime of indifference, so Colorado can lose its distinctiveness, its soul, as a community by failing to pay attention to the changes now taking place....

—FORMER CATHOLIC ARCHBISHOP OF DENVER J. FRANCIS STAFFORD,
IN A 1994 PASTORAL LETTER

The evening before the fires, Sunday night, October 18, fifteen or so mostly college-aged environmental activists sat around a campfire at the base of Two Elk Creek, five miles west of Vail, and discussed the best way to stop Vail's expansion plans. The activists, affiliated with the Boulder-based group Ancient Forest Rescue (often referred to by its initials, AFR), were revved up to stop VA by using any means available. Two days previously, a federal judge had swept away AFR's last, best legal challenge to Vail's Category Three, or "Cat III" expansion, into the vast roadless wilderness on U.S. Forest Service land adjacent to Vail's resort. By all accounts, construction was about to begin the next day, and the environmental activists were fit to be tied.

Ben Doon, a six-foot-two-inch, twenty-eight-year-old with a master's degree in creative writing from the University of Colorado at Boulder, argued that the group should begin civil disobedience the next day by blockading two key access roads. With his short-cropped hair and clean-shaven face, Doon looked more like an ROTC recruiter than an environmental rabble-rouser, and he strategized like a field general. Bulldozers and cranes could enter the Two Elk area only through a pair of access points, Doon explained as he pored over several United States Geological Survey topographical maps of the area. Block those points, and the cranes were going nowhere. Everybody agreed that when the bulldozers came, they would set up roadblocks and stage "tree sits."

AFR had been working the issue hard for more than a year. Besides the federal lawsuit, they had rallied huge crowds at county commissioners' meetings, organized letter campaigns, and drafted detailed rebuttals during the U.S. Forest Service's public comment period. AFR had argued that the undeveloped Cat III area was invaluable wildlife habitat, including an elk calving ground and potential home for the elusive lynx, which the U.S. Fish and Wildlife Service was considering listing as threatened or endangered.

AFR, which had also been protesting a divisive logging effort in the southern part of Colorado, was known for its peaceful civil disobedience, as opposed to Earth First!–style monkey wrenching of tree spikes and of putting sugar in gas tanks. Recently, on southern Colorado's Taylor Ranch, AFR had made itself a significant nuisance to a private landowner whose plans for industrial logging were being opposed by the mostly Hispanic population of the San Juan range, who depended on the water from the mountains above them for agriculture and domestic use.

Although more committed than most, the members of AFR were far from the only Coloradans concerned about their environment. Residents of all backgrounds consistently named growth, development, and quality of life as among the most important issues; even the conservatives who dominated the state legislature couldn't ignore them. With so much attention focused on the use—and abuse—of public lands, Colorado became one of the highest-profile battlegrounds in the country; Vail was one of the highest-profile places of them all. Not only did the name Vail enjoy instant international recognition, but the controversy involved more than the actions of a private company on private land. Vail is situated on a portion of national forest land where a certain amount of development is permitted; the Cat III expansion penetrates land that had been identified as a potential national wilderness area (which by law must remain "untrammeled by man"). Because Colorado was gobbling some 70,000 acres of open space a year for development, the environmentalists fervently believed the Two Elk roadless area, as the Cat III expansion area was dubbed, was worthy of protection. With controversies over growth and development raging throughout Colorado, VA might as well have painted a bull's-eye on its logo when the company decided to expand its resort into an old-growth forest.

In the months leading up to the fires, Doon had rallied with Jeff Berman, who worked for AFR out of Boulder, the university town nestled against a group of rocky outcroppings at the geographical spot where 1,000 miles of Great Plains flatness meets the Rocky Mountain uplift. Boulder, a Democratic island in a sea of western Republicanism, was Colorado's epicenter for environmental activists and progressive politics of all kinds.

Berman, a former electrical engineer for Motorola, had moved to Boulder from Florida in 1993; he quickly lost his interest (and his job) as an engineer as his passions drew him to spend much of his time doing volunteer work for environmental groups. And skiing.

A fiery orator with a penchant for confrontation, a hard-bristle head of brown hair, and an intense gaze, Berman had worked on mining issues for the National Wildlife Federation, one of the country's most staid conservation groups, before getting involved in national forest politics. Although he had hooked up with some AFR types for weekend training in civil disobedience, he mostly followed the mainstream environmentalists' credo of using strategic legal strikes to get things done. Or not done. When Berman heard about Vail's plans to expand into the Category III area, he saw an opening. Taylor Ranch was a good issue, but nobody had ever heard about it and he couldn't get the national press interested. Vail, on the other hand was, well, Vail.

Ted Zukowski, a Yale-educated lawyer who had moved from Washington, D.C., to work for the Land and Water Fund of the Rockies, had already been retained by the Colorado Environmental Coalition to challenge Vail's expansion plans. Zukowski, a bearded thirty-seven-year-old idealist, had mapped a legal strategy that focused on the lynx; this way he could use the Endangered Species Act as a forceful legal wedge. His legal challenges had failed, however, and VA was preparing to begin construction on July 1. Zukowski caught a break when he filed a successful appeal that postponed construction until at least the fall of 1998. He and Berman discussed maybe trying to generate local opposition to Vail's plans in the meantime. Although it wasn't supposed to work that way, the forest service wasn't immune to political pressure.

Thus, Zukowski led the legal fight while Doon and Berman rallied "outsiders" from Crested Butte and Boulder to go up to Vail and organize. There, Berman met Jonathan Staufer, a young Vail entrepreneur (whose father, Josef, was the businessman so dismayed by the numbers in VA's annual reports). Jonathan was a local firebrand with a rich daddy, brown and hazel mismatched eyes, and a reputation for having too much time on his hands. But he was passionate—some would say too passionate—about the environment around Vail.

The younger Staufer came by his awareness honestly because his dad had always supported sensible growth, civility, and comity. "From the beginning, he thought that Vail shouldn't be a soulless entity where people came to visit and never stayed," says Jonathan. "It needed to be a community." Josef Staufer was instrumental in getting projects such as chapels and schools and parks set up in the town. Even as he prospered from the town's remarkable transformation, Josef maintained his passion for its well-being, physically and spiritually.

After high school, Jonathan left his "ideal childhood" in Vail, where he had been skiing since he was two, and went east to Bennington College in Vermont to study creative writing. After college, he returned to Vail. His environmental awareness began budding in simple ways, first by organizing a group to plant trees along the interstate. He soon discovered the vagaries of state bureaucracies when he fought with the Colorado Department of Transportation's regulations over right-of-ways and view corridors. As he puts it: "And then there was Cat III."

After meeting Berman, young Staufer became intimately involved in the fight against Vail's expansion, to the consternation of many locals. Some, who had known Jonathan all their lives, worried that the out-of-town environmentalists were taking advantage of him. Because he was a native and a local businessman with a boutique kitchen supply store called To Catch a Cook, Jonathan was a much more appealing public spokesman for the Cat III opposition than a bunch of tree huggers from the Republic of Boulder. For his part, Jonathan did not care if he was being exploited; if he was more effective talking to Vail locals than Berman was, he'd be happy to do it.

The trio of Doon, Staufer, and Berman put together a slide presentation and headed out on the road. The first stops were the friendly milieu of the state's biggest college campuses, at Colorado State University in Fort Collins and at the University of Colorado's main Boulder campus. They also took to the hills, presenting shows in neighboring Summit County, then in Vail, Avon, and Eagle. They talked to plenty of locals, and slowly began amassing enough supporters to stuff an Eagle County commissioners' meeting with a significant public display of disapproval for VA's expansion plans. At the end of the day, however, Berman, Doon, Staufer, and

Zukowski were left, with the other Cat III opponents, staring at the wrong end of a judge's edict on October 16. By all appearances, VA had won. Cat III would be built after all.

But just because the forest service was cowed by Vail's political pressure and the judge was feckless, they figured they shouldn't just give up and go home. In the meetings just before the date Vail was to begin construction on Cat III, Staufer, Berman, and Doon presided over several gatherings where various strategies were discussed. Some argued that they should place slash piles before the blockades to slow the trucks down, but nobody was arguing for the kind of destructive tricks that could quickly escalate to violence. At least not publicly.

•

As the date for construction to begin grew closer, a group of AFR activists set up camp high on the mountain so they could better scout and plan their acts of civil disobedience. They had already done a fair amount of reconnaissance during the previous summer, before the judge's temporary stay postponed VA's starting date by a few months. Doon felt good about the group—they were all committed—and he knew most of them; he had personally incited quite a few to join the "Stop Super Vail" crusade as he roamed college campuses and showed slides of the endangered lynx habitat. "Getting people pissed off at Vail was kinda my goal," he avows. And Doon knew he had some true believers along with him, which was good because the October weather was turning nasty and it was "diehards only need apply."

When snow fell late in the week, the cold and slush sent the high-altitude camping activists down into the village over the weekend. They hung around Staufer's apartment, meeting all day, continuing their nonviolence training and strategizing. They realized they had a problem. There were only two ways that construction crews could get up the mountain—either up from town on Mill Creek Road or around the back from Minturn up the Two Elk Creek drainage. They noted that hunting season was about to start and that many of the hunters would be using Mill Creek. If they chose to blockade that road, somebody pointed out, the activists would be pissing off rednecks. With guns. After much debate, they decided that they'd stick to the Two Elk drainage: They'd rather face sheriff's deputies with service revolvers than drunk bubbas with rifles who maybe hadn't gotten their elk and might be just as happy bagging a hippie protestor.

On Sunday, the weather cleared and some of the protestors moved camp to the bottom of Two Elk drainage, near Minturn. By that time, some of the students from Ft. Lewis, Durango, and Boulder had gone home, and only about fifteen people were left to discuss what to do next.

All day Sunday, activists armed with walkie-talkies and such handles as "Lodgepole" and "Calamity Jane" had scattered around the mountain on reconnaissance missions. They had picked up the combinations to the on-mountain gates by listening to scanners. A couple of people camped farther up the creek to establish an advance camp; they lugged tents, a two-burner Coleman stove, and, among other things, a hundred Boulder Bars, a high-energy sport food. Huddled around the campfire that night, the scouts reported that despite rumors to the contrary, Vail had not begun operations on the expansion. That meant that the next day, Monday, would probably be D-Day. Word was that a crane was coming 150 miles from Grand Junction to drop a bridge over the creek so the heavy machinery could follow. "We weren't going to do anything until we saw the trucks roll," Doon says. Then, they would have to stop the crane. Somehow.

Staufer and Berman, who had been visiting the camp, went back to Vail that evening: Staufer went to his parents' house because they were on a safari in Kenya, and he spent the night with his two standard poodles, Theo and Bijoux. Berman sacked out at Jonathan's condo.

Just outside of town, Berman had posted a "lookout" armed with binoculars, a police scanner, and a walkie-talkie. He knew that his people at the Two Elk campground would see the crane going up their way. The lookout would see the crane coming up the front of the mountain. Nobody was taking any chances of getting blindsided.

Around midnight, people who were staying at the campground began dispersing into their tents, VW vans, and sleeping bags to brave the cold autumn night ahead. The lookout, meanwhile, huddled in for the night, braced for the cold under layers of fleece and down. Sometime around 5:00 A.M., the scanner started picking up traffic. Something about a fire on the mountain, maybe some gas pipe leaks. He called Berman, who told him to monitor the situation. Berman sounded tired.

Berman glanced up the mountain and thought he saw mist. It was too early in the season for VA to be shooting compressed air mixed with water to make snow, but as it was cold enough outside, Berman didn't put it past the company. Then he thought maybe the forest service was doing a controlled burn on the mountain. The lookout called back; maybe one of them should get over to the campground to warn the others. If others had gone up the trail, they should know about this.

Berman hopped into his car and drove the twenty minutes to Minturn, phoning Staufer en route. Berman asked Staufer to look outside and evaluate his snowmaking theory. Staufer was unequivocal. "That's definitely not snowmaking. That's smoke."

Within what seemed like minutes, Staufer recalls, the phone started ringing and didn't stop. He and Berman had ginned up a few contacts in the media and knew what the obvious question would be. "We knew we had to have a response to this and we needed one right away," Staufer said. "We had to say, 'We're pissed off. This is unbelievable that anybody would do this.' We knew people would look at us, which they were doing anyway."

Over at the Two Elk campground at about 6:00 A.M., Doon was awakened by somebody shouting something about a fire on the mountain. Doon, groggy, crawled out of his tent and saw the smoke plume on the ridge. He realized immediately what the implication of arson meant. "Everybody's immediate fear was that if this was arson, we'd be prime suspects," says Doon. "I expected the feds to start swarming into our campsite." Doon knew that the hunters nearby could probably corroborate their story about camping there all night, but worried about the knee-jerk conclusions that many people would jump to. "There is no way enviros did this," he says.

The fires were on the mountain and had no apparent connection to the imminent construction. The arson turned the environmentalists' organizational work to ashes, as the locals—predictably—rallied behind Vail as the "victim" and shunned the environmentalists. Besides, Doon argued, why would a tree hugger make the point that logging old-growth forests was bad by burning down Two Elk, with its 2,000 tons of wooden beams, acres of cedar shingles, and dozens of thirty-foot-high old-growth Douglas fir poles that had come from 125-year-old trees? Or, for that matter, risk a fire that might spread and destroy the forest they were trying to protect? Whoever lit the fires had an intimate knowledge of the mountain and of VA's security systems, Doon reasoned.

"It had to be," he said with conviction, "an inside job."

PART 2

USUAL —
AND UNUSUAL — SUSPECTS

8

Bummed-Out Ski Bums

Long Island Iced Tea: The Drink of Scalpers

Brad is pretty well toasted at two in the afternoon. The twenty-five-year-old arrived from nearby Breckenridge after a sleepless party night to conduct black market commerce in Vail on a sunny spring day. It's been a good one.

"I made $2,500 bucks in two hours," he says, sipping on yet another Long Island iced tea, a near-lethal mixture of rum, vodka, gin, tequila, sour mix, and a splash of cola. "It's sick. It's crazy."

Brad's "business" is as telling about the composition of a new ski area's workforce as it is about many people's attitude toward VA. Most VA employees receive vouchers for ski tickets—"comp passes"—that can be redeemed for a full-day ticket, worth $61 at full retail. Brad figured out that many of the Mexicans who work at VA's ski areas not only don't ski, they have no idea what the comp passes are for. Brad, who works as a bouncer at a local watering hole, assiduously gathers the comp passes from the Mexicans. "They just give 'em to you," he says. "They don't ski." So today, from 8:00 A.M. to 10:00 A.M., Brad sold discounted lift tickets to skiers and 'boarders who were more than happy to get a 20 percent break on a full-day pass from the lanky six-foot-six-inch blond fellow wearing a full-brim sun hat pulled down almost to his hoop earrings. "The real scam is paying sixty-one fucking bucks for a lift ticket," he says. "I'm not scamming nobody. Except Vail Associates." As if that doesn't even count.

He's got a grudge against the company because it fired him for getting into a fight with a fellow employee. A buddy got caught sneaking onto a lift without a pass, and Brad got involved. This was at Keystone, another resort owned by VA. He says they dropped all the charges, but he still got fired because he didn't show up for work during the month he was in jail. And that wasn't the end of his problems. A short time later, he "beat up a guy who beat up a girl," did some more time in Buena Vista prison, and really found himself on the wrong side of the human resources department. He wanted to get rehired as a snowboard instructor but, even after a mandatory six-month cooling-off period, was blacklisted.

Brad's an astute observer of his potential clientele. "See that couple there," he says, pointing to an impeccably dressed pair wearing matching ski suits and $150 goggles. "They're gapers"—skiers who think they can ski better than they can—"and they'd never buy a ticket from me. They'll say, 'Are you legitimate?'" Another man walks by—"too preppy"—and women in furs—"no way." "Now those girls"—he points out three twenty-something women carting snowboards—"they'll be happy to save ten bucks apiece on a ticket.

"If you live in Vail," he continues philosophically, "you gotta be rich or know somebody who's rich." He sucks down the last of his Long Island iced tea. "Or else you gotta do what you gotta do. I'll be back tomorrow. Even drug dealers in L.A. don't make twenty-five-hundred bucks in two hours."

When an FBI and an ATF agent showed up at Roby Peabody's door in the weeks after the fires, the pair of investigators didn't seem altogether impressed with his excuse that he was in bed sleeping—alone—on the night in question. But after a few queries, they let him be. "They said they were looking for somebody who used to live there," says Roby, the prototype of a modern American ski bum. For his part, Roby was equally unimpressed with the feds and their questions, and was glad when they finally left him alone. "I don't need the police," he says dismissively. "They've never caught me for any of the stupid shit I've done," he adds with a smirk.

Roby had what is perhaps the ultimate ski bum job: Friday through Monday, from 4:30 P.M. until 3:00 A.M., with a half hour for "lunch," he drove a Canadian-made Bombardier snow cat around the mountain "making corduroy," or grooming ski runs. (He has since moved to Telluride.) Roby and his cohorts trafficked the mountain all night in snow cat *remudas*, dragging heavy flat square flaps of grooved metal that flatten and smooth the snow so that skiers would enjoy perfectly groomed surfaces resembling the straight, grooved lines of corduroy. After three years at the job, Roby made $11.80 an hour, enough for him to survive; he shared a house with three others for $1,660 a month ("that's fucking lucky"), and seemed to know every bartender in town—at least at the places that would let him inside.

I had met Roby briefly at the "Cat Box," where the night snow cat drivers congregate to receive their assignments, on a night early in the season when I rode with another groomer. Before the shift began, I told the assembled drivers that I was interested in the fires, but also in how the mountain worked, about the relationship of the town to the ski company. A few days later, at The Daily Grind, a local coffee shop by day and watering hole by night, Roby approached me and started shouting over the live music. "They're fucking taking the spirit out of skiing," he yelled. "They're trying to kill it."

"They," of course, are the executives who run VA, and Roby continued to rail about the way the whole place has "gone corporate." He railed about VA's new "cops on skis"—the "yellow jackets" who stand around yelling at Roby and people like him for going too fast or for skiing out of bounds in the secret powder stashes. He told me his favorite strategies for avoiding the dreaded yellow jackets. The simplest seems to work the best: Catch me if you can. (At the speeds Roby goes and with his knowledge of the mountain's shortcuts, usually the yellow jackets can't.) "They're taking all the fun out of it," he complains. "They're killing the ski bum. It's going to catch up with them."

On the night I meet Roby at the Grind, he's on hour twenty of a twenty-four-hour-long binge to celebrate his twenty-fourth birthday. Hunched over the bar, Roby orders another drink in an unsteady but admirably calculated attempt to regulate a combination of pharmaceuticals and alcohol that will get him through a full circadian bender. At least six feet three inches tall, with a bouncing ball of curly brown hair tucked into a baseball cap, Roby has the gleam in his eye of a young man who is livin' large and lovin' it immensely. When a friend comes up, slaps him on the back, and grabs a drink, Roby wags his gleaming, pierced-tongue ring almost like a Tibetan greeting. The prince of the Vail ski bums, holding court, in his natural habitat.

Roby is deeply philosophical, the way pitchers of Killian's Red can make a young man philosophical. "It was the initial energy driven by the fucked-up ski bums that electrified the industry," he explains. "They're fucking it all up. They're putting a governor on the fun. You're restricted to highway speeds."

Roby casually lists the mind-altering substances he has ingested or imbibed for the epic day-long celebration of his birthday. Mushrooms were indispensable for a low-energy buzz early on. "Romeo and Julio," marijuana, was an essential item on the menu. "We sparked a couple at strategic intervals," he says, now deep into the alcohol phase of the binge at eleven in the evening. He looks, glassy-eyed, around the packed bar, raises his glass in a mock toast. "Vail's a drinking town with a skiing problem." He grins.

A converted skier from Maine, Roby lives to snowboard. Roby's VA-issued season pass and night-shift weekend schedule allow him more than 120 ski days a year, if he doesn't mess up his ankle or his shoulder or some other appendage from careening too fast down a hill and flopping to a stop from high speeds on frozen, crystallized water. No matter he's worked an all-night shift, if the next day is a powder day, he's all over it. He may go to bed at 4:00 A.M., but if there are freshies to be had, he's up at 6:30 and readying himself for first tracks.

"Sleep," he says, "is optional."

Roby embodies the new blood and energy that the sport of snowboarding has brought to the entire ski industry. Although there are a few holdouts, notably Aspen Mountain, Taos, and Alta, most ski areas have embraced the snowboarder culture, even if reluctantly. For the past decade, boarding has been the lifeblood of skiing, the only significant growth area and the one that has injected vitality and the proverbial "big air" into a sport that had become synonymous with aging baby boomers. Boarding culture demands attitude as well as altitude, and it spills out in predictably rebellious ways, such as loud, baggy clothes modeled on inner-city fashions and fast, downhill assaults while exhibiting borderline control. Roby, for one, hates Vail's attitude toward what he sees as the main source of cosmic energy on the mountain—him and his "posse." To hear this poet-boarder philosophize, one would think he and his friends are the only thing standing between the pure downhill experience and a homogenized, groomed, and unexciting imitation. Roby thinks Vail, with its increasingly snobbish ways, is especially culpable. "VA is all about making money," he expounds. "They don't want the young rebels of skiing here at Vail. But that's what's driving the industry. We don't have the money but we have the energy that makes the industry go." Roby points, appropriately, to the Warren Miller–type ski films, the marketing, everything the industry tries to promote in its advertising campaigns. "Big air. Extreme this. Extreme that. Yet Vail is stifling all that to make money. It's like taking grandma's cooking and putting the federal government in charge of it."

Roby grew up in the small town of Bridgton, Maine, in the southwestern part of the state, a self-described wuss who got into a few too many drugs and a little too much trouble in high school. He had to get out or spend the rest of his life pumping gas. "I just didn't like the people. Too conservative." An uncle worked at Telluride, and Roby came out to visit one year. He sold his skis, bought a snowboard. And stayed.

For two years in Telluride, he was the classic ski bum in a ski town where self-control was a rare commodity. He worked as a lift operator ("liftop") for a while, which he describes as "the most thankless job ever. Be kind to lift operators." He learned to drive some of the snow grooming machinery, and parlayed that experience into driving a Bobcat in the summers, when he worked at landscaping. Even Roby knew he was living a little too large. "I spent the whole summer on mushrooms," he says. "I had to move."

Vail appealed to him. He had friends who had migrated there, and he knew the place was so big that he could probably get his dream ski-bum job as a night snow-cat driver. He remembers his first meeting with the snow cat supervisor, Marvin Gray, an ex–rodeo rider who wore cowboy boots when he wasn't wearing ski boots. Roby came in, tongue pierced, hair in dreds, and sporting a Grateful Dead tie-died shirt. "You know, some people in the company wouldn't take a liking to your looks," Gray deadpanned.

Roby was hired nonetheless, removed the tongue stud before his shifts, and learned the cat-driving ropes the hard way. "The first year was hell," he recalls. He was hazed by a couple of old-timer cowboy types, who sandwiched him in the middle of their armada of three snow cats for eight hours at a time. "It was like, they were watching my every move," he says. "At one point I just said fuck it and went in. I came back the next day, though, and I coulda swore that I saw some money exchange hands between the two of them. One of them bet that I wouldn't be back."

He blew out his knee in 1996 in a boarding accident. "I totally destroyed my right one," he says, nonchalantly. "ACL, MCL, both meniscus." The complete list of Roby's career injuries is as long as his string-cheese legs: concussions (no, he doesn't wear a helmet), shoulders, ankles, wrists, ribs, both knees. Snowboarding can be a high-impact sport.

For all his rebelliousness, Roby knows his grooming cold; he's willing to do the devil's bargain to keep his dream job. He says he never shows up to work high, never drinks on the job. The cat-driver culture is strict, and if you make a mistake, you have to pay fines in beer to the other drivers. "I almost ran over a mechanic who was under the cat when I started it up," he says. "That was a case of beer."

But even if Roby doesn't fire up on the job, he makes no secret that his off-hours proclivities occasionally include the ingestion of contraband, despite the drug-testing policy. What about the drug testing, I ask. "If they happen to catch me on the wrong week, I might be out of a job," he says, but emphatically states that it would be "insane" to be high while driving his rig on the mountain. "If they get me after I've been polluted, I have to take responsibility for my actions."

He doesn't think the drug testing is that big a deal, except when the company uses it as a club to punish people. "It's supposed to be random," he says, but he knows somebody who "got randommed" after he got into a tiff with his supervisor. "It's a filtering system to keep people in line if your attitude sucks," he says. "They can random you any time they want." He points out that VA isn't too heavy-handed about drug testing because the company's insurance has to pay drug rehab bills for a first offender. But if anybody screws up and breaks something, it's testing for sure. "If you do over five hundred dollars in damage, you gotta go pee."

Many of the longtime employees on the mountain had become fed up with the new régime—with drug testing, poor pay, stricter dress codes that include no facial hair, and a general feeling that the ski bum life was tanking. Used to be that the drudgery of working in the ski world's service economy was offset by the perks of living in a ski town that unofficially declared powder days after big dumps. But that was changing dramatically. The ski bums were bummed out. Some of them wondered whether dramatic action wasn't required before it was too late.

●

When a group of ski instructors at Vail asked some union reps from the United Auto Workers to pay a visit to the ski area, Harold P.* knew that

---

* "Harold," who still works for VA, asked for a pseudonym because he feared losing his job and benefits.

things were pretty bad. A twenty-year veteran of the Vail professional ski corps, Harold and his ilk were the last of the great freelancers; they spent their summers in Belize or New Zealand, and lived to the hilt the idealized life of the professional ski bum. In normal times, nobody had thought much about unionizing.

But when VA went public two years previously, things began to change for the worse. Some of the instructors were getting fed up, and the situation was going beyond the normal late-night bull sessions over margaritas at their favorite bar, ironically named Vendettas.

For Harold, VA's latest maneuvers had pushed him to the brink. The year previously, the cost of private ski lessons went up appreciably, but the base salary of instructors didn't. Why the hell should VA pull in $435 for an all-day private lesson, when the junior ski instructors were paid less than seventy-five bucks of that? VA would make instructors hang around for hours, even if they didn't end up with enough students; then VA would throw the instructors a lousy ten-spot. In 1998, the ski-instructor supervisors had received a hefty raise, but the rank and file got a zero percent raise in their base pay. Even small perks, like ski passes for Harold's wife and kids, were being slowly whittled away. VA was cutting back on child care for workers, as well. "Goddamn," thought Harold. "The whole feel of the place has changed. Conditions and pay were never great, but at least the place used to be fun."

The ski patrollers, too, had faced the end of an era when the resort ownership changed. Patrollers pride themselves on their training and ability to brave avalanches, adverse conditions, and idiotic skiers to save anybody who needs help. The group had become legendary for everything— from saving visitors' lives with defibrillators at 11,000 feet to winning a bet by having sex in a toboggan while being taken down the mountain by fellow patrollers. In the old days, the patrol and assorted hangers-on would snowmobile to the top of the mountain with cases of beer and settle in for a wild night of partying. They regularly cranked up Chair 5 and skied the back bowls by moonlight. As recently as the mid-1990s, patrolmen could quietly ask their supervisors for permission to head up to PHQ with a girlfriend or a couple of buddies to party atop the mountain. But that changed after a food service guy hit a patrolman's snowmobile loaded with cases of beer. Kevin Latchford, a thirty-six-year-old patrolman known as "Latch," says that these days, "nobody even bothers to ask." Latch moved to Vail when he was eighteen, planned to stay for a year, and ended up a classic ski bum story: "Seventeen years later, I'm still here." Latch had been scheduled to move into the apartment at PHQ that burned down, a primo mountaintop pad with a zero dollar rent; he had intended to spend the weekend before the fires up there putting the final touches to his on-mountain apartment.

VA was cutting back so far that the patrollers were being asked to clean the patrol shack's bathrooms, an indignity that most patrollers considered unpardonable. One patrolman reports that his former boss said, "Employees are like toilet paper on a roll. There's more where that came from."

The clients weren't much better. Many of the wealthy patrons expected the patrolmen to help them put their ski boots on the correct feet and call on the patrol phones to have the emergency dispatchers make restaurant reservations; these clients saw the patrolmen as little more than on-the-mountain babysitters and event coordinators. With the advent of Adventure Ridge and such gimmicks as laser tag, corporate special tours, and pricey private "first tracks" programs for VIPs and the like, "it's more like Disneyland every day," says Dennis Mikottis, also known as "Buffalo," who started in 1965 and has the distinction of being the longest-running patrolman on the mountain. "Guests don't treat you with respect. They think you're their tour guides," he says. But whatever the patrolmen thought about the current ownership, not many mourned the passing of PHQ, according to Buffalo: "Hell, we used to think we should just burn it down so they'd build us a new one."

Harold the ski instructor was clinging to a small home as real estate prices were driving property taxes and his expenses through the A-frame roof. He had attended some of the meetings in opposition to Vail's expansion, but had the sense that he shouldn't be seen there because VA's spies attended the meetings. "I feel I can't speak out for fear of losing my job," he complains. He needed the rare space in subsidized day care for his child, and he knew of VA employees who had been subtly dissuaded from environmental activism. Everywhere Harold looked, the Vail he loved was almost unrecognizable.

It was predictable that some of that animosity would be directed at Adam Aron and the New York owners of Vail Resorts. In many ways, Harold felt, Vail was not unlike a West Virginia company coal town where the paychecks were delivered in scrip for the groceries purchased at the company store. The cost of living, even in company-subsidized housing, was eating their paychecks. Everything, from gas to milk, was more expensive, but wages were stagnant. And tourists were increasingly being fleeced by VA's ever-expanding reach. "Of every dollar that comes into this valley, the majority of the pennies end up in their pocket," says Harold. To his eye, VA's vertical integration simply wasn't appropriate. "In a small market like this where people have started their lives in a small economy, it's not as ethically viable."

Ski instructors, of course, knew the mountain cold. So did the professional ski patrollers. All the on-mountain people—lift operators, snowmakers, groomers, and lift mechanics—knew where the gasoline caches were. Where the avalanche control dynamite was hidden. Who was on the mountain, and when. And how to get around the mountain at any time of the day —or night.

Harold wonders aloud whether it was just a coincidence that the fires happened at a time when Latch, the on-mountain ski patrol caretaker, happened to be gone for a week. The time the fires started was probably the only window in the entire year when somebody wasn't on the mountain. Not many people knew that.

"Kind of peculiar," says Harold with a bemused look. "Don't you think?"

■

On the morning of the fires, Roby says he got an early morning call from a friend: "Take a look at the mountain, it's burning." Roby, who lives on the north side of the valley and couldn't see the mountain from his pad, drove to Potato Patch across the valley and gawked. "It was like, sweet," he told me later. "Right on. Someone stood up against those fuckers."

Roby had his own reasons for opposing the Cat III expansion. Normally, the idea of having more shreddable terrain was a no-brainer for the likes of Roby. If there were more powder runs, there'd be more freshies, more secret stashes to hoard. But he had heard that VA, as a mitigation measure to appease the Colorado Division of Wildlife, had agreed to limit access to the East Vail Chutes and Mushroom Bowl, both existing locals' caches of out-of-bounds powder that were like magnets for Roby and his clan.

On the strength of the Mushroom Bowl closure rumor, a local powder hound named Adam Heller organized a ragtag group of skiers and boarders who were targeting the Cat III expansion for selfish reasons. "It was pure, greedy ski-bum mentality," says Roby. "I didn't want to see any terrain taken away. The chutes are the steepest, gnarliest terrain we have out there; I didn't want to see 'em lock it up." The 11th Mountain Alliance was conceived and organized at the eleventh hour; two months before the fire, Roby joined up. "I paid my twenty bucks and attended a coupla meetings," he says. "Then the fires happened."

9

What about the Little Guy?

Do we want to develop Colorado as a national tourist Mecca, par excellence, or do we want the state to deteriorate into just another second-rate industrial complex with too little water, too much smog, too many people and all the scars and blight that industrialization inevitably brings?

—VA's FIRST VICE PRESIDENT FOR PUBLIC RELATIONS,
BOB PARKER, WRITING HIS "PARKER PENS" COLUMN IN THE *VAIL TRAIL*, 1/13/67

For many local business owners, the first empire-building moves of the ski area's new régime exacerbated long-standing tensions between the town of Vail and VA. For Kaye Ferry, owner of The Daily Grind, the locals' favorite coffee shop in Vail Village, the anger boiled when she decided to expand her restaurant by knocking out a closet to add more seating. When she made her applications, she was in for a rude surprise. The town of Vail was asking $16,000 in mitigation for adding a table for four, which included paying into a parking fund. Ferry agreed that the need was there for parking, but was angry anyway. "VA doesn't have to do this," she reasoned. "They don't have to pay into a parking fund. They don't pay city sales tax. It's not fair."

Because VA operated on leased federal land, all the company's on-mountain businesses were exempt from the town's 8.5 percent sales tax. VA also owned much of the land and many of the buildings for its off-mountain businesses, which meant the company wasn't paying the same extortionate rents that Ferry had to pay. To operate the Grind, Ferry paid a typical $145 a square foot for her space on the prestigious Bridge Street in the heart of old Vail Village. That's about four times the price of some of the best retail space in Denver's equally prestigious Cherry Creek. "I would be very surprised if there were five coffee shops in the U.S. that pay more than I do in rent," she says. "And I'm only in business half the year."

When Ferry got wind of the fires, she didn't seem surprised at all. "If they had set out three years ago with a mission statement saying, 'We're going to do everything we can do to ruin our reputation in the Vail Valley,' they couldn't have done a better job," she explained. "They've pissed off so many people on so many levels. You could put a dart board on the wall to take your pick of suspects."

As president of the Vail Village Merchant's Association, Ferry knew a lot of business owners who were ticked off. She thought about the owners of the Red Lion, the local watering hole that was suffering because of Vail's cut-rate prices for on-mountain cocktails and après-ski fare. Who wouldn't want to take a free gondola ride to have a discounted drink atop the mountain? "There are people who are out of business or are afraid of going out of business because of the competition with VA," says Ferry, a fiery silver-haired fifty-eight-year-old with ice-blue eyes. "You can't compete fairly with them."

Ferry is one of Vail's more colorful civic participants—and some might say she's a gadfly. An heiress of a Chicago-area car dealership fortune, she moved to Vail in 1988 after a divorce, and didn't look back. Because she can be seen making cappuccinos at six in the morning when one of her employees—she calls them "my kids"—has a hangover or just blows off work, many people in town don't understand what league Ferry is in financially. She has also been a VA ski instructor for years, mostly filling in from time to time and making herself available when preferred clients come to town or during the Christmas rush. "I've got to be the hardest working person in Vail who doesn't need a job," she says. "I can play with the big boys," she remarks modestly, and isn't afraid to jet off to Cabo San Lucas for a long weekend to escape the winter's tedium. "But I care about this place, and they're fucking it up. It's enough to make you give up on democracy."

Ferry owns several homes and lots around the Vail area, and may have the most expensive employee housing in town. Her second house, on the golf course, is worth at least $2 million, and is where she puts "her kids"—the workers who pull the cappuccinos and mochas for her customers. The "kids," mostly in their early twenties, are indoctrinated into the ways of Vail by a volatile combination of Ferry's rants about the civic ineptitude of VA and the underground rebellion of the Roby Peabody crowd. Her other house, where she lives with her one-eyed cat, Holden, is a modest (by Vail standards) two-story duplex in East Vail. The Grind itself is a coffee bar by day and a bar with music by night—where Roby spent part of his birthday bender.

Ferry is especially tired of VA's not taking responsibility for its enormous impact off the mountain. "In the late sixties, they gave the city two pieces of mud for parking lots," she says, dismissively. "The town now has a $22 million debt for the parking structures, and parking is a constant problem. VA says they gave the town the land so they have no further responsibility besides paying two dollars per lift ticket into a free bus shuttle system that their customers use." For Ferry to put a small addition into her coffee shop, she's looking at paying $22,000 per space. "What I'm thinking about is how many cups of coffee I have to sell to make that worthwhile," she says.

For Ferry, it was VA's arrogance that really got to her. She once raised the sales tax issue at a town council meeting and was met with shrugs. Afterwards, VA's Porter Wharton III gloated: "By the way, Kaye, we're never paying sales tax. Ever."

•

Ferry was the most vocal but not the only merchant upset with the way things were going. Packy Walker, one of the town's most notorious characters, is a grown-up ski bum who's made a pretty good living out of Vail—and he was fed up, too.

Walker's legend dates back to the early 1960s, when he wanted to know whether people would miss him if he left. So he arranged for his own funeral. He disappeared for a few weeks, then climbed into a coffin in the back of a 1957 black Chevy convertible and held a wake. He painted his face white, got high inside the coffin, and placed a rubber duck on his chest. As he "lay in state" at the Pig 'n Whistle watering hole, he suddenly had the urge to pee. So he got up and gave a speech to the three hundred people who attended, then headed to the bathroom.

Walker and many of the old-time locals bemoan the loss of "fun" from the place in its current incarnation. It's not that he pines for the days when he and his buddies would regularly steal the Vail Police Department's cruisers, or commandeer a city bus to go drinking in Minturn—but maybe a little more frivolity wouldn't hurt. Not that he hasn't tried. At a Fourth of July parade the year after the fires, Walker dressed in his kilt and painted a sign saying, "Save the Links." The authorities told him there was to be no political grandstanding, and Walker raised his hackles. "Somebody has to stand up for the golf courses," he said. When Walker refused to beg off his mock protest, he was arrested. "I don't know if the cops could spell," he deadpans.

Walker owns the Lift House condominiums, and has watched rising rents and competition from VA make life more difficult for the independent business owner. "You might make your landlord's mortgage payments, but you can't make yours," he complains. All in all, he says, things appear to be going to hell around him. "The corporate world hasn't done very much for this town," he says.

■

A few months before the fires, Ferry's antagonistic relationship with VA became heated. Ferry had been in partnership with a couple of other people at The Daily Grind, but they had decided to sell out. Ferry had reluctantly agreed to put the Grind on the market. Almost immediately, Starbucks came in with an offer; the partners all agreed that it was reasonable and that they would probably go ahead.

A few days later, VA's president, Andy Daly, called Ferry and told her, "You won't be getting an offer from Starbucks, Kaye." Daly explained that he had just gotten back from New York, where he had met with "Leon and Adam"—Leon Black and Adam Aron—and that VA had forged some kind of exclusive arrangement with Starbucks in Vail. The long and short of it was that VA had the right to veto the location of any Starbucks store in Vail, and they had decided that The Daily Grind would not be sold to the Seattle coffee chain. Although Ferry appreciated Daly's reasoning—"I am not going to be responsible for putting out of business the only place the locals call their own," he told her—she was nonetheless aghast that VA would throw its weight around like that. "They did this and I *know* about it," she says. "You have to assume that this is not an isolated incident."

Ferry's confrontations with VA, both personal and by proxy, were almost a weekly occurrence. Local journalists knew that Ferry was always good for a no-holds-barred quote on any subject. Just a few months before the fires, Ferry had spoken her mind at a community meeting in the Municipal Building. To VA's company line that the town had better work more cooperatively with the ski area's owners because "a rising tide raises all boats," Ferry snorted. "You know, we all sink together, too," she said.

Ferry was especially concerned that ever since Vail Resorts had packaged themselves as four separate destinations (Breckenridge, Keystone, Beaver Creek, and Vail), they weren't putting as much effort into marketing Vail as a unique entity; they were getting entirely too big for their ski britches. After the meeting, Robin Litt, an assistant to Daly, came up to Ferry and delivered a message from her boss. Litt told Ferry that VA wouldn't support merchants' projects—such as an employee training program—Ferry recalls, "until Andy and I ironed out our differences." "Is this intended to be a threat?" Ferry replied. "Tell whoever sent you that I am not threatened by Vail Associates."

After the fires, Ferry expressed a local's dismay that the mountain had been vandalized, but wondered whether the event would take down VA's arrogance quotient a notch or two.

And where was Ferry on the night of October 18?

"I don't remember," she says. "But I can't even remember where I put my glasses, either."

10

Mink Liberation

Earth Liberation Front Guidelines:

To inflict economic damage to those who profit from the destruction and exploitation of the natural environment.

To reveal and educate the public on the atrocities committed against the environment and all the species that cohabitate [*sic*] in it.

To take all necessary precautions against harming any animal, human and non-human.

—FROM AN ELF LINK ON THE ANIMAL LIBERATION FRONT'S WEB SITE

Nearly five hundred miles from Vail, across the Rocky Mountains, the western slope of Colorado, and the Wasatch Range that marks the beginning of the Great Basin in Utah, Agent Lee Perry of the Utah Criminal Investigations Bureau perked up his ears. The initial news reports of the Vail arsons had hit the national airwaves early Monday morning, and Perry was a lot more interested than your average citizen in Vail's misfortune. In his Salt Lake City office filled with colored plastic chairs and imitation wood grain institutional tables, Perry turned to one of his colleagues and said, "I bet our guys had a hand in that."

"Our guys" was a loosely knit group of anarchic arsonists in Utah that Perry and a task force of Salt Lake area and federal law enforcement officials had been watching carefully and prosecuting occasionally. They had nailed one, Josh Ellerman, for bombing the Utah Fur Breeders Agricultural Co-op in Sandy, which provides food for the state's $20-million-a-year mink industry, and some other punks they had eventually convicted for "liberating" minks from a fur farm in Salt Lake County. (Jacob Kenison, one of the mink liberators and a strict vegan, had also set fire to a leather store in Murray, Utah.) Something was familiar—and fishy—about the Colorado fires. Although the first reports weren't *saying* arson, Perry had a hunch that it was.

Perry had been hard at work amassing a profile of so-called "straight-edgers," an odd subculture that spawned a no-drinking, no-smoking, ska-music-listening crowd of radicals, who not only were vegetarian but refused to wear leather or to use any animal products. The straightedge movement had started on the East Coast, but had taken an unusually firm hold in Mormon Utah, which saw more body piercing and tattoos than drug use and free sex and was a natural place for a rebel subculture to take root.

The more radical fringe of the straightedge crowd called themselves "hardliners" and aligned themselves politically with the militant—and violent—animal-rights group known as the Animal Liberation Front, or ALF. These were the true believers, and Perry thought them capable of just about anything. The ALF, with its roots in the British antivivisectionist movement, had been implicated in or had claimed responsibility for a series of worldwide sabotage efforts that targeted animal research labs, fur farms, and the meat industry with what they called "actions." In similar arsons, mink "liberations," releases of laboratory animals, and explosions using nail-spiked pipe bombs, the ALF had left its mark all over the United States and Europe.

One of ALF's signatures, a macabre calling card, was to leave at the scene swaths of graffiti in red paint, which appeared to be blood. The movement had also developed a pattern of issuing detailed claims of responsibility; these were circulated anonymously over the Internet and then released to the media through "spokespersons" who maintained plausible deniability of firsthand knowledge of the crime or its perpetrators.

The ALF was not alone. Ever since Edward Abbey's novel, *The Monkey Wrench Gang,* inspired such radical groups as Earth First! to forsake the national conservationists' strategy of lobbying and filing lawsuits to change environmental laws, a sporadic guerilla war of so-called ecotage has targeted the traditional extractive industries that industrialized the West. The actions peaked in 1986, when so-called monkey wrenchers cut power lines to a nuclear power plant in Arizona. The radical group drew the attention of the FBI, which launched a two-year probe that "pretty much beheaded the radical environmental movement," as Susan Zakin, author of *Coyotes and Town Dogs: Earth First! and the Environmental Movement,* told *Mother Jones.*

With the 1990 arrest of Earth First! founder Dave Foreman and four other members—and the subsequent car bombing of two other Earth First! leaders—Zakin said that "people realized that if they called themselves Earth First!ers, they might as well have an 'Arrest Me!' sign on their back. It sobered them up." Some, as Foreman did, abandoned the group; others, convinced that illegal direct action was the only sure way to further the cause, went underground.

Meanwhile, North American animal liberation groups, ALF among them, stepped up attacks on fur farms, meat packers, and animal laboratories. Inspired by England's antivivisectionist and animal rights radicals, ALF leaders started calling for the joining of forces with the radical environmental movements.

Perry had noted that the ALF had recently been linked to a strange sister organization that called itself the Earth Liberation Front, or ELF. The ELF, which had publicly affiliated itself with the ALF in a joint communiqué issued on September 22, 1993, before claiming credit for burning a U.S. Forest Service pickup truck in the Willamette National Forest in Oregon a month later, was still relatively unknown. Some of the ELF claims were tangential, at best, to their environmental message; for example, in an action on June 28, 1998, the ELF claimed credit for spraying red paint on the Mexican Consulate in Boston to protest the treatment of peasants in Chiapas, Mexico.

The ELF had claimed responsibility, or co-responsibility, for a release of horses and a failed arson at a corral owned by the Bureau of Land Management in Rock Springs, Wyoming, just weeks before the Vail arson; ELF had also claimed responsibility for destroying several of the U.S. Department of Agriculture's animal damage control buildings the previous June, in Washington State. The U.S.D.A.'s Wildlife Research Center hit by ALF allegedly euthanized wild "pest" animals—thus a natural target. Wisconsin suffered a mink and ferret "liberation" of some 170 animals in July 1998, and the U.S. Forest Service had been targeted in 1996, when a vehicle was set on fire. The ALF and ELF had also claimed joint responsibility in the winter of 1995 for burning an Oregon corral to protest the roundup and slaughter of wild horses.

Agent Perry knew that if the ELF was anything like the ALF, they would soon be a force to be reckoned with. The ALF didn't shy away from its intent to wreak as much havoc as possible. Its Web site held forth about various levels of civil disobedience and not-so-civil disobedience, including a step-by-step arson lesson: "Your guide for putting the heat on animal abusers everywhere." One detailed page explained how to set fires by using plastic jugs filled with a diesel-gas mixture and stuffed with gasoline-soaked sponges.

Trouble was, investigators knew that these days just about anybody with a modem could have taken the advice—and that really meant just about anybody.

Perry also knew that these people were growing smarter with every action. Increasingly, they operated in secrecy, in small cells that had no equivalent of a "Mr. Big" calling the shots. Once a small group decided on a plan, members kept their chores separate; this way, they could never testify against one another. As did drug kingpins, the activists often enlisted "juvies," or underaged activists, to light the match; if the kids were arrested, they'd never do time. The groups may not have had a mink-loving John Gotti running the show, but Perry knew even the loosest groupings had a code of enforcement against rats that was "about as close as you can get to the Mafia." Perry's point is well taken, even if it's overstated; ALF defectors were more likely to get a beating from the group's self-styled "Justice Department" than a pair of cement overshoes.

Via sophisticated Web-site primers containing how-to lessons in encrypting e-mail or staking out targets, the ALF had fashioned the ultimate dis-organization—an amorphous collection of radicals whose beliefs and Internet connections were all that bound them together. Every time law enforcement busted one of the activists because he or she had made a fatal mistake, somebody else learned the lesson and posted it on the Internet.

The resulting ultraloose structure has confounded law enforcement agencies, which have solved only a handful of the dozens of illegal actions claimed by the ELF and ALF since the early 1990s. Radical animal rights types don't keep membership lists, require annual fees, apply for grants from the Pew Foundation, or put out glossy monthly magazines. Anyone logging on to ALF's Web site is told that "someone 'joins' the ALF simply by doing ALF actions." The site implores potential adherents to take matters into their own hands rather than look for the next annual meeting or local chapter cookout. An example is a posting from a young woman who claims to have sabotaged a McDonald's restaurant. "At one point, I wrote an animal rights group letting them know I would be willing to help them raid a lab. Needless to say, that letter went unanswered. Would anyone who put hundreds of hours in planning a covert, illegal direct action that could land them in prison for years risk asking a basic stranger for help simply because he or she is a vegetarian or belonged to a local animal rights chapter? No! So how did I, or how do you, end up joining the ALF? That's easy! Come up with your own plan!"

Labeling the groups "domestic terrorists" on par with the Unabomber and convicted Oklahoma City bomber Timothy McVeigh, U.S. Justice Department officials and antienvironmentalists such as Wise Use movement founder Ron Arnold have lobbied Congress to redirect millions to fight the so-called ecoterrorists. Unlike the government's earlier success in neutralizing such groups as Earth First!, investigators have been largely unable to infiltrate the animal liberationists' disconnected cells or to decode their ciphered e-mails. Instead, they've gone after aboveground ALF spokespersons, one of whom is Rod Coronado, a thirty-two-year-old Yaqui Indian who kept tabs on the Cat III fight from an Arizona prison while finishing a fifty-seven-month sentence for aiding the torching of a Michigan animal lab. Craig Rosebraugh, the Portland, Oregon–based mouthpiece for the "Liberation Collective"; and Katie Fedor, a Minneapolis-based spokesperson for ALF "actions," also drew attention from authorities. Rosebraugh and Fedor had maintained a strict discipline in distancing themselves from those who committed the actions. At least so far.

To Perry, Vail made sense as a target. After all, to save the animals, these new animal rights activists figured, you also need to save the land the critters live on. Jeff Long, Salt Lake City's fire inspector, had worked with Agent Perry in solving the ALF arsons, and had the same first hit that Perry had. "It didn't surprise me that they picked an area that was so remote," he says. Still, Long didn't want to jump to conclusions in the days after the fires. "Eliminate the obvious first," he had said, and explained that he'd start with disgruntled employees or others who had an obvious beef with the ski area's owners. Arson was generally a property crime committed in the heat of the moment, so to speak. Of all insurance claims for fire damage, about half the fires turn out to have been deliberately set. Of that half, nearly 40 percent are committed by property owners.

One thing was clear to the Utah law enforcement types: No matter who these ALF or ELF radicals were, their people did their homework. One convicted Canadian ALF activist, Darren Thurston, in a lengthy interview on an Internet site, said he had staked out a University of Alberta facility for several days and nights to familiarize himself with the routines; he had noted when employees came and went, who lived there, what security was present. He had borrowed road maps and aerial maps of the area from the public library. He had picked a night with a new moon and little activity. (The Vail fires took place on a moonless night, also.) Before he and his team went in, they had familiarized themselves with the area, with the plan, and with alternative escape routes. The night before the raid, they filled a duffel bag with drills, radios, and scanners. They took a supply of their signature "blood"—thinned red paint contained in plastic two-liter soda bottles. Thurston got caught, however, when a woman in charge of "re-homing" the liberated lab cats turned in the liberators.

Perry wondered whether the investigators at Vail would catch a break like that. If they didn't, nailing the culprit might be tough.

11

Footprints in the Snow

Vail has now reached the stage where it should no longer be a "company town" and the main problem would be how extensive should the corporate limits be....

—2/4/66 EDITORIAL BY GEORGE "THE SKIPPER" KNOX,
WHO FOUNDED THE *VAIL TRAIL* IN OCTOBER 1965

We're not really the masters of our destiny. We are a company town.

—FORMER VAIL TOWN COUNCILMAN MERV LAPIN, 1/27/89

Despite the airspace closure for civilians, a Denver news station got through and began beaming images of Two Elk's eerie skeletal remains—the kinds of images that were already leading Agent Perry in Salt Lake to his own conclusions.

Up on the mountain, the fire department and the sheriff's department were busy hashing out a difference of opinion. The fire guys wanted a helicopter with a drop bucket to make sure the blaze was completely extinguished before it had a chance to spread should winds come up. But Sgt. Mike McWilliam from the Eagle County Sheriff's Department told them that available Hueys wouldn't be able to transport much water at this altitude, and that he preferred to use the Air National Guard chopper to do some recon. McWilliam won the argument; an Air National Guard pilot and a spotter wearing infrared goggles flew the perimeter of the fire area scanning for suspects, scanning for anything. But they saw nothing but forest.

McWilliam had arrived at Two Elk by about 6:30 A.M., before Two Elk was completely engulfed. The east side was roaring, but the west, north, and south sides were still catching on. It didn't take long from then. By 7:15 A.M., Patrol Headquarters simply, but loudly, collapsed; and an hour later, Two Elk followed suit—a stunning crunching of glass and timbers and flame. At 8:43 A.M., two sheriff's deputies reported spotting cross-country ski tracks in the snow and fresh footprints. Other 911 calls came in reporting the unusual vehicular traffic that people had seen that morning. One report of a white male who "wasn't a hunter" and who was wearing a gray wool hat, blue jeans, and a blue frame pack and tent sounded promising. Maybe.

The morning after the fires, Neil Sebso, the hunter who had been sleeping in the bathroom at the top of the mountain when the fires were set, remembered something haunting that he thought he had dreamed. He remembers being startled at some point during the night when he thought the door to the bathroom was pulled ajar. "I swore I heard the door open,"

Sebso recalls. He thought perhaps it was his friends trying to scare him, so he went to the window and checked but saw nothing. Sebso wonders whether the outhouse would have been torched as well if those who started the fire hadn't found out he was in the building. And, he thought with a shudder, there was no guarantee that he would have gotten out alive.

Dave Alt wondered whether maybe the authorities were having second thoughts about the hunters' role in the fires. On Wednesday, he and his buddies were asked to show up in Avon to talk to some more law enforcement types. Each of the four hunters was assigned an FBI and an ATF agent, interviewed separately about the night's events, and fingerprinted. Steve told his questioners that he had seen a Ford or a Dodge truck on the mountain Friday night, which was unusual because the truck wasn't a company vehicle; to drive onto the mountain, the driver had to get through a gate. The truck was green and two young men in their twenties were inside: one Hispanic, one Caucasian. They had said they did contract work on the mountain, so they knew the combination to the gate lock. "They said they were just driving around," Steve recalled to the feds.

Later, the feds took them up the mountain, again separately, and made them walk through the evening's events. Where had the fires started? Where did it seem to be the hottest? Were the flames low or high? What parts were more on fire than others? "Steve's pictures helped," says Dave Alt.

Media types, satellite trucks, and rumors were all pouring into town, fueled by the mass and macabre adrenaline of a nationally breaking story. One rumor had it that the huts where dynamite was stored for avalanche control had been broken into. Were the fires just a decoy? Was there reason to believe more was to come? Paul Cacioppo, a self-styled local journalist and one of the strangest of the town's gadflies, asked questions about bombs at the morning press conference. He had heard there had been a bomb scare, but no confirmation came from law enforcement.

For Kim Andree, who had been the sheriff's department's point person for the media when a $9 million Air Force A-10 Warthog fighter plane had inexplicably veered off course during a training flight in Arizona in 1997 and crashed in Eagle County, the rumors, and the throb of the national press, were eerily familiar. Then, she had to contend with the suspicion that the pilot had secretly landed and all the ordnance on the plane had been spirited away by antigovernment militia members. "Here we go again," she thought.

Investigators were starting to wonder about the timing. To pull this off during the first days of hunting season must have been a calculated gamble. Enough people were roaming around the mountain that a few more wouldn't draw much attention; yet that meant there were a number of potential witnesses, such as a young hunter sleeping in the bathroom.

And why wasn't the patrolman at PHQ that night? Normally, a full-time caretaker lived in an apartment inside the Patrol Headquarters. The digs were a great perk for one lucky ski patrolman who didn't mind waking up at 4 A.M. every morning, checking snow conditions, and alerting the avalanche control people whether they needed to do some blasting before the lifts opened. The views were unbeatable, even if you had to be there seven days a week.

The authorities learned that Latch had not yet moved in. Two weeks earlier, Mark Hillman, the patroller living at PHQ, had vacated. Trying to get settled in, Latch had made three trips with the bulk of his stuff over the previous two weeks. That weekend, he had planned to go up one more time with his mother to get that maternal interior decorator's touch. But he didn't. "If it hadn't snowed that Friday night, I would have been up there," he recalls. "That would have been my last trip up before the season."

Latch says that nobody knew of his plans—either to go up or to not go up—except his mom. "Nobody knew I had plans to go up there—and nobody knew I had canceled those plans." Still, he can't help but think that somebody might have noticed that his truck wasn't there, and that the coast was clear.

Latch may be the only true personal casualty of the fire. "They burned all my stuff," he points out, including irreplaceable family pictures. It wasn't just the loss of his belongings that left Latch despondent. "I had plans for the next two years," he says. "You can save money by not paying rent; that can get you ahead in this valley. Those plans got canceled by other people."

But Latch says he was never interviewed by the FBI or ATF. Nor were the two patrollers who had lost out to Latch in the competitive PHQ apartment selection process, Colin Berry and Justin Leitz.

•

"All I know is that I wasn't there," Latch says.

Late in the morning of Monday, October 19, hunters Dave Alt, Neil Sebso, and the Gaal brothers were worried that the warming sun would begin to rot their elk kill, and asked if they could drag the carcass down the mountain. They had written down statements, and packed their gear, because they knew hunting season was over for them. They asked Eagle County Sheriff A. J. Johnson whether maybe one of the VA trucks could help get them and their elk off the mountain. A VA guy interrupted. "We can't take them down," he said. "It's against procedure." Apparently, VA had a rule against guns in their vehicles, and against giving rides to nonemployees.

"You're gonna break the rules today," A. J. told him. The Gaal brothers, Alt, and Sesbo hopped in.

VA's ingratitude seemed suspect to the hunters, who after all had reported the fires. "You know, we never got a thank you from anybody at VA," grumbles Steve Gaal. "Dave saved Chair 11. Maybe they didn't thank us because they wanted to rebuild that one, too."

■

Most of the morning, three photographers from the *Vail Trail* were trying to get up the mountain. Peter Fredin, a longtime local, had originally tried to get a friend to take him up in an airplane to take some aerial shots, but found out that the airspace had been closed. He then raced to the far eastern part of the mountain because his colleagues were trying the two other most obvious routes from town: a straight assault up the road, and a less-traveled western approach. On his way there, he saw something unusual, but he didn't think about it until much later: At the foot of the mountain, near one of the main roundabouts, some men drove up in a VW van and stopped at another vehicle that was waiting. Several guys jumped out and switched vehicles. Fredin didn't pay enough attention to notice other identifying characteristics, of the men or of the car.

Fredin started out from Golden Peak on foot at about 11:30 A.M.; as he climbed, he tried to piece together what might have happened. His first thought when his wife had woken him up with news of the fire was eco-tage. "Without batting an eye, my thought was 'Monkey Wrench Gang,'" recalls Fredin.

At about the top of Chair 12, he met a couple of VA employees who warned him that he'd be stopped and detained if he was caught farther up. "Fine," thought Fredin, and gave the pair one of his business cards. Just in case.

He stuck to the edges and fringes of the slopes, then began climbing Highline, a ski run noted for its steepness and relentless mogul fields. When he stopped and unzipped his pant legs, stripped to shorts, and took some breaths, he noticed a National Guard helicopter circling. Though he was in his late forties, and his hair was tinged with gray, Fredin was in good shape. "Boy," he thought, "anybody who hoofed it up this mountain through the thin air must've been acclimatized." You couldn't just show up here from sea level and do what he was doing.

On his way up, he saw elk and coyote tracks in the snow, but nothing else. Looking back, he could see Mill Creek Road and a line of vehicles that had stopped by a sheriff's department Blazer. On the ski run Flapjack, where the mountain starts to flatten out, Fredin saw more tracks: human tracks. There, in the snow, were the fresh tracks of people walking five abreast, moving to the east across the ski run. To Fredin's photographer's eyes, they were not typical huntsman boots—more like running shoes or light hikers. "The thought I had was, 'This is the exit dance,'" Fredin recalls. "These weren't hunter tracks." He paused to take photos. From where he stood, he could look up and see the remnants of Two Elk smoking.

Fredin made it up to Camp One, a picnic area near Two Elk that the locals still referred to as "Far East," its previous name. It was in cinders. Chair 14 was charred, too. At about 1 P.M., he made the top and saw two more VA employees sitting in a truck. "They said, 'You'd better get out of here,'" and Fredin replied, "I'm on my way." Soon, he ran into Andy Daly and Paul Testwuide cruising the area in a VA truck, and also saw people from the Colorado Bureau of Investigation, the U.S. Forest Service, the Eagle County Sheriff's office, and others from VA security. Fredin knew a lot of them. He told one sheriff's deputy, whom he didn't know, about the five sets of footprints he had seen on the way up.

Fredin was approached by a man wearing forest service khakis whom he also didn't know. The man approached him and asked who he was. "I'm from the *Vail Trail*," Fredin replied. "Oh, shit," the man said. "You stay right here."

But nobody shooed him away; he took more pictures, and eventually hitched a lift with Daly and Testwuide. "It was the quietest ride down the mountain," he recalls. Then Daly asked Fredin for copies of the photos—and later on, so did the FBI. There might be a chance that the sharpies at the FBI lab could make something out of the pictures of those five sets of footprints; but it wouldn't be easy. Fredin hadn't thought of including a marker in the photographs—a pen, for example—that would have given the prints some scale. Without it, law enforcement would have a hard time matching the footprints with anybody. Before long, the sun melted and erased the tracks, leaving nothing but Fredin's inadequate photos and his own memory.

12

Minturn: "We Won't Surrender"

Overheard at a restaurant:

On a brilliant sunny day in the middle of winter, two fifty-something women are picking at salads at Pepi's Gasthof Gramshammer, one of Vail's oldest continuously running inns. They are talking about how difficult it is to find household help these days.

"I've got this girl who comes in and I pay her $10 an hour."

"That's all? I just can't find anybody who will be reliable. I'd be willing to pay twice that if they didn't always have excuses like their car broke down or their kid was sick."

"You know, they're all trained by the hotels. Don't you hate it when they fold the toilet paper into those little triangles?"

They giggle at the joint revelation.

"Yes, and the way they fold the napkins? It drives me crazy."

They laugh, sip their Chardonnay.

Isn't life just funny sometimes?

Almost immediately after the fires, the joke in the neighboring town of Minturn was that soon five arrest warrants would be issued: one for each of the small town's councilmen. Just months before, Minturn had been involved in nasty water rights litigation with a consortium of water districts that had been spearheaded and partially bankrolled by VA. Hardly a person in town didn't believe that Minturn had been steamrolled by VA, with its deep pockets, armada of lawyers, and insatiable appetite for water to fuel ever-expanding development plans and snowmaking dreams.

Robert Kelley-Goss counted himself among those in Minturn who thought that VA was composed of a lying, cheating, stealing, Machiavellian group of ruthless and unprincipled businessmen. In 1996, the thirty-four-year-old had transplanted himself to Minturn from Arkansas, where his grandfather had been one of the last Dixiecrat congressmen. Within three years of moving to town, Kelley-Goss had followed in his grandfather's political footsteps, after a fashion: By running on a vehemently anti-VA platform, he got himself elected to the town council in the first election after the arson.

Though he had moved to Minturn only recently, the pony-tailed Kelley-Goss took to defending the place with the zeal of a convert. He first got a job working as a reporter for the *Vail Trail*, and it didn't take long for him to develop a strong distaste for VA. His editorials frequently ragged on VA for one thing and another. Kelley-Goss's great-great-great-great-grandfather was Patrick Henry, and to the reporter, VA looked as tyrannical as the colonizing English bastards ever were.

Sandwiched in the deep, narrow valley between Vail and Beaver Creek, Minturn is an island of habitation located in a steep, narrow valley hemmed in on two sides by national forest hillsides, the other two by the narrowness of the valley itself. The century-old railroad and mining town sits on the Eagle River just a few miles down valley from Vail and a few miles south of I-70. The clapboard siding on the bungalows is original, the picket fences are authentic, and people hang laundry on real clotheslines. Its three-block stretch of Main Street boasts little more than a couple of restaurants, a handful of curio shops, and some kitschy art galleries that sell more trinkets than masterpieces.

In the arid West, water is more valuable than gold, and by that standard Minturn was a very wealthy place. The town had laid claim to senior water rights from the Eagle River back in 1916, enough water so that Minturn could, if it wanted to, grow significantly larger than it had by the mid-1990s. To VA, Minturn's water rights appeared excessive, especially to a company that could put the water to better uses, say, by upgrading snowmaking capabilities or for irrigating putting greens. A VA-backed consortium of water agencies demanded that Minturn relinquish its water rights by 80 percent. Minturn refused, arguing that under the "great and growing cities doctrine," which essentially says that municipal water owners could save their rights for future growth, they had every right to keep their water in the stream bank even if they weren't using it yet. Besides, water law in Colorado was governed by one overriding concept: "first in time, first in right." Minturn was indisputably first in time.

For most of Vail's history, Minturn had been something of a no-man's land where many second- and third-generation Mexican and Hispanic immigrants settled. For many years, Anglos steered clear of Minturn, thinking of it as "the seedy side of the county," says longtime Minturn resident Sean Gallagher, the current fire chief and son of the former mayor. "Minturn was considered a place where you didn't go," which was just fine to Gallagher and many of the residents who preferred a quieter, less glitzy existence than that of the ski area a few miles away. Gallagher, as did many Anglo residents, enjoyed a perfectly amiable coexistence with his Hispanic neighbors and friends.

By the late 1960s onward, the town had no particular claim to fame except that it wasn't Vail. Houses didn't include seven bathrooms and black-bottomed lap swimming pools. Cracked sidewalks provided the means for locals to cruise down to the post office and talk to just about everybody in town along the way. So what if the roads were repaved every twenty years instead of every ten? It was a small price to pay to live in a place with real character. Minturn wasn't Vail; it was the anti-Vail.

But things are changing. Kelley-Goss owns the Windwood art gallery plunk in the middle of Main Street; a signpost sits on the front lawn telling visitors where they are in relation to everywhere else: London, 5,377 miles; Boston, 1,998; Miami 2,107; New York, 1,794; Rio, 5,894; Tokyo, 12,830; Sydney, 14,044; Denver, 111. Kelley-Goss sits on his front porch on election day more than a year after the fires as he campaigns by smoking cigarettes, drinking black coffee, and waving to anybody who walks by. Minturn, he says, has been struggling, as 1,000-square-foot homes already fetched more than $320,000 and property taxes were rising commensurately. The inexorable march of Vail, and the money it attracted, would almost certainly engulf Minturn. But if Goss has anything to say about it, that day was going to be postponed as long as possible.

Many of the old owners are still hanging on, Kelley-Goss says, but only because they're betting that property values are *really* going to skyrocket one of these days. The Union Pacific railroad owns sixty-two acres at the lower end of town, which used to house extra engines to haul freight over Tennessee Pass. Almost everybody figures that when U.P. decides to develop the rail yard, VA will stick its chubby fingers into the pie. Kelley-Goss is sure that the company plans to use the U.P. foothold at the base of the mountain as a "portal" to Vail Mountain, connecting to the ski area by a funicular or gondola. This idea had been floated before, but in less incendiary times; in the late 1980s when George Gillett was still running Vail, Gillett had approached then-mayor Michael Gallagher about building a gondola or lift from the rail yard that might eventually link Minturn with Vail's skiing, as well as, potentially, to Beaver Creek on the east. At the time, the town government showed little interest, and decided to preserve Minturn's funky railroad culture and maintain its integrity and heritage.

If Minturn becomes a portal to Vail, Kelley-Goss figures, he might as well move back to Arkansas.

◆

Around the time of the water wars, Minturn residents had become increasingly more vocal about their antagonism for VA. Bumper stickers that read

"Stop Vail Expansion!"; "EVAIL"; Minturn 99"; and the most direct "No More Fucking Rich People" began appearing on the beat-up trucks and aging Subaru wagons that plied Main Street in Minturn.

Before the fires, Minturn's town council had already approved more than $1 million to repair and upgrade the town's ailing water system, and had attempted to buy a small reservoir south of town to augment its ailing domestic water supply. But the pond sat on a 6,000-acre private tract on Battle Mountain, which was just a mile or so from Vail's planned Cat III expansion. That tract was not owned by a Minturn-friendly local. Some former EPA lawyers had formed a company called Turkey Creek Limited Liability Company to buy tax liens and foreclosure rights on the property, a move that could give them ownership—and development rights—when it emerged from bankruptcy. The lawyers who now owned the land in question had bankrolled their plan, in part, by selling a 50 percent option to VA.

Minturn's town manager then made a strategic mistake. In Colorado, tensions had been increasing between the "Western Slope" communities on the west side of the Continental Divide and the "Front Range" communities on the east side. The Front Range was growing unchecked, and critics warned that soon one long strip mall would stretch along the I-25 corridor from Fort Collins in the north, through the Denver metropolitan area, south to Colorado Springs and on to Pueblo. These Front Range communities were thirsting for water, and many western-slope towns were enticing targets for more water acquisition.

In the arcane world of western water law, Minturn could pretty much bank on maintaining its senior water rights to provide for the community if, or when, it grew. But when the Minturn town manager started peddling the town's temporarily excess water around, VA's slick attorneys saw an opening. If there are two major tenets of western water law, the first is that senior rights are rights forever, no matter what they're used for. The other, however, is that the water has to be put to "beneficial use," which earned the lay translation "use it or lose it."

The Vail Consortium, a group of water users including VA and two valley water and sanitation districts, sued Minturn for what VA's lawyer, Glenn

E. Porzak, claimed were excess and unused water rights. If the water wasn't being *used,* what good was it?

To Kelley-Goss, the suit represented all the worst aspects of VA. For years, the company had been quietly buying up water rights all over two counties, and had amassed more than enough to service all its development dreams of the moment. (In Colorado, water rights are considered property that can be sold independently of the land associated with the water. Ranchers or mining companies who no longer needed their historical allotments were selling out to Vail and other developers, who paid top dollar.) Kelley-Goss was one of many who were apoplectic because VA could keep buying water rights and sucking the rivers dry for snowmaking during the critical late-autumn months—just so that thoracic surgeons from Atlanta and investment bankers from Chicago could be guaranteed skiing at Thanksgiving. "I personally believe that VA's only concern is to put snow-making on every acre of skiing on Vail Mountain," he says.

If VA couldn't get something done with the brute force of money, the company did it subtly. Up and down the valley, virtually every town council, water board, and sanitation district had been stacked with VA employees and those sympathetic to the company. For just about any significant political decision in the valley, it was hard to maintain an arm's-length relationship from VA. Vail's mayor worked for the Beaver Creek Development Company. A former mayor and current town council member was Rod Slifer, a founding partner of Slifer, Smith and Frampton / Vail Associates, the largest real estate business in the valley and a joint venture with VA. The Avon town council had a couple of VA employees. Testwuide, a VA senior vice president, was on the Eagle River Water and Sanitation District board, as was Rick Sackbauer, who also worked for VA. VA's own water lawyer was Porzak, who had earned the derisive nickname of "Prozac" among the anti-Vail faithful. Porzak just happened to be the main counsel for one of the water districts as well.

In meetings with Minturn, Porzak made it clear that VA and the water consortium were not going to back down. Minturn had screwed up by trying to sell their water, he intimated, and VA would win, one way or another. But even though the legal fees were mounting and the small town was already having to cut back services, the prevailing opinion in Minturn was to stand up and fight. The desperate townspeople begged the Sierra Club to come to their rescue with a cavalry of pro-bono lawyers, and when that failed, they sent a letter to Oprah. Vail's lawyers made it clear to Minturn's attorney that VA had lawsuits backed up like United flights at O'Hare if the company's first approach failed. "These are not nice people we are dealing with," said former mayor Mike Gallagher (Sean's father), echoing the prevailing opinions. But after Gallagher finished his term, the new mayor, Gordon "Hawkeye" Flaherty, decided it would be too costly to fight VA in court. So Minturn settled. Defeated, one of Minturn's lawyers proposed putting up a banner in Vail that would greet visitors to the 1999 World Alpine Championships: "VAIL '99: Snow Provided by Stolen Water from Minturn."

Kelley-Goss admits he's paranoid about VA, but wonders whether it's appropriate to be paranoid when everybody's watching you. "I really did see a black helicopter in Beaver Creek," he says earnestly. "I saw it and thought, 'Holy Shit, I can't believe this!'" Turns out it wasn't a mirage: The helicopter belonged to the Secret Service, which was whisking Vice President Al Gore away after his stay at Adam Aron's house. "Which tells you something right there," Kelley-Goss says, raising an eyebrow.

Kelley-Goss is convinced that some of his paranoia was justified. After a town council meeting during which the council agreed to sign a memorandum of understanding with VA regarding a possible future "portal" from Minturn up to the ski area, Kelley-Goss was desperate. "We just signed our own death warrant," he says.

•

The morning of the arsons at Vail, Fire Chief Gallagher recalls, he dispatched Big Bird, his six-wheeler wildlands fire truck, to the top of the mountain. Then he sat in the back of his truck listening to the radio traffic. When he realized that the fires were under control and that all the firefighters were safe, he started laughing. "That's good," he thought. "Somebody actually did it."

Gallagher, who had worked for VA in the shipping and receiving department for years, had nurtured a growing distaste for the current owners of the ski area. "When the [Leon] Black group took over, it completely changed the character of the company," says Gallagher. "It killed employee morale right away." VA instituted an invasive drug-testing policy "to change the image of the pot-smoking ski bum," which ticked people off. Gallagher, who has no patience with people who get high at work, was fiercely opposed to the policy. "Skiers don't have to worry about being boarded on the lift by somebody who smokes pot on the weekend." VA also changed the dress code—a dress code in the mountains, for Chrissakes—and told people, even in shipping, that they couldn't have beards or facial hair. Talk about ridiculous.

After the fires, in an EMT refresher course with the Eagle County Sheriff's Department's lead investigator, Mike McWilliam, Gallagher was even asked jokingly, "Where were you the night of October eighteenth?" He threw his hands up in mock horror. "Arrest me!" he exclaimed, and some of the others in the room thought the joke was a little too close for comfort. Gallagher didn't mind. "Hell, I understand it. I've spouted off about the way VA does things. I'd probably be called a disgruntled ex-employee." Gallagher says that several law enforcement agents had serious discussions about who in Minturn might have lit a match against VA. After all, just a few months before the fires, the *Vail Daily* had run a banner headline about the water wars: "Minturn: We Won't Surrender."

"And we mean it," says Kelley-Goss, before clicking his lighter and putting the flame to another cigarette and grinning cockily all the while.

13

"No Tenemos Nada"

Letter from a Vail second-home owner from Dallas opposing an employee housing project near his exclusive Potato Patch home. The letter raised such a furor in town with its racist and classist tone that the writer eventually apologized.

•

Dated March 21, 1996, and addressed to the Eagle County Commissioners, the Town of Vail, and Vail Valley Consolidated:

Upon hearing of the proposed high density employee housing project under consideration on Red Sandstone Road, we have jotted down a few reservations and questions:

1. Would the inevitable loud rap music and clouds of marijuana smoke adversely effect the deer, elk and wildflowers on the nearby hillside?
2. Is the current price of recycled aluminum cans sufficient to avoid a "can jam"-caused flood on the creek?
3. Can a sidewalk be constructed clear to the Frontage Road capable of sufficiently accommodating vast hordes of skateboarders, rollerbladers, bicyclists, and the "rolling stoned."
4. Has a Federal approval and funds been secured to have signs placed along I-20 warning: "Idiots Crossing." Would you simply make them a gate instead of forcing them to tear down the fence as they have further west?
5. Would speed bumps on Redsand Stone Road cause lowriders to rip-off their oil pans—polluting Gore Creek, the Colorado River and ultimately the Pacific Ocean? What about the whales?
6. Would this oil from the lowriders running down Redsand Stone Road make the street too slick for Emergency Vehicles to get up "The Projects" to answer rape and domestic abuse calls, carry off drug overdoses and fight balcony fires?

7. And regarding access and lowriders, how many legal holidays (besides Cinco de Mayo and 16th de Septembre) would Redsand Stone Road be closed or clogged due to parades??? Saint Paddy's? Martin Luther King's? June Teenth?? When does it end, the closures that is—Cinco de Mayo Parades seldom go far, but can last a long time....

8. Will each employee/resident be required to own his own set of jumper cables? Will their be onsite tire repair?

9. Which brings up the question of how many tires, batteries, appliances and dogs will be allowed on each unit's porch or balcony?

10. And speaking of dogs, will there be a reasonable limit of say 10 per unit? Will the boys' rottwielers and the girls' huskies and dobermans chase away the elk and deer on the nearby hill? Or, since we already scared them away with music and smoke, will the dogs be over at the Potato Patch Club hunting for small children and making yellow snow?

11. Also, will there have to be an onsite tamale maker to control the population of cats? Are there Federal Guidelines on proper Dog/Cat/Rat ratios? Do rats have Civil Rights like dogs and cats? Will they all get their own Federal Holiday?

12. And speaking of rats and hordes of "diverse" people living in close quarters, does bubonic plague negatively impact the tax basis?

13. Are the police going to have a substation in "The Projects" in order to be closer to the action? Or maybe they would like to rent a Potato Patch Unit across the street—provided they could stand the neighborhood. (The Town of Vail would likely be too smart to buy real estate for a police station in a declining neighborhood.)

14. Finally, does the downgrading of this site from sewer collection to high-density employee housing require an Environmental Impact Study?

On the positive side, you wouldn't have far to go for tamales or ... to buy back your stolen skis.

Author's note: This letter has been reprinted here as it was received, the writer's spelling, punctuation, and style intact.

Gerardo and Olivia Diaz's double-wide trailer commands an inspiring view of Interstate 70 from its perch in the Eagle River Village. From their front porch, the family can listen to a symphony of car and truck stereos booming bass in the Rocky Mountain night. The Diazes' home, squeezed among four hundred other trailers fifteen miles or so west of Vail in the town of Edwards, sits in an area that might as well be called Little Mexico. The Eagle River Village is like immigrant communities across the United States: a place of hope and a place of desperation.

Gerardo, forty, is a maintenance worker at the Vail Racquet Club, and Olivia, thirty-five, works as a maid at the Hyatt at Beaver Creek. They both come from a tiny village in Xacatecas, Mexico, where there were only two problems, according to Gerardo: "Finding water and food." In 1978, Gerardo moved to Chicago, where he worked sixteen hours a day in a restaurant as a busboy. In 1985, he and Olivia moved to the Vail area from Chicago before their first daughter was born because Olivia's sister was there and had told them there was plenty of work.

In many ways, the Diaz family became the vanguard of a great change in the service sector of the Vail economy. In the old days, the transient workforce consisted mostly of college-bound ski bums wanting to take a year off before taking their rightful place in white-collar society. Now, the Eagle Valley has been flooded with Mexican, Salvadoran, Honduran, and other Central and South American workers who have heard that there is plenty of work for those smart enough to at least pretend to be legal. All that it entailed was to pay a visit to Denver and fork over several hundred dollars for a fake green card. Everybody knew that employers eager for workers were loathe to question the authenticity of residency documents.

The Eagle River Village trailer park is also the home for busboys at Two Elk restaurant, the sandwich-makers at Subway at the base of the gondola, the checkers at Wal-Mart, and myriad low-paying service industry workers.

Statistics are sketchy or nonexistent, but the best guesstimates of local officials suggest that about half the low-wage service sector jobs are filled by Hispanics, a marked increase from, say, twenty years ago. The valley's economy would likely tumble, if not collapse, without its Hispanic workers. Increasingly, Hispanics have become foremen, subcontractors, and entrepreneurs in the burgeoning construction business; however, virtually no exchanges between the Hispanic and Anglo cultures occur in the valley besides "Do you want pinto or black beans on that?" In the trailer park, with often from eight to twelve people living in a two- or three-bedroom trailer, a parallel universe to Vail's ritzy façade conducts its own business. "Here, it's like Mexico," says Diaz. "There are the very rich and the very poor."

Although the Diaz family is legal and has been working in Vail for fifteen years, from their point of view, things have only become more difficult for them. Wages are virtually stagnant because of the seemingly endless waves of workers arriving from Mexico who are willing to labor for entry-level pay. Meanwhile, everything gets more expensive. Olivia rides a public bus past Adam Aron's house on the way up the hill to the Beaver Creek Hyatt. Her frustration with trying unsuccessfully to get ahead seeps out of her otherwise sweet, long-suffering demeanor. Every time Olivia asks for a raise, she says, or for a Sunday off to go to church, she is told that her job is a take-it-or-leave-it proposition. When hotels don't have work, they send people home without paying them. If they have work, employees must be there twelve, fourteen hours a day. She says she'd love to take some night classes to study English, but between working and caring for her daughters, her days are long. "There is no time to study, to get ahead," she says. Gerardo says he has a better understanding with his bosses when he needs to attend to such matters as fixing his car or taking his daughter to the doctor. But he has seen many of the newcomers struggle with their anger over the conditions. "The young employees are very mad," says Gerardo. "They live with nothing." Indeed, Gerardo describes working for VA the way a miner might have described working for Peabody Coal in West Virginia. "What is called 'affordable housing' is a joke," he says, in thickly accented but very passable English. "You pay $450 a month, live with a bunch of roommates you don't even know, and when you get your check at the end of the month we don't have anything.

"No tenemos nada."

The Diaz family, which includes Gerado and Olivia's two girls, is one of the rare families at the Eagle River Village who try to live alone in a trailer without cramming in relatives or boarders. It's not easy, and Gerardo says he's going to look for somebody—maybe a couple—who can rent one of their three bedrooms to help defray the twelve hundred dollars a month in payments and rent. And they still might be forced out at any time: The trailer park where the Diaz family lives is being eyed by the toney Cordillera development as a prime location for yet another golf course. "Where are we going to go then?" Diaz wonders.

Ironically, many of the Hispanics, whether they are here legally or illegally, are so fearful of the U.S. government that they eschew services they are entitled to. Michael Wasmer, an Anglo who worked with Catholic Charities in the Vail area, says that organizing the Hispanic community is difficult; and persuading the powers-that-be to spend political capital to help this cadre of workers so vital to the local economy is equally as difficult. The closest thing to a community gathering spot is the Wal-Mart in Avon on Saturday nights, where Mexican workers dressed in their finest and looking for mates cruise the electronics aisles.

Gerardo wistfully says he wouldn't have minded being the one to torch the mountaintop. "I wish I did. But if people thought I did it, they'd find out by now." He looks at his wife, sips his instant coffee. "If we protest about conditions too much, they'll think we did it." He sits back, breathes a deep sigh of resignation. "We're the ones that make VA rich and they don't give anything back. They don't even like us." A car drives by the trailer, booming bass, and Gerardo doesn't seem to notice. "Here, everybody's scared of the government," he says. "And here, VA is the government."

14

I'm the Sheriff Here

When original *Casino Vail* owner Bill "Whitey" Whiteford joined the ski instructor cadre early on, he quickly got into trouble with his supervisor. One day, Whiteford drank a beer at the top of the mountain "because there wasn't any water and I was thirsty." He was fired on the spot.

One of the other instructors took pity on Whiteford and told him to follow his boss down the run called Riva Glade after lunch. Whitey knew that, hidden from view from the runs, someone had set up an old Army canvas tent, affectionately known as the "Tuck 'Em Inn." The tent had a brass queen-sized bed, satin sheets, a chandelier, floor boards covered with throw carpets, a deck outside, and a battery-operated phonograph with a keg of beer sitting next to it. Whiteford followed at a careful distance until he could hear a woman's voice beckoning. "Oh, hurry up and get in here, it's cold."

Whiteford waited a few moments until he heard the unmistakable sounds of hanky panky before skiing up and sticking his ski tips inside.

"Goddammit!" screamed a male voice.

"It's me," said Whiteford. "And I want my job back."

"Okay," his boss grumbled.

"And I only want to give private lessons," he added, pressing his advantage.

"Okay."

"And I want to pick 'em," grinned Whiteford, pushing his luck.

"All right, all right," he capitulated.

Whiteford beams, triumphant, more than thirty years later. "I owned his ass the rest of the year."

Eagle County Sheriff A. J. Johnson was in Salt Lake City in Utah at a police chief's convention when he got the call. Because the fires took place on Vail Mountain and beyond the town of Vail's boundaries, the sheriff's department was the default lead agency, and A. J. the default head of the investigation. He took the first plane he could get back to Vail. He knew that because the fires had taken place on federal land managed by the U.S. Forest Service and leased by VA, there was potentially a federal crime here. But the fires had been set in Eagle County, and A. J. was still the law in these parts. Until and unless somebody wanted to make a federal case out of it, the arson was his baby.

As A. J. started back from Salt Lake, he called the Colorado Bureau of Investigation; he knew his guys would need help processing the crime scene and doing follow-up, especially with the budgets he'd been getting recently. The feds would probably come crawling onto his turf, and A. J. hoped he wouldn't see a repeat of the debacle that had occurred when an Air Force A-10 fighter plane had slammed into the New York Mountains, not far from his office in Eagle, the county seat. Then, the Pentagon had practically taken over Eagle County, and they couldn't even figure out why their own frigging pilot had changed course over the Barry Goldwater Bombing Range in Arizona and flown due north in a fully armed Warthog before running out of gas and crashing in Eagle County. They never found the goddamned bombs, either.

During that time, A. J. had seen the rumors fly and the national press run with them. With the fires, he'd once again have to talk with those dumb-shit media types from New York who didn't even know what county they were in.

After the Pentagon fiasco, A. J.'s disdain for all things federal went to the FBI and pretty much continued on from there. The ATF still had a solid reputation, at least their line officers did, as straight-up arson investigators, but you had to wonder about what they *really* did at Waco. Still, A. J.'s general attitude was summed up by a militia-like comment he made after the fires: "That's what you get with a government of the government, by the government, and for the government."

Johnson moved to Vail in 1975 from Omaha, where he had worked on the police force after serving a tour in 'Nam and a stint as a fuel-injection mechanic. He had skied a couple of times in Colorado, and ended up chatting with one of the local cops during a trip. He joked about maybe working for the Vail Force sometime, but laughed it off almost immediately. But the officer pursued him. "Would you be able to take a polygraph today?" A. J. did, and within a couple months was hired.

He did various jobs on the Vail force, and then quit to become director of security at Beaver Creek in 1982. In 1983, he saw an opening to run for sheriff, and "won healthy" as an independent. Over the years, he's earned a reputation as a prickly man who rewards his friends and sticks it to his enemies. Opinionated and blustery, he nonetheless took the little people's side in a lot of disputes. When the fires came, he didn't seem all that surprised. "There's been a change in our whole valley—housing issues, employee issues, the infrastructure. Frustration levels are up. All these things boil down to the fact that we've been in a pretty fast growth pattern with a lot of dollars. It's frustrating whether you're on the top or the bottom of the ladder. The economic split is phenomenal. That creates a lot of resentment."

En route back to Colorado, A. J. knew things were in good hands with his investigator, James Van Beek, as the incident commander. Van Beek was sorting through the initial reports when an FBI agent from Glenwood Springs, Ken Jackson, arrived. Van Beek knew Jackson from other cases, but he hadn't asked for the FBI's assistance. He was damned sure that A. J. hadn't, either.

"Who called you?" Van Beek asked Jackson. "I dunno," the agent replied. "I just got a page from the Denver office to come up here." Van Beek, who has since left the sheriff's office and now does security for VA, recalls wondering what in the name of "interagency cooperation" was going on. "I was pretty surprised," he recalls. "Nobody was thinking terrorism yet. It didn't even cross my mind at first that it might have been environmentalists. There were so many others to think about."

Van Beek started thinking about the tense relationships he knew about in the valley. He knew that a huge hunk of money had been involved recently in the Turkey Creek deal at the Gilman tract. There had been duplicate deeds, strange claims to mineral rights, people who said they were getting screwed by the deal. "I didn't like the way that went," says Van Beek, and neither had A. J.: He had been ordered by a judge to conduct a public auction of the property just weeks before the fire. "It was screwed up and very clouded."

•

Vail Police Chief Greg Morrison was at the same International Association of Chiefs of Police meeting in Salt Lake City when he got the call. Although technically not his jurisdiction, the fires would require his attention. As Morrison sped back in his Saab, he felt prepared for this kind of tragedy. Because Vail would be hosting the 1999 World Cup Championship ski races, he had been working with a preparatory task force consisting of law enforcement agencies of every type: FBI, ATF, forest service, sheriff, and Colorado State Patrol, as well as fire, medical, transportation, emergency response, and the Federal Emergency Management Agency. Only one week before, he had attended a seminar in Washington, D.C., about domestic terrorism, sponsored by FEMA and titled, "How to Survive a Terrorist Attack." "It was an awesome school," recalls Morrison, with briefings about everything from the Oklahoma City bombing to the possibility of anthrax attacks. There was "real-time tabletop stuff," says Morrison, with mock-CNN broadcasts, command posts, and quick decisions. Ironically, says Morrison, the Eagle County Sheriff's Department had been invited but didn't go.

Morrison had already set up the skeleton of what would become his command post during the Worlds, when VIPs from around the globe would converge on Vail. He had begun to install video surveillance cameras all over the village and the mountain, and had borrowed communications equipment from the Pentagon, including a video wall with eight screens and joystick controllers that allowed him to zoom in to a face in the crowd and take pictures. Morrison offered the room, and soon the incident command center switched from the fire station to the Vail Police Department in the municipal building.

■

As far as A. J. was concerned, though, there had been some fires in his county and he was the chief law enforcement officer and was in charge. Period.

Soon after arriving on the scene, A. J. called together all the law enforcement agencies, facilitated by Van Beek. Before the meeting, A. J. told Van Beek, "Don't give those FBI guys an inch, they'll take a foot." At the meeting, A. J. wore his cowboy boots; the FBI guys showed up in suits and ties. Van Beek introduced the sheriff and made it clear that it was A. J.'s case. "Then the FBI started talking and telling us what was going to happen," Van Beek recalls. "They said, 'We have the SMART system, et cetera.' They basically said they were taking over. 'This is what we're going to do.'

"And A. J. said, 'No way.'"

◆

Because the fires had been lit on federal land managed by the U.S. Forest Service, the investigation was at least partly a federal case. And Tommy Wittman, supervisor of the Bureau of Alcohol, Tobacco and Firearms western regional response team, had the same thought as the other investigators when they arrived at the top of Vail Mountain to begin the investigation: This wasn't an accident.

Though official information was tightly controlled, Governor Roy Romer unequivocally called the fires "an act of terrorism" before Wittman and his crew officially called it arson. "I know that mountain quite well and it is inconceivable that this is a natural occurrence," said Romer, who had once been part owner of a now-defunct ski area called Geneva Basin. Looking around the mountain, Wittman had little doubt that the governor was right.

Wittman's crew brought seven teams of "accelerant-detecting canines" to the site and watched the hounds have a field day. The dogs are rewarded with food when they find traces of accelerant such as gasoline, and Wittman, with classic bureaucratic no-speak, was willing to acknowledge to reporters only that "the dogs have been wellfed."

Reporters who did manage to get on the hill that day noticed a can of fuel that resembled a Coleman gallon container of white gas sitting below burn marks on the Chair 11 lift shack. The gas can was a classic smoking gun, thought Kelly-Goss. It was so obvious, he thought, it almost seemed as though it had been planted there to guarantee it would be easily found. "It really bothered me the way it sat there," said Kelly-Goss.

ATF had activated two of its four National Response Teams to come to Vail, the same mobile arson investigation units that had been busy in the past few years: the bombing of a federal building in Oklahoma City, set by a disaffected Army veteran; the World Trade Center bombings, pinned to Islamic terrorists; and the TWA 800 crash off Long Island and Olympic bombing in Atlanta, both unsolved. Now there were the Vail fires, maybe set by some radical domestic ecoterrorist group. Or maybe not.

One of the NRT team leaders, Harry Eberhardt, was also in Salt Lake City at the same law enforcement convention attended by Sheriff Johnson and Police Chief Morrison. Normally, NRT gets a heads-up when there's an incident that might require their services. Initially, Eberhardt got a call telling him about a fire on Vail Mountain. "Why the hell is somebody calling me about a forest fire?" he wondered, as he hung up the phone. Then another call came in to clarify things. No forest fire, but plenty of structure fires.

At first, officials would not elaborate on whether the seven fires were set simultaneously, although they did confirm that fire detection devices in Two Elk lodge and from the Patrol Headquarters did sound alarms to the town communication center. The timing of the alarms could be important because the two sites are a mile and a half apart atop an 11,200-foot ridge and may have required a well-organized team to pull it off. Wittman said that no signs of explosive devices were found, and implied that the arson may not have been a sophisticated job. "It doesn't take a rocket scientist to start a fire," he said.

On the mountain, chemists, photographers, and fire suppression experts performed their meticulous work. They established a perimeter, and people leaving the scene washed their boots and cleaned their tools. To avoid contaminating the scene with outside gas, the investigators powered their drills and saws with their own generator located outside the perimeter in an ATF truck. For the most part, concrete foundations and charred wood were all that remained to investigate because the fires had burned so intensely. The next day, as they sifted through the still-warm remains of the once-elegant Two Elk lodge, the investigators realized that they'd have to be really lucky to find enough physical evidence to figure out who did this.

•

In town, Vail began to look like the law enforcement gathering that Sheriff A. J. and Vail Police Chief Morrison had just left in Salt Lake City, but without the camaraderie. It didn't take long for tension between the local law enforcement heads to surface. Morrison, a straitlaced, barrel-chested, affable, and ambitious small-town chief, liked to play with the federal big boys. A. J., a short Vietnam vet who railed against the New World Order and the impending federal government's takeover of practically everything, wasn't cottoning to another federal grab of his turf as had happened when the Warthog went down. According to one fed, who spoke on the condition of anonymity, the FBI didn't like A. J.'s *attitude* much, either. "A. J. pulls an Al Haig, you know: 'I'm in control.'" The FBI went nuts when A. J. shot off his mouth at a press conference and let it out that investigators had found footprints on the mountain. "People tend to throw their sneakers away when they hear something like that," said one fed, shaking his head.

The mutual disapproval club had many members. A. J., sensing that he needed to assert himself to maintain the lead role, decided to pull out from the command post at the VPD headquarters in the town's municipal building and set up shop at a sheriff's substation nearby. He put the word out that "somebody with authority" from each federal agency meet him there. "At some point it became us versus them," says Eagle County Sheriff's Department spokeswoman Kim Andree.

The turf battles began on multiple fronts, just as the fires had. Early on, Andree and Jeff Atencio, the Vail Fire Department's public information officer, argued that it was time to quit the charade and just say it was an arson. They were overruled. A. J.'s troops quickly became short-tempered with what they saw as the FBI's prevailing attitude, which the sheriff's people dubbed MOSS: the Mystic Order of Secret Shit. Some of these freshly minted Quantico replicas wearing their suits and ties looked as out of place in the Rocky Mountains as Tarzan would look wearing his loin cloth in Manhattan. Within days, says Andree, "the information flow stopped. It made me feel they didn't trust me. It was our investigation. We know the terrain, the people, the village. We know our area well. It almost felt condescending."

The FBI is "arrogant and disrespectful," says Andree, not mincing words. "When they arrived, many people clammed up. The intimidation factor was clearly there. They took information and didn't inform us. Our deputies gave them every piece of information. It felt like a playground where people weren't interested in sharing toys," she added. "It makes you sit back and say, 'I understand what some of these antigovernment people are saying.'"

■

On Wednesday afternoon, Colorado Public Radio and the *Vail Trail* each received a strange e-mail. A group calling itself the Earth Liberation Front was claiming credit for the fires "in the name of the lynx." The communiqué arrived via a series of "anonymizers" to a Colorado Public Radio affiliate in Fort Collins, and to the *Vail Trail*. David Williams, the editor, passed it along to law enforcement, which had gathered in the sheriff's substation in Vail. The anonymizer, police figured, may have traveled around the world, from the sender to maybe Australia, to Europe, and to God-knows-where before it ended up in Colorado.

The communiqué, especially as it arrived two days after the fires, was suspect. There was nothing in it, not a single detail, that wasn't already in the public domain. For Van Beek, something wasn't sitting right about the note. "For your safety and convenience, we strongly advise skiers to choose

other destinations until Vail cancels its inexcusable plans for expansion."
He asked around. "Isn't this phrased pretty weird?" he wondered.

There appeared to be similarities between other ELF claims and the Vail
arson, but there were significant differences as well. At a protest against a
prairie dog hunt just north of Denver in July, police had found a plastic jug
full of a diesel-gas mixture, with a sponge on the end and a crude timing
device that hadn't worked. Maybe the arsonists had learned a lesson from
this and several other recent failed attempts. Or maybe it was another
group entirely.

The FBI's linguistic experts had their go at the communiqué, and compared it to previous letters sent by the ELF. The similarities didn't jump out
at anybody. In former arsons, the ELF had given specific details about
points of origin, how many fires were set, and other information. This
communiqué was vaguer, and strange in its language inviting people to ski
at other areas.

In his office in Eagle, A. J. started spending time on the Internet educat-
ing himself about what he saw as a concerted effort by environmentalists to
collaborate internationally to shut down forests for human use—what he
calls an "Earth Plan." "It's almost like a cult," he says. The whole World
Trade Organization, he continues, is part of a plan to create a secondary
government "that's above the federal government." Proposals to limit
motorized recreation on public lands are just one more example. "The
handwriting's on the wall," he says. "Everything starts to fit a picture." That
picture, according to A. J., is of an organized group intent on creating a
world army, just as the European Union is intent on controlling Europe.
The Rockefellers, the Pew Foundation, the Tides Foundation—"they're all
tied together," he says. He just doesn't understand what motivates these
people. "What's their reasoning? Did they really think they were going to
stop Vail from putting in more lifts? They just got more sympathy for VA."

◆

In Portland, Oregon, inside the offices of the Liberation Collective, then
twenty-six-year-old Craig Rosebraugh knew the feds would soon be after

him. In the collective's cramped offices, with the slogan "The FBI are the real terrorists" displayed on the walls, Rosebraugh says he had fielded an anonymous request from the ELF to claim credit for the fires. This had happened before. In 1997, Rosebraugh had received a communiqué from the Animal Liberation Front asking the collective to claim credit in ALF's name for the largest release of minks—10,000—from a fur farm in Oregon. More recently, the ELF had claimed credit through Rosebraugh for the failed arsons in Wyoming and Colorado, both with four intended points of origin.

But the Vail fires, with about two dozen points of origin, were in a different league entirely. And the nature of the cyber-beast was that even Rosebraugh couldn't be sure the anonymous request regarding the Vail fires really was from the ELF. Could it be that someone was going to an awful lot of trouble to set the environmentalists up? But who?

15

Bunny Huggers Meet the Tree Huggers

We take inspiration from the Luddites, Levellers, Diggers, the Autonome squatter movement, ALF, the Zapatistas, and the little people—those mischievous elves of lore. Authorities can't see us because they don't believe in elves. We are practically invisible. We have no command structure, no spokespersons, no office, just many small groups working separately, seeking vulnerable targets and practicing our craft.

—FROM AN EARTH LIBERATION FRONT'S WEB SITE

Away from the initial investigation that targeted the "usual suspects" of Ancient Forest Rescue activists and terminated-with-prejudice Vail Associates' employees, federal investigators began taking an interest in a figure on the forefront of animal rights politics in Colorado: Nicole Rosmarino. Rosmarino was a twenty-eight-year-old Ph.D. candidate at the University of Colorado at Boulder who had befriended Rod Coronado, the notorious arsonist and animal rights activist who had been convicted for his participation in the 1992 ALF raid on Michigan State University's Furbearer Research Facility. Investigators thought that Rosmarino was worth a hard look: She had possibly been in Portland in December 1998, when some fires were set at a logging industry building. Agents tried to link her either to the attempted arson near federal horse corrals in Rock Springs, Wyoming, just before the Vail fires, and/or to the 1998 failed arson at a Wray, Colorado, gun club. The club had hosted a prairie dog shoot in 1996, and Rosmarino had protested that event. After the fires, Rosmarino recounted how a federal investigator told her ominously that she "seemed to have a habit of turning up in the wrong place at the right time." She says she wasn't in Rock Springs or Wray in 1998, and she wasn't in Vail at the time of the fires, either.

Even with all the investigative fervor focusing on Rosmarino, she didn't back away from provocative rhetoric condemning Vail. "I believe in exhausting all reasonable efforts first," she said. "But when you're shut down at every turn, there's no reason why fires shouldn't be set." Unlike the AFR activists, who loudly denounced the fires, Rosmarino commended the arsonists. "It was one of the most beautiful acts of economic sabotage ever in this state," she said.

A strict vegan who not only doesn't eat meat but doesn't use leather or other such animal products, Rosmarino grew up in upstate New York in the heart of its hunting culture. She stopped eating animals while an undergraduate, became increasingly involved in animal rights issues, and soon began protesting the use of animals in scientific research. But saving lab animals seemed to be off-point for her energies. The natural next step for her, she says, was to become active in wildlife issues, "because those are the animals that still have a fighting chance." Rosmarino, in effect, represents a new breed of activist. "I have absolute adoration, even quasi-worship, for wildlife. So habitat protection quickly became my struggle," she says. "We pride ourselves on seeing the links between individual animals and their habitats."

Rosmarino calls herself an animal liberationist and a "bunny hugger," and believes she is helping to bridge the divide between animal-rights activists and environmental activists. Rosmarino had been part of the original group that sued to list the lynx as an endangered species, and also attended several Vail protest meetings, including a passion-filled county commissioner's meeting in March. "I see skiing as just another extractive industry," she says. "We are letting these guys get away—literally—with murder." As far as Rosmarino is concerned, after the legal remedies were exhausted, "there was nothing left to do but break the law. I was ready to do acts of civil disobedience to slow down the loggers. But what transpired was more effective than anything I was prepared to do. This sends a message to Vail, but it also serves as a lesson to all of us who were too afraid to light the match ourselves."

She says she was alone at her house, about an hour's drive from Vail, on the morning of the fires. Sometime in the morning, she recalls, she went to a neighbor's house and saw a television report about the fire (she doesn't own a television herself). When she saw the news report, she said, she was "jumping up and down with delight. I was so excited. What a little present that somebody got their act together." Up to that point, Rosmarino says, she had been getting disenchanted with the Vail protests because so many of the participants were unorganized younger college students. "I thought, 'I don't have to do anything, because somebody did it for me.'"

Before the fires, Rosmarino's efforts to marry the bunny huggers to the tree huggers were as problematic as persuading a mountain goat to mate with a grizzly bear. Rosmarino's group's hue and cry was "Extinction stinks! Save the lynx!" whereas Ancient Forest Rescue's Berman and his cronies were hammering on VA's real estate greed, a message that had a wider appeal, especially among the locals, who tended to believe that there weren't many lynx in them thar hills anymore. Indeed, Berman needed to appeal to Vail's fur-coat-wearing crowd if he hoped to succeed, because they were the ones who had the real power.

As the two disparate groups sought common ground, their world views collided. At one point, members of each camp were walking in Vail Village when they passed a fur store. A woman emerged wearing a mink coat, and one of the Rocky Mountain Animal Defense protestors yelled, "You'd look a lot sexier without sixty-five dead animals on your back!" Little did he know that when fur protestors had descended on Vail in a previous year, the two fur shops in town had done record business. The wealthy, it seems, have their own methods of sending a message.

Berman didn't want to alienate potential allies, and asked Rosmarino to calm the fellow. She declined. "I had no problem with him telling that lady off," she told Berman. "That's why the lynx are in the shape they're in. And I'm disappointed in environmentalists who can't see that."

Rosmarino's link to Rod Coronado was especially disconcerting to law enforcement. Coronado was seen as a powerful, savvy, and radical influence on the entire animal-rights subculture. Vail became a magnet for the two movements to converge, Coronado told *Mother Jones*, because Vail is typical of a new kind of environmental threat. "It's an example of the power wielded by corporations against animals and the environment," Coronado explained. "In the Northwest, it's timber. In the Midwest, it's the livestock industry. And in Colorado, it's the ski industry. Even though it's based on recreation, people are realizing that it's just as exploitative as the timber industry, so it's an excellent target for the younger generation that now finds itself holding the reins of the environmental and animal liberation movements."

Long a target of federal investigations, Rosmarino says she's accustomed to being followed. "I'm in a perpetual state of harassment," she says of the ten times she's been stopped by police and questioned since the Vail fires. She even met with U.S. Attorney Ken Buck in a Denver brew pub, accompanied by her lawyer—but the meeting barely lasted ten minutes before

Rosmarino left. "The police are always harassing me, but I have the luxury of not having any knowledge," she says. For Rosmarino, plausible deniability is apparently intact.

After the fires, while all the other environmental activists were distancing themselves from the arsonists at Vail, Rosmarino praised them to a reporter from the *Colorado Daily.* "I hope it was an environmentalist who set those fires," she said. "I hope that someone that good would be on our side. In terms of the damage that Vail is doing to the earth, this is war. Property destruction is not violence—especially when it's directed against property that has been illegally constructed on public lands. That's particularly abominable, and Vail should be burned for that."

Schussing with the President

Pepi GRAMSHAMMER
From Innsbruck, Austria. Austrian National Team star. IPSRA professional. A great racer who can improve any skier's technique.

Morrie SHEPARD
Native New Englander, former asst. director Aspen Ski School. Chief Examiner, Rocky Mtn. Ski Instructors. Master of deep powder.

Roy PARKER
Lives in Georgetown, Colo. Former director Loveland Basin ski school. Skilled, patient instructor—the epitome of elegance in deep powder. Assistant school director.

Ricky ANDENMATTEN
Hails from Zermatt, Switzerland, where he was nationally certified instructor, mountain guide. Specializes in wedeln and parallel skiing.

Manfred SCHOEBER
Talented guide, mountain climber and ski teacher from Bavaria. Returns to Vail from expedition to Asia's Hindu Kush range. Leads top class in high speed skiing.

Rod SLIFER
Native Coloradan, former top instructor at Aspen, permanent resident of Vail. An experienced all around teacher who doubles as assistant school director.

EXPERTS—learn deep powder and wedeln on America's most challenging slopes.

INTERMEDIATES—improve your technique on Vail's wide, well-packed trails.

BEGINNERS—master the fundamentals in one day on Gopher Hill . . . then ride the gondola to exciting Swingsville.

LEARN THE AMERICAN TECHNIQUE AT VAIL

SKI SCHOOL

CERTIFIED INTERNATIONAL INSTRUCTORS TEACHING THE NEW AMERICAN TECHNIQUE

RATES: One day class $6.50—Two day class $11.50—Six day class $28.50—One hour private lesson $10.00 by appointment.

JOIN YOUR CLASS DAILY AT THE SKI SCHOOL BELL—9:30

It wasn't pictures of skiers defying gravity through deep powder or even the allure of rubbing ski tips with the world's elite that got Vail into the national lexicon. What put Vail on the map was a skiing president.

House of Representatives Minority Leader Gerald Ford and his family had been quietly coming to Vail since 1968. When Ford took over the presidency after Richard Nixon was forced out of office, President Ford continued to visit Vail under heavy Secret Service guard—once enough Secret Service agents could be found who could attach six-foot fiberglass boards to their feet without falling on their guns and breaking their ribs, as one agent did. Ford was vacationing in Vail over Christmas 1974 when the *New York Times* broke the story that the CIA had been illegally involved in domestic espionage. After CIA Director William Colby flew to Vail, Ford acknowledged that he had had "partial knowledge" of the program when he was vice president; he then ordered the CIA to cease and desist on U.S. turf. Every news organization in the country began sending datelined stories from Vail, Colorado.

Wherever that was.

It didn't take long before people were referring to Vail as the "western White House," which doesn't do much harm to anybody's marketing strategy. "Guess Who's Coming to Ski?" *Newsweek* wrote at the end of 1974. "Skier Ford Helps Vail Find Place in the Snow," read a *Los Angeles Times* headline from 1975.

•

Ford wasn't the first high-level Washingtonian to discover Vail's slopes. Whiteford recalls that back in the early 1960s, Robert McNamara, President John F. Kennedy's secretary of defense, was a keen skier and loved coming west to vacation. McNamara visited the new resort soon after it opened, and he liked what he saw. Vail was a lot closer to Denver than Aspen, and the developers appeared to be creating an atmosphere more like that of a country club, which wasn't happening in the old mining town where McNamara had skied before. The big open bowls on the back side of the mountain were damned impressive, he noted while being given a private tour. McNamara told one of the original investors (Whiteford says it was Caulkins; Caulkins doesn't recall the conversation) that he'd be back, and he'd bring the Kennedys next time. McNamara's tour guide, surprisingly, balked. "You're welcome as the flowers in May, Robert," somebody told McNamara, as Whiteford recalls. "But don't bring those damn Kennedys. They loused up Hyannisport, and we don't want them to louse up this place, too."

•

In 1976, a cable carrying Vail's famed gondola cars severed and crashed to the ground. Four people died and eight were injured on March 26 after two cars fell 127 feet from the tower to the hard-packed snow below. Another 175 skiers had to be lowered to safety from at least thirty other cars. The U.S. ski world had never seen tragedy on that scale.

The gondola collapse was symbolic of Vail's failure to bring that year's Winter Olympics to Colorado. VA would have liked nothing better than to host the Games. The company had lobbied hard to get them, and apparently had won; its executives were so supremely confident of bringing the Games to Colorado that they laid ambitious plans to expand Beaver Creek. At the end of the 1972 Sapporo Olympics, the ritual see-you-in-four-years sign read "We Meet Again in Denver '76."

VA had jumped the starting gate. State legislator Richard "Dick" Lamm, who went on to become governor, fought hard against bringing the Olympics to his state because, he suggested, the Games would create an environmental nightmare and hasten overdevelopment in the high country. Colorado voters agreed with him and passed Amendment 8 in 1972, which forbade spending state tax money on the Games. That sent the 1976 Olympics packing to Innsbruck, Austria.

Despite the presidential seal of approval, the magic bubble that had surrounded Vail began to leak. And it kept leaking when the economy turned south.

Back in 1966, the original Vail owners had taken the ski area public. Pete Seibert had remained chairman of the company, but before long others were calling the plays from the sidelines. After the Olympic failure and the mid-70's gondola accident, with its prospect of some $50 million in lawsuits, Vail's board of directors decided the company was something of an albatross and put it on the block. Twentieth Century–Fox showed some interest; but in those pre–*Star Wars* days Fox wasn't flush enough to outbid a Texas oilman named Harry Bass, who bought a controlling interest for $13 million in late 1976. (After the success of *Star Wars*, Twentieth Century–Fox bought the Aspen Skiing Corp. for $48 million, the next year. Aspen was subsequently sold to the Crown family of Chicago.) Bass had made money with his family firm, Goliad Oil and Gas, and reminded some of the autocratic Larry Hagman character, J. R. Ewing, from the TV show *Dallas*. Soon after Bass took over, Vail founder Pete Seibert was put, rather unceremoniously, out in the cold. Bass, by most accounts, was a detached yet stormy owner who treated Vail as erratically as early season snowfall. He built hundreds of condo units in Beaver Creek that weren't selling well during Colorado's mid-1980 oil bust, when Texans were about as popular in Colorado as New Yorkers are anywhere but New York. Although the gondola litigation didn't turn out to be as expensive as had been anticipated, by 1984 Bass had suffered an internal family coup and lost the resort when his children pulled enough stock rank to force him out. At the time, VA continued on as a public company, traded on the American Stock Exchange.

With the coup, Vail's majority stock went on the block. After one deal was aborted, a Wisconsin-born entrepreneur named George Gillett entered the fray. Gillett was a second-tier wheeler and dealer of the high-flying Reagan era, his interests in everything from low-cholesterol beef to mid-market network-affiliated television stations. "I've tried not to go head-to-head with the big guys," he says in a self-deprecating way that rings mostly true. "I try to find unique niches."

The son of a prominent surgeon in Racine, Wisconsin, Gillett fought hard to not follow in his father's métier. He dropped out of Amherst College and made his way to Aspen to become a ski bum before working his way into the business world as a sales rep for Crown-Zellerbach. After being rejected by Harvard Business School, Gillett set off on his own and, by the time he was twenty-three, had made a small fortune developing loan software for banks and investing in Wisconsin farmland. He parlayed those successes into an even more profitable venture into the meatpacking industry.

He made one of his first major moves into more glamorous businesses when he became business manager and part-owner of the Miami Dolphins in 1966, when the team drafted what would become their franchise player in quarterback Bob Griese. A few years later, Gillett invested in the Harlem Globetrotters and became their president and general manager. During his tenure, Gillett helped pioneer the merger of sports and entertainment when he popularized the Globetrotters by teaming with Hanna-Barbera to produce a successful cartoon show about the basketball wizards and clowns.

Gillett moved into broadcasting in 1978, and eventually owned eleven television stations, many of them CBS affiliates. The Gillett Group was, at one time, the largest non-network television company in the United States.

A longtime skier and visitor to Vail who had bought his first home there in 1977, Gillett had been biding his time for years until he could make a pitch for Vail. When he got his chance, he pounced. In October 1985, the Gillett Group purchased the area for $131 million. Gillett bought as much stock as he could, then called in the rest and took the company private once again.

The short, gray-haired Gillett, sixty-two, looks like everyone's favorite uncle with his large horn-rimmed glasses and quick smile. At Vail, he was known for his affable, slap-your-back and shake-your-hand and ask-about-your-wife-and-kids-by-name style. He'd dress as Santa Claus and hand out dollar bills to kids in the lift lines, and have long conversations with VA janitors who didn't know who he was until later. He had the uncanny ability to remember lift operators' names (he instituted a policy of having them wear nametags with their hometowns on them) and started an open-door policy to all employees. Calling himself "Director of Quality Control," he'd slide around his snowy empire on skis and wear a name tag that said "George: Racine, Wisconsin"; and he once rescued the injured editor of *People* magazine by carrying him down the mountain piggyback.

Most winter days, Gillett was out on the slopes, like the football team owner who loves to mingle with the players on the sidelines, and Vail was on a roll again. It was named *Ski* and *Skiing* magazines' number one ski resort in North America and the world, respectively, and held that spot during all of Gillett's tenure. Before long, Gillett had made a name for himself in the snow world and had infused the industry with flair and a high profile: He was part P. T. Barnum, part grown-up ski bum. One year, to prove that the resort was indeed a family-friendly place to vacation, he displayed his showmanship at a New York City–based ski show when he rented the entire FAO Schwartz store in Manhattan and invited the national ski media for a meal of minihamburgers and M&Ms. In 1989, when he was at the epicenter of the ski industry, he hired the Gatlin Brothers to play at the National Ski Areas Association meeting. He was on the board of the U.S. ski team, and rode the wave of success from Vail when he was named host to the 1989 World Alpine Ski Championships, the first time the prestigious event had come to the United States in more than forty years. Viewers of his television stations located strategically around the country were treated to an onslaught of come-to-Vail advertising. "People were saying, 'This guy's fucking great,'" says Bill Jensen, now the chief operating officer at Vail Resorts, who worked for Gillett as president and CEO of Gillett's post-Vail ski venture, Booth Creek Enterprises.

The affable Wisconsin meat-packing and media magnate poured his money into Vail. He approved a multimillion-dollar plan laid out by former VA president Harry Frampton to put in one of the industry's great technical revolutions, the detachable high-speed chairlift. With the faster lifts, which could whisk four people at a time up the mountain, the industry's albatross of lift lines was banished. Gillett also spearheaded a massive terrain expansion into China Bowl on the back side of Two Elk, which was tactically unveiled when the ski resort hosted the 1989 Worlds in front of international media coverage.

That expansion, almost as large as the current Cat III controversy, went off almost without a whinny of protest. A few top management people took Gillett skiing one day and pointed out all the terrain they could open up on the back side of the mountain with just one new lift. "I said, 'Buy the lift,'" Gillett recalls, and it was done. Gillett had also overseen the construction of Two Elk, which became an icon of Vail's increasing decadence and lavishness. His wife, Rose, decorated Two Elk after scouring the Four Corners area for Indian petroglyph images to use as the restaurant's motif.

For Gillett, being Vail's owner gave him a cachet he had never had before. Although the Gillett Group was listed number 111 on *Forbes* magazine's 1988 list of the 400 largest private companies in the United States, owning Vail was the feather in this Bartholomew Cubbins's hat. He says that he remembers telling a beautiful woman at a cocktail party what he did for a living at the beginning of his tenure. "I kill cattle," said the meat packer and beef processor, "and I own a ski resort." It didn't take long for Gillett to drop the cow line. For Gillett, and for the subsequent owners, Vail became the ultimate trophy wife.

■

In Gillett's case, however, the marriage didn't last.

In the mid-1980s, the term *junk bonds* was just coming into the popular lexicon. Some people were making a lot of money, but few understood exactly how the high-risk, high-yield financing scheme worked, including, possibly, George Gillett. "I met a man named Michael Milken," one former colleague recalls Gillett saying. "He told me I was the smartest guy he ever met." Milken was happy to loan Gillett money over the next few years at exorbitant 18 and 20 percent interest rates to finance a television station buying spree. In 1986, Drexel provided Gillett with $1.3 million in junk bonds to bring Gillett's empire together under the corporate umbrella of Gillett Holdings, or GHI. Then Gillett borrowed another $1.3 billion to buy Storer Communications, a chain of six TV stations that many analysts said were overvalued.

But after Black Monday, when the stock market crashed more than 20 percent on October 19, 1987, interest rates for Gillett's Storer deal zoomed from 7 percent to 22 percent when investors turned skittish and money for high-risk ventures became scarce. Still, because all the GHI companies were making profits well in excess of 17 percent, servicing the debt wasn't an issue. But in 1990, CBS was hit with a writer's strike, and most of Gillett's stations were CBS affiliates. The strike hurt Gillett badly, and things were made worse when television ad revenue dropped as the upstart cable stations began their inroads into the networks' broadcasting monopoly. Now those interest rates started to matter. By the time all the notes came home to roost, Gillett had racked up $1 billion in debt.

Gillett didn't capitulate yet. Many of his notes weren't due until 1992, and he had a plan to rescue his empire. He says he was all set to refinance and restructure his debt by buying it back at a discount with the help of "a major institution" when Iraq invaded Kuwait. After Operation Desert Storm erupted, the "major institution's" international partners declared force majeure and backed out of the deal. All his companies—the Packerland meat-packing plant, the TV stations, and Vail ski area—were cross-collateralized and their debts cross-guaranteed. He turned to his colleagues and said despondently, "I don't think we can earn our way out of this." Recalling it years later still brought visible distress to his face. "When one piece started to go," he says disconsolately, "it took everything down."

◆

Around the time of Gillett's troubles, Leon Black entered the picture. Black was a Wall Street financier and former Milken protégé who had dusted himself off in the wake of the savings and loan debacle, when the FDIC had sued Milken and Black for $1.3 billion. Although Black was not convicted of anything, he agreed to pay a reported $18 million to the feds. As the head of mergers and acquisitions for Drexel, Burnham, and Lambert, Black had learned to navigate around a foundering company's ledger sheet. After Drexel tanked in 1990 in the wake of a Securities and Exchange Commission investigation, Black formed a new company, Apollo Partners, LP. Named after the Greek god of healing, the new company specialized in finding good companies that had made bad financial decisions or had been whacked by anomalies in the business cycle, and then creatively found ways to restructure them and acquire them.

Apollo is good at what they do in the same way a hyena is good at what it does. "Leon is a vulture fund operator," said one businessman who has dealings with him and admires him for his acumen and toughness. "He feeds on carrion. He eats the animals that other animals have killed." This was meant as a compliment.

During his tenure at Apollo, Black had earned a reputation for shrewd-ness backed by loads of capital and a willingness to take risks that turned heads on Wall Street. Apollo didn't seem constrained by a particular genre of business; they acquired companies as far-flung as Culligan Water Tech-nologies, Samsonite, Furniture Brands International, Allied Waste, the Spanish-language cable television Telemundo, and Berlitz International. They even went into partnership with Ted Turner to purchase the then-laughable concept of an all-cartoon cable station. Thus was born one of the most profitable concepts in cable television history: the Cartoon Channel.

In their prospectus, Apollo Management LP calls itself a "private equity investment firm with offices in New York, Los Angeles, and London.... Our reputation is one of developing creative, unconventional, successful invest-ment solutions for complex business transactions." Backed by the French banking giant Credit Lyonnais, which was in turn backed by the secretive Altus Finance, Apollo has raised more than $10 billion in equity capital through various individual funds, and had easy access to $1 billion in ready cash on their own. Black and his partners were well fanged and always scav-enging.

In 1992, the buzzards were beginning to circle George Gillett.

•

After the refinancing deal was cut short by the invasion of Kuwait, Gillett contemplated his options. He shopped his debt around, displaying his in-the-black balance sheets with his in-the-red debt obligations. He paid a visit to Apollo Partners, LP, one of the most obvious places to look for help, but they weren't interested—or at least they didn't *seem* all that interested. Nor did anyone else.

Back in Vail, panic took hold. When it became clear to the town council that Gillett was probably going to lose the ski area, the town decided to explore whether they could buy Vail by claiming eminent domain. They hired New York attorney Jack Nusbaum, who had battled Kohlberg, Kravis, and Roberts in the RJR Nabisco buyout. But even with all the money that gravitated to Vail, the idea of ponying up that much cash, even if it was a bargain, spooked the locals. After spending more than a quarter million dollars in lawyers' fees to explore their options, the city let the idea drop. "It was the greatest lost opportunity the town ever had," says Robert McLaurin, the current town manager (who at the time hadn't arrived yet from his previous job as town manager in Jackson Hole, Wyoming). "We had the opportunity to control our own destiny," says McLaurin. "Two hundred million scared the shit out of a small mountain town. Two hundred million to some Wall Street sharks was nothin'."

Once the town had bowed out, Gillett had nowhere else to go. True to his reputation, Black smelled blood in the water, and now he decided he wanted to talk with Gillett. GHI's portfolio was classic Apollo fodder: good companies, bad debt structure. Vail was making money, the meatpacking was making money, the television stations were making money. But there was too much debt. Apollo could do something about that.

Up at the Shearson-Lehman retreat at Saddle Ridge in Beaver Creek, Black, Gillett, Craig Cogut, Black's brother-in-law, and a few others met to discuss Vail's fate. "The meeting could not have been more gracious," recalls Gillett. "They told me there were 'lots of challenges' around how our assets would operate in bankruptcy," Gillett recalls. "They were very savvy," he says of the Apollo people. "They had done their homework. And Leon lived up to every promise."

But before Apollo could amalgamate GHI's debt, Black et al. had to placate several other investors holding GHI's paper. They wheeled and dealed, offering various senior and junior creditors options from cash buyouts at quarters on the dollar to complicated combinations of stock options, equity, and cash.

Buying out the bulk of the senior bonds from First Executive, the California insurance company that held much of Gillett's debt, was fairly easy. But a dissident group of bondholders, led by the quintessential cranky financier and corporate raider Carl Icahn, decided to raise a fuss. For months, the skirmish was monitored in the pages of the *Wall Street Journal*, as then-TWA Chairman Icahn held out for more. Black and Icahn were odd rivals, the types who could play poker together on a Thursday night and sue each other on a Friday. But as Black and his partner Cogut had amassed nearly two-thirds of GHI's bonds, Apollo held the better hand this time. Eventually, they upped the ante a little for Icahn and settled. Apollo had pulled off what *Colorado Business* magazine called "the best deal in the history of finance."

After the bankruptcy, Black bought GHI's senior debt notes, which had the effect of consolidating his control over Gillett's holdings. Black then sold the television stations at a nice profit, then dealt the meatpacking plant back to Gillette through Hancock Insurance. To cash in even bigger, Black immediately laid the groundwork to take Vail public. It was he who was behind the strategy to pump millions into an aggressive expansion campaign, increase real estate revenues nearly threefold, acquire two nearby ski resorts, and replace Gillett's lame-duck post-bankruptcy chairmanship with new, Wall Street–savvy executives willing to make investors a top priority.

The plan worked. On the day of the resort's initial public offering of the new Vail Resorts stock in 1997, Black's Apollo group sold $64 million worth of MTN stock, more than anyone had ever made in the ski business— before or since.

The IPO unsettled the small Colorado town for many reasons. To begin with, when the company started putting out its quarterly and annual reports, townspeople, some for the first time, realized just how much money was at stake in their bucolic mountain valley. Fear and loathing followed. "Because it's a public company, all the numbers are in the paper," says burly Senior Vice President Testwuide. "People don't like to see great big numbers with lots of zeros unless they're in back of their name."

Within a year of the IPO, the windfalls that befell VA's top executives in the form of stock options were blowing hot winds of discontent through the valley. Andy Daly, who had stayed on as president after Apollo brought Adam Aron on as CEO, had sold half his shares for $6 million. Chris Ryman, who subsequently left the company to join Gillett at his new ski company, Booth Creek, got $3 million for his shares. Almost immediately after Apollo took over, Black's group hit gold with the Bachelor Gulch development near Beaver Creek, which was almost better than any mining lode found in the West. On fourteen hundred acres, VA had built nearly eight hundred homes, creating a "private and upscale real estate enclave in a secluded and scenic valley," with a security gate system and twenty-four-hour controlled access. The first offering, in September 1995, brought $42 million for fifty-two lots, which sold in under two hours to people who had to show a certified check even to get in the door to bid. The second batch brought $7.5 million for fourteen lots in less than an hour, and the last thirty lots sold for $26 million in less than an hour and a half. The real estate bonanza piled on top of the $64 million Apollo had reaped at the IPO. At one time, Apollo held 60 percent of Vail Resorts stock. They've slowly sold stock over the years, reducing their holdings to more like 22 percent of the 35 million shares out there.

The upshot was that in the first four years, Apollo quadrupled their original investment in Vail. "This is," says current Vail COO Jensen, "the art of the deal." At the end of the day, he adds, "Leon ended up with Vail for free."

■

As for Gillett, Apollo cut him a consulting deal as nominal CEO of Vail for $1.5 million a year, and tossed in 786,000 shares of stock that eventually went out at twenty-two dollars a share. He also received another $1.5 million annually to help out the television stations for a few years. But this colorful parachute seemed fishy to a lot of locals, most of whom loved Gillett. There were plenty of people in and around Vail who would have liked to be given 3 million a year plus 17 million bucks' worth of stock as a reward for running their businesses into the ground. Wasn't it curious, people wondered, that at the time of the transition, Gillett was holding about $500 million in NOLS, or net operating losses, for the previous year? Those NOLS, they pointed out, could give a tax benefit to the new owners of about $200 million. Maybe Apollo couldn't get them without George's signature? Gillett says he is "99 percent sure" that there was no quid pro quo, as has been rumored, where he signed over the tax credit, and in return got kept on as chairman for five years and one-point-five per. Still, at the time, the deal was so suspect that the *Wall Street Journal* recounted a striking exchange between Icahn and Black. Black began by defending Gillett's salary. Icahn reportedly retorted: "I don't mind the guy, but Leon, did he marry your daughter, or what?"

Although Gillett made a fine impression on many of the townspeople that lasts to this day, he also made a few enemies. Inside the current régime at VA, frustration with his whitewashed image gives way to the moniker "Mythical George." "George thinks he can walk on water if it's not frozen," says Vail cofounder Seibert. Vail town manager Robert McLaurin sums up the feelings of Gillett's critics when he notes: "George thought he could play with the big boys. And he got fucked."

◆

Gillett emphatically doesn't ask for pity, but says he lost more than $500 million in the GHI bankruptcy. Though he was "embarrassed" by his monetary defrocking, he didn't stay down for long. Already in 1995, he had established a holding company that began to approximate the old GHI, with lean-beef packing and transportation companies. Then, in December 1996, Gillett went on to create another competing ski empire, Booth Creek Ski Holdings, by purchasing five medium-sized resorts: Northstar at Tahoe, Sierra-at-Tahoe, and Bear Mountain in California; and Cranmore Mountain Resort and Waterville Valley in New Hampshire, where Adam Aron first skied. Later, Gillett bought Grand Targhee in Wyoming, and several other small resorts. He is now the fourth-largest ski resort operator in the United States.

Gillett still has Vail roots, and the headquarters of Booth Creek are located in a modest, squat, green building west of town. (His house, however, is anything but modest, a $7 million palace in Spraddle Creek, Vail's highest-end gated minicommunity.) Gillett agrees with what most people have reasoned about the arsonists: Whoever set the fires had to know the mountain and had to have a serious grudge against the current owners. "The arrogance of the current management was felt by many," he says. "The trouble is," he says, leaning back in his chair and placing his hands together behind his gray-haired head, "the number of people on that list is in the hundreds—if not the thousands." He is sure that the effects of the fire will reverberate in ways that nobody has yet even thought of. No longer could the ski industry wrap itself in the mantle of healthy, outdoor recreation for the masses and not be open to charges that their ski slopes were, after all, nothing but clear-cuts, and their real estate developments no more environmentally sound than a strip mall. "The burning of Two Elk may be the single most significant event in the history of the ski industry," says George Gillett.

"You want to know who the real culprit is?" he asks conspiratorially. "It's Wall Street."

•

The Leon Black family bought a condominium above the lobby of the Vail Village Inn, which was impressive even by Vail's standards. Its vaulted ceilings and large glass openings to panoramic views of the mountain told the locals right away that they were entering a new era. Former Vail fire inspector Jeff Atencio recalls giving the Black place a once-over and thinking, "This is real money."

Real money no doubt. But Black and his less-visible partner Cogut, with "some public relations baggage they'd rather leave at the 'unclaimed luggage' counter in the train station of life," as a January 1995 *Colorado Business* story put it, knew they had to treat Vail differently from the way they treated, say, Samsonite or Allied Waste. Immediately after the deal was made, Black visited Vail and paid his respects to community leaders. He told then-mayor Peggy Osterfoss that Apollo was in Vail "for the long run." Osterfuss asked Black what "long run" meant to a New York investment firm. Black replied confidently, "Four to six years." That didn't placate the mayor. "What may be a long-term investment in the financial community is a relatively short-term one in a community like this," she retorted.

Cogut also knew that this wasn't just another acquisition. "Getting something like Vail is like winning the World Series," he told *Colorado Business*. "When we finally got the deal done, it was not like: 'Oh, well, we got another one.' We popped some champagne corks."

Right around this time, Vail lost its number one standing to Whistler/Blackcomb in Canada in *Snow Country* magazine's reader's poll. It would miss the number one slot the following year, too. That irked Black and Cogut. Black put the plans to develop the Category III area on the fast track. Vail would be the biggest ski area around. No matter what.

17

Battle Mountain

CANADA LYNX FOUND ON VAIL MOUNTAIN

VAIL, Colo.—Vail Associates officials announced today that preliminary results of a wildlife study recently completed on Vail Mountain this winter indicates the presence of Canada Lynx (*Fil. Candadensis*) in existing developed areas as well as in potential expansion areas of Vail Mountain.

...Joe Macy, Mountain planning manager for Vail Associates, indicated that field work for the Vail Mountain lynx study was completed last week. A final report on the study will be completed in several months. Macy said that preliminary indications are that Canada Lynx do not seem to be incompatible with the existing and proposed level of development of the Vail ski area.

...Lynx are night hunters whose diet primarily consists of snowshoe hare and blue grouse. They hide during the day and are seldom seen by man.

—Vail Associates press release, April 2, 1989

Close to the place where naturalist Kim Langmaid saw lynx tracks less than a year before the Vail arsons, a massive hunk of granite with the ominous name of Battle Mountain towers over the landscape. The site earned its blood-evoking name from skirmishes between the Ute and the Arapahoe tribes in the 1800s, when they massacred each other over rights to summer in the area once flush with elk emerging from their breeding grounds.

More than a hundred years later, the land surrounding Battle Mountain —a 6,000-acre chunk of private property sitting between what is now Beaver Creek and Vail ski areas—would become the focal point of another contentious battle. This time the combatants were VA and the current Eagle Valley locals. Instead of flinging arrows, they'd fight through the courts and the media.

Battle Mountain—AKA the Gilman tract—was one mile from the Category III expansion. It was also, many people believed, a place where VA planned to reap unimaginable profits from yet more real estate development. If VA could connect the Gilman tract with its ski area, it might have another bonanza on the scale of Bachelor Gulch.

•

When the whites came west under the flag of Manifest Destiny in the nineteenth century to claim the American West as their own, neither the Utes nor the Arapahoe fought very hard to keep their summering grounds near Battle Mountain. In an almost bloodless coup, fortune-seeking whites arrived and mining claims started stacking up by the late 1870s. The Battle Mountain area was like much of Colorado: It attracted schemers and dreamers and losers and, eventually, big Eastern investors. The first wave consisted of individual prospectors who tore all over the Rockies, notably hitting big silver lodes several passes over from Vail, near Georgetown and

Silver Plume. Lead was found around Battle Mountain, however, and a lode dubbed the Eagle Mine began producing in 1879.

After the turn of the century, when things were more comfortable and settled, the big money moved in. New Jersey Zinc started buying land in Eagle County in 1912, including a consolidated version of the Eagle Mine, and made a mint. According to several accounts, the Eagle Mine produced almost 70 percent of the lead used in both World Wars.

Later, in the increasingly mergers-and-acquisitions way of the world, New Jersey Zinc was absorbed by Gulf & Western. In 1983, a crusty miner named Glenn Miller and a partnership company calling itself Gold Fields bought the land, which had become known as the Gilman tract, from Gulf & Western, even though one corner of it contained enough contaminated mine tailings to be named a Superfund site the following year. A judge ruled that Gulf & Western had to pick up the $60 million cleanup tab because they hadn't told Miller about the problems.

Even with the paid cleanup, Miller and his partners started looking to sell, because the EPA's Superfund designation was hardly what real estate agents think of when they talk about the importance of "location," and back taxes were already starting to pile up. Selling wasn't so easy. "Nobody was stepping forward to buy this property with close to $30 million worth of liens against it and a Superfund site next door," Gold Fields' vice president, Collon Kennedy, one of Miller's partners at the time, told one reporter.

Jim Aronstein and Mike Page, two Denver-area attorneys, formed the Turkey Creek Limited Liability Company and created something of a niche for themselves by buying old mining claims and selling the land to developers. Sometime around 1991, while Miller was shopping his 6,000 acres around, Aronstein and Page strolled the property with Paul Testwuide of VA. If Turkey Creek got the land, might VA want a piece of the action, Page and Aronstein wondered?

VA definitely did. In January 1992, the company set up an agreement with Turkey Creek in which VA would front money for legal costs so that Aronstein and Page could clean up a few liens and competing claims on the land. In return, VA would take a 50 percent option on Gilman if and when the case was settled.

The Turkey Creek boys pecked around and bought up the property's tax liens and eventually bought Miller's partners out in a deal that was contested in court for years. In 1993, Aronstein and Page paid $70,000 for the deed of trust and judgment against Miller that Viacom had inherited when they bought Paramount, which, in turn, had bought Gulf & Western.

When they at last foreclosed on Miller in 1996, armed with the Apollo group's access to capital and lust for development, Aronstein and Page thought they had appropriated a modern day Klondike.

Aronstein and Page had grand visions for the land, Testwuide says with a snort: ski lifts, lots of condos, maybe a golf course. Testwuide reported back to his bosses, which now included Leon Black and Apollo Partners, that the development possibilities were there, but so were a lot of problems: The land was above 10,000 feet in elevation, had expensive infrastructure needs, and was serviced only by a narrow road that went through Minturn. As far as Testwuide was concerned, the Turkey Creek partners' idea for ski lifts at Gilman was a nonstarter; their slopes faced south and weren't even very steep. Furthermore, building a lift to hook up to Category III might be technically feasible, but it would be tough to obtain approval from the U.S. Forest Service; the ensuing public relations nightmare would make the 1976 gondola accident seem like good news. All in all, Testwuide concluded, the company should keep an eye on Aronstein and Page, but the promise of the land's development potential was being oversold.

Aronstein and Page were shrewd. They had inserted a clause into their partnership agreement with VA stating that if the company said or did anything that could be construed as devaluing the land, it would find its deep-pockets ass in court with some very tenacious attorneys.

VA had just met two characters who matched it for ruthlessness.

■

Ted Zukowski, the attorney with the Land and Water Fund of the Rockies, tried to use the lynx issue as a legal avenue to attack Vail's expansion; he compiled evidence that VA may have meddled politically to influence the federal agencies reviewing the animal's fate. Zukowski was desperate to delay the Vail expansion until the state wildlife bureaucrats and the federal agencies had their opinions on the area's biology straight. "The last thing you want to do is take the best lynx habitat and put a big industrial complex on it," he says.

Since 1991, Zukowski had pursued a legal strategy that had seen a lot of success for the Washington-based national environmental groups in the 1980s and 1990s. Using several key laws passed, ironically, under Richard Nixon's presidency—the Endangered Species Act (ESA), the Clean Water Act, and the National Environmental Policy Act—environmental attorneys had persuaded federal judges to back them time and again to stop or slow certain developments or extractive industry proposals. Zukowski had represented various groups who had been petitioning the U.S. Fish and Wildlife Service (FWS) to list the lynx as an endangered species, which would have effectively blocked the Category III expansion. But when the 1994 Republican takeover of Congress resulted in a moratorium on new ESA listings, the appeal was delayed.

With the ESA taken away from him, Zukowski tried attacking the U.S. Forest Service's environmental impact statements when the agency approved the Cat III expansion. The basic argument was that wildlife experts confessed to knowing little about the lynx, much less how the expansion would affect lynx populations. "There have been no recent records of lynx ... because no one has looked," biologist Richard Thompson wrote in one letter criticizing the Environmental Impact Statement, a government scientific report required by law before ski expansions or other development with potential environmental effects could take place. "We don't know squat about the Colorado lynx."

VA had been proclaiming that no lynx were left in the area, but Zukowski discovered that several biologists, both private and from the Colorado Division of Wildlife, had compiled lists of possible lynx track sightings in the Vail area. In the arcane legal world of the Endangered Species Act, it was critical to Zukowski's challenge that some animals remained; if the lynx was already extinct in the region, FWS couldn't act. For VA, it was critical to show that the lynx was long gone.

The enviros assumed that VA was using considerable political muscle to keep the lynx issue out of the Cat III debate. After one Colorado Division of Wildlife biologist called Vail the "last best lynx habitat in the state" in a draft Environmental Impact Statement, a lawyer from the forest service quickly sent a note to the state wildlife agency telling them "not to put anything else in writing." CEO Aron's connections to the Clinton-Gore administration made the heavy-handed federal response immediately suspect to Zukowski.

An e-mail memo from a state wildlife official that was leaked to Zukowski raised other questions about Vail's involvement. The state wildlife agency had been considering a plan to bring back lynx and wolverine to Colorado by trapping them in Canada and transporting them south. The question was, where should they put the furry immigrants? In the e-mail, sent to then–Colorado Division of Wildlife director John Mumma, the writer discussed a meeting with VA. "If VA takes the lead in securing funding for lynx-wolverine recovery, would the state be willing to release VA from all further obligations for preserving and protecting lynx habitat in the Vail ski area expansion zone?" When VA later paid $200,000 to help fund the lynx reintroduction (which happened to be well south of Vail), the environmentalists screamed "foul."

Zukowski saw mounting evidence that VA had managed to suppress inconvenient evidence and throw its political weight around. He turned up a report written by biologists hired by VA in 1989 in which the biologists stated unequivocally that "there is no question that lynx exist at Vail Ski Area and in the surrounding mountains." All the agencies that reviewed and approved VA's expansion plans had apparently also ignored the state wildlife agency's regional manager, Robert Caske, who had stated that "if there is any critical lynx habitat in the state, this is it" concerning the Two Elk area. Another e-mail found its way into Zukowski's hands; this time, a USFWS biologist complained that the agency's scientists supported greater protection for the lynx, but the decision had been made by the higher-ups. "We know we got our legs cut out from under us by Wash[ington]," the e-mail read. "We wind up looking like chumps to the FS [forest service] and Vail."

◆

Between the perceived real estate grab at Gilman and the future of the downtrodden lynx, the enviros had their two-pronged battle plan in place. When the Eagle County commissioners held a hearing in March 1998 to determine whether the county should approve the Category III expansion, the enviros from Boulder and Crested Butte kicked the hive. About three hundred people showed up at the Eagle County Commission hearings—the largest in county history, *vox populi* packing rows of benches stacked amphitheater-style in front of the three commissioners.

Although the CAT III expansion was on federal land, the enviros argued that the county commissioners should have asserted their rights to limit the project, on the grounds that all expansion on the mountain would affect the town and the county. "Ski area expansions cause development," Zukowski said. "It increases infrastructure needs, affects air quality, and increases traffic. Period. No matter what they say."

The argument devolved into a "did so," "did not" repartee: Environmentalists complained that the Cat III expansion was a ploy to develop more ski-in, ski-out property, along the lines of the "ski village" concept that Vail had been championing when it had sold houses for $4 million and up in its Bachelor Gulch development a couple of years before. Balderdash, replied the VA contingent. Cat III was about improving the skier's experience in the north-facing bowls that were far enough away from the base area to give visitors a sense of the backcountry ski experience—without the "earn your turns" grunt work of climbing the mountains personally. The area would also allow for more early- and late-season intermediate skiing on slopes that would hold snow earlier and later than the south-facing back bowls. That was the rationale.

Hooey to that, too, the opponents countered. The one thing Vail didn't need was more intermediate skiing, at any time of the year. Besides, the new area would be so far away from the existing base areas that it wouldn't be easy to connect the ski trails without making a ton more snow.

VA lawyers responded with a series of three-ring binders three feet thick that reminded the commissioners of the seven years and sixty-three studies that had gone into the project, from effects on wildlife to the impacts on air quality. There had been three administrative challenges and three court challenges, and VA had won every one. "This is the most studied ski area expansion in history" became the mantra of VA executives. They had run up a $2 million tab just doing the studies and fending off suits, and had scaled back the development by eliminating one proposed lift and a 20,000-square-foot restaurant in the backcountry acreage. A phalanx of private, state, and federal biologists had done some 6,000 miles of snow tracking, two years of snaring, and watching data from 110 remote cameras without turning up a single "Class I sighting" of a live lynx. VA also presented the commissioners with the petition of 3,000 skiers and snowboarders in favor of the expansion. "It's more PC to say you're against growth than you are for growth," VA spokesman Paul Witt said at the time. "Most of the people who are opposed to this are from Boulder." (He said "Boulder" as if the university town was an alien planet rather than a hundred miles away.)

Besides, said VA execs soothingly, nothing was new or shifty about this proposal. They flaunted a picture of Vail's founder, Pete Seibert, posed over a 3D model of the ski area in 1962; the dreamer's dream definitely included skiing in the area under dispute. "This is not an afterthought," pleaded James Mandel, VA's chief legal counsel at the time.

But the rabble-rousers were prepared for this line of attack. Jeff Berman, the environmentalist from Ancient Forest Rescue who had been instrumental in gathering local opposition, statewide support, and national exposure for the issue, railed on VA for having a 50 percent option on a 6,000-acre tract of land that was one extra ski lift away from being connected to Cat III. Though VA denied it, Berman was convinced that Gilman was destined to become another gaudy and wasteful trophy-home belt, with VA as the main developer.

Then, one by one, people representing any good detective's list of suspects trotted to the microphone. Josef Staufer took apart the "this has been on the table since the beginning" argument. Vail's master plan, he noted icily, was put into place before Keystone, Copper, Beaver Creek, and Arrowhead were even imagined—just four resorts out of many that hadn't existed in Colorado when Vail began. There were no lift lines in those days, and little expectation that the ski industry would grow dramatically. Given that other properties Vail owned commanded at least a $1 million premium for the "ski-in, ski-out" marketing moniker, he reasoned, what other motive could VA possibly have other than real estate development?

Earl Bidez, a town councilman from nearby Minturn, stood to say that he identified with the endangered lynx. "We are now feeling some affinity with the lynx as far as we, as a community, are feeling endangered." Bidez was bitter about the expensive water fight the town had just lost, bitter about the New York takeover of the nearby resort. "These are not nice people we're dealing with," he complained. "These are not the same people we were on a first-name basis with just a few years ago." David Kinney, a local schoolteacher, chimed in. "Vail is already less of a town and more of a shopping mall, less of a place for people who call it home and more a playground for the rich and frivolous."

Publisher-turned-rancher Merrill Hastings launched into a diatribe about the fate of the valley, which was being turned into an ugly conglomeration of strip malls, gigantic homes, golf courses, and trailer parks, all to service out-of-state nouveau riches who were behaving like ugly Americans with their stock market spoils. As he talked, he mentioned that the crowd "hadn't heard from a good friend of mine." Then he draped a lynx pelt over the lectern.

The commissioners, along with many other county commissioners in the rural West, weren't much disposed to limiting growth of any kind. Faced with mounds of wildlife studies, environmental impact reports, court rulings, and the approval of the landlord—the U.S. Forest Service— the commissioners approved the project.

●

The county commissioners' vote didn't stop Berman and his band of diehards at Ancient Forest Rescue. They organized a boycott of Vail through university ski clubs, and began civil disobedience training camps in the woods to teach a new breed of radicals the basics of tree sits and construction blockades, and the art of the "Batmobile"—where activists cement a pipe in the ground with a piece of rebar under it, then overturn a car with a hole cut in the roof. An activist then climbs into the car, sticks a hand into the ground through the roof, and chains him- or herself to the subterranean rebar. It was a lot more time-consuming to extricate someone from that setup than it was to cut away someone handcuffed to a bulldozer —an old trick of the enviros. But they knew that even such elaborate civil disobedience could do only so much.

The last legal gasp was a final appeal to Federal District Court Judge Edward Nottingham, who was not a disinterested party. Nottingham is the son of a homesteader who sold VA the land that is now the home of Beaver Creek resorts, and the Nottingham family still owns some of the largest parcels of private land in Eagle County. Several Nottinghams or their relatives still work for VA. But the words "conflict of interest" apparently never reared their ugly heads, and the judge chose not to recuse himself. Instead, he issued blistering attacks on Zukowski's arguments, and cleared the way for Vail to bring in the bulldozers.

Nothing was left for Zukowski, Berman, Staufer, and Doon to do.

Or was there?

18

Tequila Stunt Man

As a symbolic, if fruitless, act of rebellion, the moment was perfect. After midnight, Roby stood at the top of the half-pipe he had meticulously groomed until it was nearly as smooth as a bowling alley. Alone on this part of the mountain, he winched two snow cats into place and pointed their headlights down the hill, flooding the massive snow trench with light. Listening for sounds of other cat drivers or snowmobiles, and hearing none, he pulled his snowboard out of the snow cat and strapped it to his boots. The pipe was beautifully buffed, the lips at just the right angle, the snow fresh corduroy. "It was sweet," he recalls. He hopped into position and pointed the board into the pipe to begin an unobserved, solo snowboard ballet. He dropped down into the pipe, then felt the centrifugal force tighten his tendons as he gathered speed, then rose up the almost vertical side, caught air off the lip, and landed clean. His momentum building, he crossed to the other side, then flew off the lip and sensed a sublime moment of free-floating, antigravity suspension. While floating, he grabbed the side of his board like a bronc rider holding the reins, the other hand waving free. He was in rhythm now: down the pipe again, big air on the other lip, another grab. Back down and again and again, a rolling, rocking motion that defied time and gravity and everything else for maybe forty seconds. He hit the last jump, cruised to a stop, felt his heart beating and the exhilaration start to mix with fear. "I'm thinking, 'Don't wanna get caught, don't wanna get caught.'" The only way back up is on foot. "I never climbed back up a half-pipe faster in my life."

One snowy night the year after the still-unsolved fires, I decided to groom all night with Roby. We set out in a *remuda* of cats, which would spend the night trailing up and down the mountain either "flapping" or "tilling," depending on the snow.

When Roby greets me, he is wearing a tie-died Woodstock T-shirt; I note that his "do" is looking pretty much like a "'fro" this late in the season. "If I keep it off my shoulders, it's regulation," he says. If his hair were wet and straight, it'd hit his shoulders. He and the other cat drivers have to wear black or blue pants, even though the clientele rarely sees them. "Must have conformity in the ranks," he says, saluting.

Roby's charge tonight is to groom the half-pipe so beloved of snowboarders. A half-pipe is just what it sounds like: a curved, wide snow trench roughly the size of a thirty-foot-diameter drain pipe. In the past few years, virtually every major resort in the United States has built terrain parks for the snowboard set, a grouping of jumps, lips, and half-pipes where riders can get big air and perform tricks. To do his "pipe cutting," Roby drives a snow cat with a hydraulic monster called the Dragon (an ingenious $60,000 machine that sports a conveyor belt with cutters) attached to the snow cat. For all his bravado, Roby is a perfectionist and carefully examines his work after each run, spending twenty minutes making multiple passes on a few feet of pipe.

Roby is an astute observer of the changes among his tribe of ski bums, and in the past few years, he's noticed that he's a vanishing breed. He resents the "North Dakota boys"—farm boys recruited from the frozen north to drive tractors on snow instead of on fields. "They don't even ski or board," says Roby in disgust. "They play 'no-friendo' [Nintendo] all day long, drink Bud, and ride snowmobiles around." There are way more Mexican immigrants than North Dakota boys working in and around the valley, and almost none of them ski or snowboard, either.

"They give out visas like they're candy," he adds, and they don't always play nice with their *Gastarbiters.* One friend of Roby's had his visa held over his head after he came to the country ready to work—but before the people at VA were ready to put him on the payroll. The friend couldn't leave, but couldn't find work elsewhere, either.

To Roby, it all seemed part of a complicated, almost conspiratorial, VA plan. First they make the jobs lousy enough, the living conditions ugly enough, and the pay paltry enough; then they complain they can't attract U.S. employees, and therefore deserve more visas for foreign workers. The more migrant labor they get, the lower wages and living conditions go, an ever-widening vicious circle. Or, if all you care about is the bottom line, perhaps not so vicious.

As he rides the snow cat in a snowstorm, Roby explains his theory of the fires. He whips out his employee gas card to demonstrate how easy it would have been to break into the gas caches—one located close to PHQ and another close to Two Elk. "All you need is one of these," he says, holding up what looks like a plastic rectangular hotel key. "You punch in your employee number, the vehicle odometer reading, and bingo, the gas flows." But then you'd leave an electronic trail that could be traced, wouldn't you? "Anybody who works here knows that there's a gas card in the cowling of every snowmobile on the mountain," he says. The employee numbers aren't always traceable, he adds, because VA issues a lot of duplicates. "Do you know how many employee numbers are 0000?" he asks rhetorically. What about the odometer readings, I wondered. "The machine doesn't know how many miles are on your snow cat."

Later, over hot chicken wings ($3.99 a dozen) and discounted pitchers of beer at Garfinkle's, Roby's Tuesday night ritual meal, he sits with a couple of buddies to quaff brew and shoot the breeze. Other ski bums come in and banter with Roby, exchanging news of a friend who blew out a knee or the latest edition of condo rental roulette. As I write down Roby's last name and his telephone number, his drunken friend leans over.

"I thought you only had one name, dude," he says with astonishment. "You know, like Madonna."

Roby guffaws. "Self-control's a beautiful thing, but not everybody's got it." He points to the friend who made the Madonna crack. "Tim here is a perfect example of what happens when you have no self-control in a ski town."

More pitchers flow, and there's talk of heading across town to 8150, the latest wee-hours gathering spot, now that midnight is approaching. Roby is dared to do a "tequila stunt man," and I, as usual, am baffled. Roby explains: You snort the salt, drink the shot, and squeeze the lemon in your eye. Why would anybody want to do that, I wonder aloud. If you have to ask ...

We hop on one of the free shuttle buses that travel across town, and I witness a classic clash of local and visitor, the meeting of otherwise parallel universes. Roby stands next to the bus driver, slapping skin and jabbering about getting up early for first tracks in the morning. On the bus, a beautiful Argentine visitor shifts uncomfortably in her seat and tucks her mink coat a little more tightly around her. She is bemused and a little frightened by this species of ski bum, and will no doubt recount her adventure to her friends. The driver has the Pink Floyd tune "Money" playing at slightly higher-than-official decibel levels. "Get your hands off my stack," wail the bus speakers. Roby sways on the metal pole, standing just in front of the yellow line that says, "Please stand behind this line while bus is moving."

At 8150 this particular Tuesday night, the drinks continue to flow and Roby holds forth. The place is just filling up. A band called Blister 66 is playing, the lead singer in a skull cap, no shirt, and pec-to-pec tattoos. There are young men in ponytails—the real, long kind, without accompanying receding hairlines—and lots of backward baseball caps and men with buzz cuts. One man wears a hairdresser's frock with the name "Elaine" stitched on his right breast. Wafts of pot smoke drift through the cavernous nightclub, all industrial I-beams and high ceilings. The place is filling up as if a sports event were about to begin; virtually no customers under the age of twenty-five are to be seen. The predominantly male crowd slouches around, Coronas in hand, tonsorial combinations abounding: goatees and close-shaven heads, retro sideburns, and highlighted blonds in the style of white rapper Eminem. The list of coming attractions means something to most of them: Bands such as Project Lojic, Das EFX and Blacksheep, Hyroglifics, Groove Collective, and Deep Banana Blackout are all visiting in the winter of 1999.

This is the ski industry's underground, the necessary evil that keeps the lifts running, the slopes groomed, the rental skis fitted, the muffins sold, the hot tubs cleaned, the buffets piled high. Roby feels unappreciated. "The millionaires who come here don't get it that it's us ski bums that are the ones waiting on them!" he screams over the cacophony of Blister 66's angry white suburban teenager tunes. I ask about the current mating rituals of the ski bum, and he complains that the male-to-female ratio is disconcertingly high, as evidenced, he gestures with a sweep of his arm, by the turnout tonight. "Here you don't lose your girlfriend, you just lose your turn," he says. Roby's roommate Ann, cocktail in hand, shares the female perspective: "Here, the odds are good. But the goods are odd."

Thankfully, there remain a few time-honored, almost picaresque traditions of ski-bum life that have remained unchanged through the decades. For instance, an honorable ski bum "never pays full price for food, except at McDonald's," intones Roby in the manner of someone reciting scripture. (Thou Shalt Not Pay Retail seems to be the unofficial religious dogma of the ski-bum tribe.) "Everybody's tapped for cash who lives here, so you hook each other up," he says matter-of-factly. There are buffets to raid, and hot tubs to poach "every night of the week if you want to." Hot-tub poaching is almost a civic sport among Roby's ilk. The test is simple. Go to one of the ubiquitous outdoor tubs in one of the equally ubiquitous condo associations, hotels, and clubs. Check the security by opening a gate, slamming it, and waiting in the bushes. If nobody comes, the coast is clear and it's party time. Similarly, there are steam rooms, workout facilities, baskets of croissants, thick slices of prime rib, and an abundance of other animal, vegetable, and recreational freebies. All for the taking. But if people are helping each other in unofficial quid pro quos, I ask Roby, what does he have to offer? "I'm the one who's grooming the pipe," he says. "They all know that. Sometimes those landings need to be taken care of. I'm their man."

At the end of the season, I join Roby and his posse for another piece of irrepressible ski-bum ritual: the BB&B. Nobody is sure what the letters stand for, or about the exact provenance of the springtime rite; but everybody *is* sure that the BB&B is an unsanctioned, on-mountain bacchanalia that takes place in a secluded picnic area surrounded by a grove of trees and out of sight of the tourists. As I arrive in the late afternoon, the scene appears to be a twisted ski-bum version of a Rainbow gathering (the roving bands of latter-day hippies who congregated annually on forest lands around the country) mixed with Mardi Gras. Young women stroll by with glitter eyes and pink boas; men in duderific snowboard pants, backward baseball caps, and brews in hand watch the parade, nodding as if listening to an invisible rhythm. The music blares from speakers in a tree and people gather in dugout pits that look like snow-cave living rooms, some with buffets spread out on ice tables.

Members of the snow-bum tribe chat and share smokes, occasionally aiming a snowball at a few buck-naked skiers who cross an unofficial no-man's-land in a small clearing. The smell of pot and Marlboro Reds fills the great outdoors, where more than a thousand of Roby's clan has gathered, carting minikegs, cases, talls, six-packs, and beer bongs; pipes and bowls and papers and the means to spark them up; mushroom tea and psyche-delics of all stripes. "All these people, they serve the tourists all season long," Roby exults, his hair curls wild, tongue ring again intact, and blaze orange United Airlines mechanic's vest hanging over his brightly colored shirt in vertical stripes of primary colors. His neck garlanded with Mardi Gras beads, Roby looks around the encampment in the ponderosa pine groves at the droves of revelers, then lifts a Bud in salute. "Today, the mountain belongs to them." Somebody unleashes a round of firecrackers into the crowd, which erupts in whoops and hollers with each incendiary flare.

Roby and his posse decide to take a couple of runs before the lifts close at 4:00 P.M. They strap into their snowboards and take off in a pack of eight, cruising the mountain at high speed, bobbing and jumping off each lip, cornice, and bump. I feel as though I am swimming with a school of dolphins, or playing in a torrent with river otters. The boarders gracefully pop up, weave close to each other, but sense each other's moves as they swerve and streak down the mountain with abandonment. They are high. It is their day.

Later, I ask him about the sociology of the assemblage. There seem to be a lot of young kids driving some pretty expensive SUVs, I've noticed. Roby nods knowingly, then tells me he doesn't begrudge the trust-funder ski bums, or "Trustafarians," who don't have to work. "That's what I'd do if I had a check coming in every month without having to work for it." But he's cynical about the way Vail came into being, and wants to know, when I tell him I'm writing the history of Vail, whether I'm "gonna write about how Pete 'n Earl swindled the poor farmers out of their land." Even the ski bums know about Vail's dubious origins.

The next time I visit Roby, he is busted up. In a little more than a month, he has sprained his wrist, broken his foot, turned three vertebrae, and generally banged himself up big time. "I had a coupla crashes," he says matter-of-factly. "I just splattered." Then he grins that grin again. "VA's health plan kicks ass."

Talk turns to the arsonists again. He thinks that whoever set the fires made a pretty dumb choice. "If you're going to hurt somebody, hit 'em where it hurts. Spike every tree. Put sugar in their gas tanks. Blow up roads. Buy the *Anarchist's Cookbook*.

"I don't understand the targets at all," he says, his brow furrowing. "Burn down a restaurant? C'mon. There's only about fifteen others. What a pathetic gesture. It was a pretty senseless act. If I was an ecoterrorist, I'd do a better job."

What else did he think about the placement of the fires?

"Well, somebody had to know the mountain pretty well," he says with grin.

"You know the mountain pretty well, don't you?" I say rhetorically, goading him a little. His grin is sloppier than before, a little more telling. He shakes his head so hard his curls bounce. "I'm a cat driver. I know where that shit is." He holds up his hands and turns one of his palms in to his face.

Suddenly serious, Roby points to the back of the hand that is now facing me. "There's the mountain right there."

19

What the Poodles Knew

Arson is a very serious crime, so before considering it you'd better be aware of the possible consequences if caught. Fire is also terribly dangerous, so the utmost care is needed when starting one. It's necessary to be positive that no human or non-human animals will be hurt in the blaze. It is also dangerous media-wise. Arson carries the heavy tags of "terrorism," and must be used wisely as not to discredit the entire movement. As dangerous as arson is, it is also by far the most potent weapon of direct action. One of the first arson attacks in the U.S. was against a new research lab at U.C. Davis doing over four million dollars in damage.

When constructing your incendiary device, be careful!

—FROM THE ANIMAL LIBERATION FRONT'S WEB SITE

As the fires died out, two Eagle County sheriff's deputies arrived at the Ancient Forest Rescue campsite and methodically wrote down the names and addresses of about thirty activists from Durango, Boulder, and Fort Collins, along with their driver's license numbers and phone numbers. The deputies learned that a small advance group of AFR protestors had spent the night higher on the mountain to establish a forward camp so they would be ready to blockade the crane if it came early.

The deputies took off up the trail with the list of camper-activists they had just compiled. Then, inexplicably, they lost the list. Later, when a federal grand jury investigated the arson, the lost list would come back to bite law enforcement right in the sitzmark.

After the deputies took the campers' names, most of the AFR protestors decided not to stick around and get accusatory fingers pointed in their faces; when it came time to round up the usual suspects, they knew they'd be in the mix. Most headed off, despondent and a little scared, for their respective homes scattered around the state. Congenitally distrustful of authority, with many of the younger hotheads among them ready to believe that the FBI might have set the fires themselves as a way to crack down on radical civil disobedience, soon the activists were gleefully giving the impression that they weren't cooperating with law enforcement.

As far as the feds were concerned, the attitude itself was suspicious. Did the group, or somebody associated with it, have something to hide? If they wouldn't talk now, there were always ways to make them talk later—like the threat of a federal judge's contempt charge and a few months in jail.

Perhaps more than any of the known activists, Jonathan Staufer found himself squarely at the point where the red laser sight formed an "X." But Staufer, along with many of the locals, believed that the honchos at VA *were* Machiavellian enough to have set the fires themselves. Parroting the line from *"All the President's Men"* about Watergate, Staufer asked, "Follow the money. Who paid for it? Who profited from it?" Red Tail Lodge near Beaver Creek burned down the previous year, after Vail had been denied a permit to expand. They rebuilt it, and bigger. The same deal with Two Elk: rebuilt with insurance money, bigger and better. "Most arsons *are* self-inflicted," he says.

But does he *seriously* believe VA did it? "I just thought those were interesting coincidences," he tells me over coffee, smirking and pulling on a fresh American Spirit cigarette. "I'm sure they asked, 'How are we going to get anything done if we've got the whole community against us?'"

What about the claim of responsibility by the ELF? "They're a convenient scapegoat, aren't they?"

What pisses Staufer off is his belief that public opinion had been turned firmly in the right direction before the fires. "People here were beginning to realize that Category III is the biggest snow job ever to come to Colorado," he says. "Vail Resorts clear-cutting 885 acres of old-growth forest—that's ecoterrorism," he says resolutely.

"As far as an alibi," he adds, "I guess I don't have much of one. I was at my parents' house, alone." He pauses, defensive, then feigns indifference. "I know where I was."

The smoke spills out from his mouth, and he aims a mischievous smile across the table. "My poodles know where I was."

●

As the FBI, the ATF, the Colorado Bureau of Investigation, the Eagle County Sheriff's Department, the Vail Police Department, and a few other law enforcement agencies fanned out into the Vail area and around the state, the leads started pouring in—563 of them. One report—false, it turned out—had it that bombs had been set to go off at the restaurant complex on the mountain called Mid-Vail. There was the more credible sighting of a suspicious "hunter" whose truck, which had Oregon plates, had been stuck in the mud; this turned out to be a hunter from Oregon whose truck had been stuck in the mud. As well as the usual crank calls, there were the well-meaning calls that were goose-chasers from the get-go.

Nothing terribly promising.

But almost every lead was pursued. Early on, Vail President Andy Daly received a nervous call from somebody who claimed to have information about the fire. The caller had a tape recording of a phone conversation between two Boulderites that was apparently quite incriminating. Daly convinced the man to call back, and had an FBI psychologist/profiler listen to the call on a speaker phone. The FBI tried to trace the call, but couldn't. The man said he had overheard conversations between a pair of activists in Boulder, and had a tape recording he felt was critical to the investigation. Suddenly nervous, the man cut the conversation short and said he wanted an attorney present for the next talk.

After the call, the psychologist debriefed Daly. The caller was between twenty-five and twenty-eight, the psychologist conjectured, and some of the idioms he used identified him as having an East Coast upbringing. The man was probably the son of a lawyer, the profiler told Daly, because of his knowledge of certain arcane legal concepts. The psychologist believed the man was acting out of conscience, and was willing to betray confidences because he felt morally bound to share the information. This could be important.

Eventually, the FBI talked to the man's attorney, heard the tape, and decided there was no value in the tip. "It was a wild-goose chase," says Daly, frustrated. "There were a lot of people who could take credit for the incident but who weren't necessarily involved in it."

The day after the initial ELF communiqué arrived, the FBI's supervisory special agent in Denver, John Kundts, worried that solving the arson would be difficult. "There was no fire fighting effort. Those buildings were burned down to nothing. That could be a problem." Later, when a VA employee received via e-mail a second possible ELF communiqué that said, "We're going to do it again," VA called the FBI immediately. But for some inexplicable reason, the FBI didn't immediately try to track the message back to the Internet service provider. (Apparently, if the trace isn't started within the first forty-eight hours of receiving the message, there's no hope at all of finding the server on which the message originated.)

C. Suzanne Mencer, a former FBI domestic terrorism expert based in Denver, had never heard of the ELF at the time of the fires. She also thought it dangerous to take the claim at face value, especially since the initial e-mail had arrived some sixty-plus hours after the fires were set. "It's unusual that they waited so long to claim credit for it," she told me. She noted that the communiqué seemed "pretty well written," which also was unusual. There were double spaces after the periods. Terrorists were "not usually very well educated. This doesn't sound like the usual militia-type individual."

Still, she wasn't dismissing the possibility of an ELF strike's being real. "It's the people that become too radical for their own groups and splinter off that are very dangerous. How do we find out about those people until they commit a crime?"

And how do you prove they've committed a crime if they have?

Up on the mountain, Eagle County Sheriff Department Sgt. Steve Huskey gave his canine, Cash, a workout searching for footprints or the scent of suspects leaving either of the fire sites. A single set went from the Two Elk area to the PHQ area along the ridge road, but Cash didn't detect anything suspicious entering or leaving the sites. There were several sets of hunters' tracks, and the fire trucks had obliterated the snow on the ridge road. On the morning of the fires, the sun had melted most of the footprints that weren't shaded. By mid-morning, there was no contiguous snow around the place, only a helluva lot of mud. For the next few days, K9 Cash and Sgt. Huskey, who endured his share of good-natured doo-doo for having a name like that on the canine squad, searched the entire front of the mountain along with several other K9 units. But no evidence. Nada.

■

Two of ATF's four National Response Teams had arrived and split up, all business: One took the area around PHQ, which included the charcoal heap that used to be the restaurant called Buffalo's and the charred Lifts 4, 5, and 11; the other team corralled the Two Elk area, which included Camp One and Chair 14. Each team had several certified fire investigators, an explosives enforcement officer, a fire protection engineer, a forensic chemist, a canine accelerant-sniffer and its handler, an evidence technician, and a few agents cross-trained in several disciplines. They looked for "pour patterns," tried to assess the areas of most damage where the fires burned longest or hottest, analyzed the portions of buildings and lifts left standing, interviewed eyewitnesses, and sifted through tons of debris, layer by layer, for any clue that might help, such as the remnant of a timing device or, better yet, an unignited incendiary device. They mapped the site and ran computer models to simulate the fire scene.

Many of the agents who had come from sea level were already having a hard time with the town's 8,000-foot elevation. Those who had work to do at 11,000 feet felt it even more, and had to guard against dehydration and mild altitude sickness. It was hard to believe somebody could just bop up from sea level and pull this off.

After digging through the ashes for nearly a week, agents identified about two dozen points of origin by using dogs to sniff out pockets of unburned fuel buried in the soil or in hidden crevices, then analyzing the finds with sensitive chemical tests: gas chromatography, mass spectrometry, and a carbon spectrophotometer. They sent agents to canvas local service stations. It was a long shot, but sometimes you could find a gas station attendant who remembered selling diesel to guys who weren't driving a diesel truck. After all, the feds tracked McVeigh in the Oklahoma City case by finding a piece of a vehicle's identification number amongst the smithereens and tracing it to a rental agency. You never know where you're gonna get your break.

They did have a few things going for them. The time of the fires was, more or less, a known factor, because of the alarms and the first eyewitnesses' accounts. Certain pieces of arson investigations were a matter of applying pure, immutable laws of physics: glass melts at about 925 degrees, aluminum at 1,100, and copper at around 2,000. Generally, fires that don't have the help of an accellerant top out at about 1,500 to 1,600 degrees. This fire, which had melted the copper in the electrical wiring, had had petrochemical help.

It wouldn't have taken much fuel to coax Two Elk to catch. At a minimum, somewhere between five and eight two-liter plastic soda containers filled with a diesel/gas mix might have been enough. (Gasoline alone is too volatile for a good arson, and diesel not volatile enough.) If you tripled that amount to account for all the other fires, you still didn't need anything more than one, maybe two, strong young bucks with backpacks to get the fuel up the mountain. At 7.75 pounds per gallon, 90 pounds of fuel could've done the whole thing easy. A piece of cake for two strong hikers. Even easier if you got it up on a truck.

With their devices strategically located, the pyros would need nothing more sophisticated than gas-soaked sponges as a starter. At Two Elk, once they placed the devices strategically under the eaves, it would be as simple as lighting the sponges with a sparked-up punk and watching the fireworks display. As the sponge burned, it would slowly melt the plastic. The liquid would spread by gravity, ignite, and catch onto the wood structure. As the wood caught, the fire could then race up into the eaves like an incendiary vine on steroids. The fire would burn the rafters made of twenty-inch-wide plywood I-beams called TJIs, and catch the ceiling paneling, which would collapse before the sprinkler system could go off. By the time the sprinkler heads started up, when the temperature reached 165 degrees, they'd be as effective as a Supersoaker on a forest fire.

The timing was a key to determining whether there had to be two teams of arsonists, or whether one team, or even one person, could have pulled it off. Investigators knew that although the alarm at Two Elk had gone off a half hour after the alarm at PHQ, it would have taken longer for the alarms and sprinklers to get hot enough to go off at Two Elk. Who knows what the actual sequence of events had to be? They had the hunters' witness testimony. They knew that the first VA and fire people who went up arrived before Two Elk had collapsed. But unless they could find better answers with more forensic detective work, how could they tell whether there had been separate groups of arsonists, or whether one group, maybe even a solo firebug, could have traipsed the mile and a half between the two groups of fires? They started looking for evidence of a timing device, like the ones that had failed in Rock Springs and at the prairie dog protests. They also took the gas can found near Chair 11 and dusted it for fingerprints. No luck. It had probably just been left on the mountain by VA employees who used it to fuel the snow machines, anyway.

These Vail arsonists were good, but not first-rate pros. An expert would have disabled the alarm and sprinkler systems first, without leaving any indication that anything was amiss. But even if the arsonists weren't first-class firebugs, they had managed to light a first-class fire. If it had been the ELF, how did they improve their skills so quickly after those failed attempts in the previous weeks? Did they really learn from their mistakes? Or were they just lucky to set fire to a huge, kiln-dried tinderbox in a place so remote that they could take their time without worrying about detection?

At the interagency law enforcement briefings and over beers at night, one operating theory of the crime gained credibility: Somebody with local connections had to have been involved. Maybe not the one with the match, but the strategic thinker. Somebody had to have known the mountain, where to strike, how to get on and off undetected. "Joe Schmoe off the street wouldn't be able to pull it off," one investigator concluded. The enemy, they realized, was almost assuredly within.

20

The Toniest Resort in the World

VAIL-SAFE

You'll hit the slopes in style with this exclusive Vail Resorts vacation featuring five nights in a three-bedroom penthouse suite at the Lodge at Vail and two nights at Trapper's Cabin, a mountaintop retreat at Beaver Creek. The package includes three days of skiing at Vail Mountain with a private instructor, one day of skiing the powder at Ptarmigan Pass via Sno-Cat, and three days' skiing at Beaver Creek. You'll also be well-equipped for the slopes with his and her Fila ski suits, TAG Heuer sports watches, Bolle sunglasses and goggles, Volant Ti Super skis, custom-fitted Nordica Grand Prix Exopower ST boots, and Marker bindings. Other amenities include en suite breakfasts, gourmet dinners at Vail's finest restaurants, first-class air travel into Vail/Eagle County Airport, limousine transport to Vail Village, a spa pass to the Allegria Spa in Beaver Creek, seats for performances at the Vilar Center for the Arts in Beaver Creek, and a hot-air balloon ride. $37,725.

—FROM THE DECEMBER 1998 ROBB REPORT'S "ULTIMATE GIFT GUIDE"

From its inception in 1962, Vail Associates intended to cater to the wealthiest people in the world with a combination of cachet, comfort, and Colorado champagne powder. Each successive owner upgraded the services and the image of this exclusive mountain retreat—providing a meticulously groomed mountain, first-class on-mountain amenities, and the sense that visitors would become walk-on actors in the most elegant façade in the West. A ski vacation at Vail, and even more so at its younger, more upscale cousin, Beaver Creek, was designed to be the ultimate ski resort experience. All the visitors needed to bring was money.

All major credit cards accepted.

At Beaver Creek, which is essentially a boutique private resort clustered around public lands, VA has created an even more exclusive destination than Vail proper. Vail, is, after all, located on Interstate 70 and is, in the words of a local doctor, "still only a day's Greyhound ride away from Las Vegas." Vail occasionally sees the odd drifter or mental patient who was given a one-way ticket and ends up wandering into the medical center emergency room looking for morphine derivatives, thereby lending the tiniest frisson of danger to the town. The past several New Year's Eves, including the Y2K celebration, the police have even had to arrest unruly revelers who came up from Denver to party.

Beaver Creek remains much less touched by anything resembling the real world. A visitor to Beaver Creek leaves I-70 in Avon, about ten miles west of Vail. After driving quickly past a Denny's, a few real estate offices, a Wal-Mart, a grocery store, and a few restaurants, and through a couple of roundabouts that constitute Avon proper, the entrance to Beaver Creek appears. Instead of a simple electronic gate, visitors must pass through a kiosk manned by amiable but wary minders who are alternately obsequious to the owners and well-heeled visitors, or suspicious of those with dirty older-model cars and multiple facial piercings.

Although the mountain is owned by the U.S. public, not many of them can afford to go up there. According to the National Ski Areas Association, the median household income of all skiers nationally is $96,000 per year. Vail weighs in at $145,000 per year, and Beaver Creek at $155,000 per year. Already, skiing survives by attracting from the richest 3.5 percent of the U.S. population, about 10 million skiers nationwide. Vail and Beaver Creek skim the top percentile of the top percentile.

Heading up the hill to Beaver Creek, one sees Adam Aron's house on the left, and then progressively more expensive houses and condos that culminate in the vaunted ski-in, ski-out properties that sell for fifteen hundred dollars per square foot. Aron had written a "Why-can't-we-all-get-along?" letter to the editor of one of the local papers, in which he wonders, looking out his picture window at elk grazing, bees buzzing, and the creek babbling, why people who live here amidst such beauty should have to fight so much. Locals responded angrily that it was a lot easier to enjoy life up there from the deck of a $3 million house than from the crowded living room of a double-wide.

The village of Beaver Creek is a much grander testimony to Disney-like imagineering than the funky town of Minturn—or even Vail—will ever be. There are heated escalators that cost $1.5 million to build, and heating elements under the main plaza to keep it clear of snow, which ran another $1.5 million to install. The oversized Bavarian-style wood lintels are a bit too oversized, and the copper roofs and copper flashing could only be more expensive if they were made of gold leaf. In the center of the village sits a $15 million ice skating rink named after either Apollo partner Leon Black or the deadly film of frozen water that forms over asphalt: Black Ice.

Beaver Creek is decidedly a money-is-no-object kind of place. You can rent Trapper's Cabin, an on-mountain chalet at 9,500 feet, where, as a brochure coos, "your private chef and cabin-keeper will attend to your every need." For visitors to Trapper's, gourmet appetizers of rare ahi tuna on a bed of jicama and tangerine slaw with wasabi aioli await, followed by entrees of pan-seared elk loin. For $750 a night at high season, visitors enjoy a Swiss-inspired interior decorator's wet dream, including a taxidermist's idea of communing with nature. A wrap-around deck features a hot tub situated nearly two miles above sea level, a full bar with only top-drawer spirits, and of course de rigeur terrycloth bathrobes for tubbing with a glass of Grgich Hills Chardonnay in hand. Ski concierges dry your boots at night and carry your skis to the lifts in the morning. Helmut Fricker plays Bavarian music on the accordion, or sounds the alpenhorn while you check your rented global positioning tracking device, which tells you how many vertical feet you skied before lunch. A few C-notes get you VIP "first tracks" down the mountain after a stellar snowfall, complete with private ski patrol accompaniment. And don't forget the vaunted (and patented) "Village to Village™" skiing, where schussers with a taste for long, uneventful traverses can go from Beaver Creek to Bachelor Gulch to Arrowhead—all principally owned by Vail Resorts.

If you've joined the Beaver Creek Club, a private society with a $30,000 initiation fee and a $2,500 annual fee, you have access to an enclave where, "because everything is planned, every detail addressed, members are just left to indulge." Members have exclusive access to a pair of five-star, on-mountain private lunch clubs, as well as a health club in town, Allegria, which has been cleared by feng shui experts as a great place to get a massage.

In the evening, the hoi polloi who can't afford to stay *on* the mountain are pulled up in sleighs to Beano's Cabin for a meal of buffalo carpaccio, grilled breast of pheasant, beluga caviar, and grilled loin of venison with sweet potato puree, roasted figs, and gooseberry reduction. Don't forget a glass of port. Prix fixe. If you have to ask …

At Beaver Creek, as at Vail, the tales of visitors' excesses are legendary. Local gossip: Did you hear about the Mexican millionairess who plunked down her platinum American Express card to buy $165,000 worth of watches, or a grateful CEO who slipped his ski instructor a five-grand tip after a week's skiing? People who regularly buy three or four bottles of champagne for lunch, at two hundred a pop? The business mogul who routinely racks up a $70,000 annual bill for private lessons? Not counting tips.

Oh, and the skiing is pretty good, too.

◆

In the end, the skiing at Beaver Creek and Vail is only as good as the snow. To provide snow, even if Mother Nature doesn't, VA has installed sixty-one miles of underground pipe at Vail alone that transport 2,000 gallons of water each minute out of Gore Creek and another 2,000 gallons each minute from the Eagle River, twenty-four hours a day, seven days a week, from late October until, usually, after New Year's. The slopes look like an enormous prairie dog village, crisscrossed as they are with subterranean tunnels of sixteen-inch-diameter air lines, ten-inch water lines, and twelve-inch compressed-air lines, connected by welded steel pipe and attached to 555 hydrants that spray snow around the mountain with an industrial roar. A Minnesota boy, Dave Techolke, head of snowmaking, doesn't seem to mind the zero degree weather as he installs me on the back of his snowmobile for an early-morning tour of the mountain. "It's basically just frozen water," he says, showing how the water and the compressed air mix together to make artificial but serviceable fluff. "The colder it is, the better the snow is."

Global warming is an issue nobody wants to talk about in the ski industry. But globally, the 1990s were the hottest decade ever recorded, with five of the hottest years on record since 1880, when recordkeeping began. The year of the fires, 1998–1999, and the following season, were both below par for snow—and for Vail. Skier visits declined and the incentive to buy more water rights and obtain permission to make more snow only increased.

Snowmaking started in the 1950s with a rudimentary system that essentially took crushed ice and spread it around the mountain. Skiers in those days took good years and bad years in stride, and the mountain moguls who ran the resorts did the same. But for Vail, the winter of 1980–1981 was disastrous; VA started investing seriously in snowmaking machinery and purchasing water rights from abandoned mining claims and ranchers who had decided to cash out.

Environmentalists have long questioned the effects of snowmaking on the water quality of rivers. The resorts say they never draw too much water; they assert they preserve what has been euphemistically called minimum stream flows—meaning they leave just enough water so the fish don't have to learn to breathe oxygen. Biologists are especially concerned that the bulk of snowmaking takes place in the season of the lowest natural water flows—

autumn—and that the downstream effects include a buildup of mineral concentrations that degrade the water quality.

Vail spends at least $750,000 in power alone during two months of solid snowmaking, with the aim of opening the season before Thanksgiving, whether or not enough natural snow has fallen. Vail hires thirty-five snowmakers, and runs three shifts, twenty-four/seven, and pays operators about nine dollars an hour starting. Not much is left to chance, except for Mother Nature's ability to lower temperatures enough to make snow. Everything about the snowmaking process is computerized and monitored from a central location on the mountain called "Snow Summit." The snowmakers follow the performance of every valve on the mountain, and watch a computer screen that tracks air pressure, water pressure, temperature, humidity, flow rates, and wet bulb temperature.

Snowmaking, in this business, is the equivalent of alchemy; it turns plain river water into white gold. And VA can make a lot of white gold. The company's enormous snowmaking facilities and rapacious water consumption are much in keeping with its approach to life: Nothing—not even the weather—is going to get in our way. In addition to making snow, the company regularly seeds clouds to bring more snow. Perhaps more than a few environmentalists grinned at the irony of VA's greedily consuming so much water but having none when it could have used it the most—to extinguish the fires.

21

Biggering

Overheard at the Two Elk lunch counter register:

The father and his two children, maybe ten and fourteen, wait in line to pay for their lunch at Two Elk, the cavernous and elegant lodge that was burned down and rebuilt even larger than before. The dad has already forked out sixty-one bucks each for lift tickets, no discounts for the kids—not to mention the cost of lodging, transportation to get here, and buying the thousands of dollars of ski equipment—nothing particularly top end—that he and his children needed for the mountain: skis that retail for five hundred bucks, bindings another couple hundred, boots at three hundred, graphite ski poles at two hundred a pair, goggles at another hundred, two hundred for the parkas, and let's say another few hundred in long underwear, ski socks, ski pants, ski gloves, ski hats, foot warmers. All times three for Dad and the two kids, assuming Mom was a nonskier and not just somewhere else on the mountain. These didn't seem the types who got everything at ski swaps.

The tray he brings to the cashier is modest. There's a salad and coffee for him, two soft drinks for the kids, a package of Starburst candies. The cashier rings it up. "That'll be twenty-four dollars, sir," she tells him with a sprightly voice. The man looks down at his tray and seems to crack.

"You gotta be fucking kidding me," he says.

He leaves the tray and walks away.

As the investigation kicked into high gear, nobody in law enforcement knew how to treat VA: as suspect, as victim, as investigative partner. They needed VA's cooperation to look at employees' records, to learn how the mountain worked, to find out such details as whether the on-mountain gas caches had been raided recently. But they weren't ready to let VA's execs into the twice-daily investigators-only briefings.

VA knew right away the image it wanted to project: The company was a victim, all right, but a victim with a positive attitude. With Aron in Florida, VA's President Andy Daly became the company's most visible spokesperson, which was just fine with the imagemeisters at VA. "Andy's been in the ski industry forever," one VA insider says, off the record, at Daly's first press conference. "Adam is Wall Street. He's not the person we want out there."

In truth, Daly wasn't used to seeing anybody else run the show. He had made a certain peace with Aron and allowed him to do the liaison work with the Apollo people; but in Vail, Andy called most of the shots. Yet even Daly felt helpless and uncomfortable around the law enforcement types who conducted the press briefings. Rumor control became increasingly important to Daly and the VA team. Bloomberg Business wire put out the wildly inaccurate story that thirty-one lifts had burned down at Vail. Not to be outdone, one radio station in the East told listeners that the entire town of Vail had gone up in smoke. With the season opening just a few weeks away, and World Championships scheduled from January 31 through February 14, those kinds of stories wouldn't do; VA spokesman Witt says the company had to nip them quickly. "Operational damage control started Monday," he says. "Corporate damage control started Tuesday."

Aron flew back from Disney World the first afternoon after making sure that nobody had been hurt, that the fire hadn't spread to the trees, and that it was contained. "By noon the first day, the issue wasn't the fire, but the aftermath," says Aron. CNN kept repeating the story of the fires, complete

with pictures, every hour on the hour. Thanks to media saturation, complains Aron, "Two Elk was on fire for five days, and it was still on fire when
Newsweek came out the next Monday."

Calls started flooding the VA reservation switchboard, and receptionists
were given a list of Q&As aimed at knocking down the preposterous stories.
By Wednesday, says Witt, "Adam, Andy, and I made a decision to be more
vocal about what it meant to us as a company." The public message was
"business as usual." Daly put out the word that their insurance would cover
the loss of business and would fully pay to rebuild the lifts and structures.
The news evidently placated Wall Street: Every day that first week, MTN
stock went up.

Even after Aron came back, Daly took most of the media spotlight. During one pivotal news conference, he choked up, broke down, and cried. The
image of the president of Vail Resorts in tears on national television
cemented the already growing impression that the ski resort owners were
victims. Daly emphasized that plans to open on schedule on November 6
were unchanged, and plans to repair damaged lifts and build temporary
structures would be complete in time for this season's visitors. Then Daly
put his chin forward and vowed to get the place up and running by opening
day. "We have a reputation for doing the near to impossible," Daly told
reporters, "and we're going to live up to that reputation."

The damage wasn't insurmountable. Two Elk restaurant was on the
easternmost part of the mountain, and Chair 5 serviced the back bowls,
neither of which were part of the traditional opening strategy. (The early
season snowmaking focused on the front, westernmost part of the mountain, and the lifts opened from west to east as more snow fell.) "Other than
PHQ, we didn't need anything for opening day," Daly said optimistically.
Experts from around the country offered their technical assistance,
mechanical expertise, and spare parts. It turned out that Beaver Creek had
a decommissioned lift that was almost identical to Chair 5, and they could
pilfer parts from that. They planned to erect a yurtlike tent that would serve
as a temporary restaurant for the coming season: It would be called "One
Elk."

VA had to move fast with its upbeat message because October and

November are busy booking months for the ski world. Plenty of other resorts were ready to accommodate a family made skittish by the odd suggestion in the e-mailed ELF communiqué that "for your safety and convenience, we strongly advise skiers to choose other destinations until Vail cancels its inexcusable plans for expansion." VA sent out letters to more than 200,000 people on their direct-mail lists, reassuring potential guests that Vail's ability to open on schedule *and* host the World Alpine Ski Championships would not be affected. "We hope you won't allow this unfortunate event to cause you to consider not visiting Vail this winter," the letter pleaded. While preserving an air of can-do calm, the resort argued that the fires didn't hurt anybody, didn't damage more than a few buildings, they'd open on schedule, and everybody in the valley was pulling together in the wake of the tragedy. But Kim Andree from the Eagle County Sheriff's Department and Jeff Atencio, the public information officer from the Vail Fire Department, began chafing at VA's heavy-handed attempts at spin control. At one point, Adam Aron came up to Andree and Atencio and told them, "This is what we want you to say." The pair of PIOs balked. "It was quite an assumption on the part of VA," recalls Atencio.

•

Much as a death or an illness can bring a squabbling family together, the fires had the immediate result of getting the fractious Vail community to rally almost as one. Jonathan Staufer and other local enviros condemned the arson, disgruntled employees showed up at town meetings to show support for rebuilding efforts, and something of a cease-fire prevailed. Some of the locals discovered, almost in spite of themselves, that the mountain meant a lot to them. They had been married on it. Laid on it. High on it. Threw their friends' ashes on it. Rode their mountain bikes on it. And VA, they had to admit, despite its reputation as the "evil empire," knew a thing or two about operating ski areas. The predominant feeling was that if anyone could put the pieces back together in time to open the season, VA's corporate beavers would pull it off.

VA took the town's welling sympathy and ran with it. Almost immediately, Daly called an employees' meeting to squash rumors and spread the victim message. "It was an opportunity for people to share information and some of the emotional outrage," he told me. "They felt they'd been personally violated." Later, VA hosted a "town meeting" in the Karltenberg Kastle, a lavish brew pub at the mountain's base, where steins of free lager pepped up a lot of people. "Don't let the bastards get you down!" Daly exhorted the cheering, overflow crowd of some four hundred supporters. Daly attempted to put a line in the snow between the contentious days of yore—before the fires—and the present, when the community pulled together as one. The fire starters, he proclaimed, "have, in a way, stolen our innocence."

They hadn't, however, stolen VA's resolve. At the town meeting, Daly showed pictures of the fires and vowed that they'd rebuild in time to open the season as scheduled. Offers of support, even free labor, poured in. "If there's a bright side, it will pull the community together," Aron said just days after the fires. All the tension in the valley, he seemed to think, from the underpaid ski instructors to the mutinous merchants, had gone up in smoke with the Native American artwork at Two Elk. "I think those issues are ancient history," he proclaimed. "People who were complaining about us four days ago are offering to rebuild with their bare hands." Perhaps a little carried away, he enthused, "This whole valley is united again."

Still, things were edgy. The ELF communiqué had warned that the radical group "will be back if this greedy corporation continues to trespass into wild and unroaded areas." On Halloween eve, a security guard noticed a suspicious-looking briefcase near the bottom of the gondola—and the resort's administrative offices. Sheriff's deputies took a look, and soon called the Denver bomb squad up there. The Kevlar-suited bomb tech faced off with the briefcase and eventually discovered that it contained a typewriter.

Ironically, the amount of public support for Vail after the fires only fueled the VA-did-it conspiracy theories. "See?" they seemed to say. "VA *knew* it would turn the tide of public opinion in its favor by setting the fires itself." Much later, when profitable Two Elk was rebuilt even larger than before, popular Buffalo's restaurant was rebuilt even cozier than before, unprofitable Camp One area wasn't rebuilt at all, and Vail emerged not only whole but bigger and better, locals' sympathy turned inexorably toward cynicism and suspicion. Aron is aware of the innuendo. "Some ludicrous people thought I had done this in some Machiavellian scheme," he says, snorting disgust. "For the record," he insists, unprompted, "we didn't set them."

22

Barking up the Wrong Tree Hugger

IF YOU ARE CONTACTED BY THE FBI OR POLICE:

1. You do not have to talk to FBI agents, the police or any investigators. You do not have to speak with them at your house, on the phone, on the street, if you've been arrested, or even in jail. Only a court or grand jury has legal authority to compel testimony.
2. You do not have to let the FBI or police into your home or office unless they show you an arrest or search warrant which authorizes them to enter that specific place.
3. If they do present a warrant, you do not have to tell them anything other than your name and address. You have a right to observe what they do. Make written notes, including the agents' names, agency, and badge numbers. Try to have other people present as witnesses, and have them make written notes too.
4. Anything you say to an FBI agent or other law enforcement officer may be used against you and other people. The FBI and the police have jobs to do, and they are very skilled at them and at getting information from people. Attempting to outwit them is very risky. You can never tell how a seemingly harmless bit of information can hurt you or some-one else or some organization. Thus the best advice is that if the FBI or police try to question you, on the phone or in person, or try to enter your home or office without a warrant, is to JUST SAY NO.
5. Lying to an FBI agent or other law enforcement officer is a crime.
6. Giving the FBI agent or police information may mean that you will have to testify to the same information at a trial or before a grand jury.
7. The FBI or police may threaten you with a grand jury subpoena if you don't give them information. However, you may get one anyway, and anything you might already have told them will be the basis for more detailed questioning under oath. If you do get a subpoena, you may be able to fight it as well, with the help of a lawyer. Contact the National Lawyer's Guild or local sympathetic attorneys for help. Don't be intimidated by the agents saying, "We know what you have been doing, but if you cooperate it will be

all right." If you are concerned about this, tell them you will talk with them only with your lawyer present.

8. If you are nervous about simply refusing to talk to them ("I'm sorry, but I don't speak with the FBI...."), you may find it easier to tell them to contact your lawyer. Once a lawyer is involved the FBI and police usually pull back since they have lost their power to intimidate.

9. If you are contacted by the FBI or police, take notes and keep careful records of what they said and did. Tell others they contacted you.

Further, if an activist does talk, or makes some honest error, explain the serious harm that could result. Be firm, but do not ostracize a sincere person who slips up. Isolation only weakens a person's ability to resist pressure. It can drive someone out of the movement and even into the hands of the police or FBI. If the FBI or other government agents start to harass people in your area or community, alert everyone to refuse to cooperate. Warn your friends, neighbors, parents, children, and anyone else who might be contacted. Make sure people know what to do and where to call for help.

—"HOW-TO" ADVICE ON DEALING WITH FEDERAL AUTHORITIES,
POSTED ON THE INTERNET

When the ATF and the FBI didn't find a smoking match in the initial investigation, the U.S. Department of Justice decided to convene a federal grand jury to tackle the Vail arson case. With a grand jury's subpoena power, the U.S. attorney's office in Denver could deliver a dose of jurisprudential heavy-handedness where the usual dose of FBI intimidation had failed. Prosecutors know that all but the most committed people tend to talk when the alternative is spending a year and a half in a federal pen on a contempt charge.

According to the activists' network, the first person to receive a grand jury subpoena was approached in Boston while visiting her parents during the Christmas holidays. She was confronted when she was taking garbage to the dump and was wearing only pajamas and an overcoat; her summons said she was to appear in court on January 28, 1999.

Activists then reported that the FBI approached two women who worked for a University of Colorado environmental group. When the pair refused to cooperate, the agents questioned their supervisor. After that meeting ended, the feds apparently told the supervisor, "You can tell those girls we are not going away." Another activist targeted by the agents reported that they had questioned her friends, her boss, and even her professors; one professor was asked to turn over the student's work from the previous semester.

In Vermont, one environmental activist received a call that began with "I'm-from-the-FBI," followed by the ominous opening: "Do you know why I'm calling you?" The Vermont activist, like most of the others, wasn't eager to cooperate.

Although most of these activists were too young to remember much of the FBI's history, the elders in the environmental movement had tutored them in the subject, especially in COINTELPRO, a domestic covert action program exposed in the 1970s that had for decades targeted social activists in the United States, including the American Indian Movement, Martin Luther King, the antinuke group SANE-Freeze, and the antiwar American Friends Service Committee. In the environmental community, especially on the radical fringe, nobody believed that the FBI's bad old days were over. Most took as a matter of faith that a May 1990 bomb that nearly killed Earth First! organizer Judi Bari and fellow activist Darryl Cherney was planted by the FBI to discredit the radical environmental group. (The pair insisted the bomb had been planted in the car; the FBI claimed that Bari and Cherney were transporting the bomb as a prelude to some kind of felonious boom-boom. But few, if any, in the radical environmental community doubt Bari's word: In the past, she had denounced tree spiking for fear it would harm innocent mill workers. She wasn't the Weatherman type.)

For the feds, the attitude that *they* were the enemy was frustrating. They were simply trying to figure out who torched a ski area, not gratuitously harassing harmless college-aged greenies who wanted to save the whales or the owls or whatever. But the "we're-from-the-federal-government-and-we're-here-to-help" line was a hard sell to Doon, Staufer, Berman, and Nicole Rosmarino. Even the twentysomething CU students who had barely dipped their toes into the green political waters successfully stonewalled FBI agents or hid behind their pro-bono do-gooder lawyers.

It wasn't just the Vail investigation that was frustrating law enforcement officials. Elsewhere in the country, the feds were getting tired of working their butts off to nail arsonists and animal rights liberationists only to watch them wiggle off the hook with relatively minor sentences even when they did prosecute them. In Utah, the feds had turned two brothers into informants against several others who had set fire to a feed store, but lost the cases against their coconspirators when a jury failed to convict. In Wisconsin, they unsuccessfully tried some animal rights activists under an arcane federal law called the Hobbs Act; the Act put crimes such as mink farm releases into the category of economic sabotage and could give a culprit some real time, maybe twenty years. Maybe they could try the economic sabotage angle at Vail; but first they needed a suspect.

The U.S. attorney put on the case was a wily character named Ken Buck, a Republican who had cut his teeth in Washington, D.C., during the Iran-

Contra hearings. Buck had already been lied to by the best of 'em. Vail's district attorney, Michael Goodbee, was sworn in as an investigator, as were two of his deputy district attorneys; all three had to pass extensive background checks.

By late January, the first Ancient Forest Rescue members were making their appearances at the same federal courthouse in Denver where Oklahoma City bomber Timothy McVeigh had been convicted.

The first subpoenas had taken aim at peripheral Ancient Forest Rescue members. Buck was obviously trying to force the less-experienced members to squeal before going for the main agitators. It was an old tactic, and had been wildly successful in RICO prosecutions: Tell the underlings that they were in serious trouble, but that trouble might be overlooked if they would just answer a few questions. Despite an offer of immunity to those who testified, however, nobody was talking. Either they didn't know anything or they were adept at keeping secrets.

■

After Buck had interviewed several AFR members who had been at the anti-Vail protests before the fires, he floated an interesting story. Somebody, Buck asserted, had told him about a meeting of Category III opponents in which the idea of arson had come up; the meeting had taken place just before October 19. The witness couldn't recall who had mentioned arson, but Buck started running the story past others who were purportedly at the same meeting.

None of the principals who had attended most of the meetings could recall any such thing. The group was well aware of the government's propensity to infiltrate radical environmental groups; indeed, the participants would have immediately suspected anybody who advocated violence or arson of being an agent provocateur. "There was nothing, nobody, who ever said or did anything that could remotely be construed as advocating sabotage," Doon says. "I feel I would have known about it." Berman and Staufer say they don't recall any such comment, and both say that such a searing proposal would have stuck in their minds.

Soon, the AFR activists were publicly accusing the U.S. attorney's office of harassment and intimidation. Doon figured that Buck had probably invented the arson comment rumor in a prosecutorial whaling expedition in the hope of bluffing his way to some real information.

Why couldn't the feds see they were barking up the wrong tree hugger?

◆

In April 1999, two teenage boys ran amok in their high school in Littleton, Colorado, killing twelve students and a teacher and wounding several dozen others before turning their sawed-off shotgun and TEC-9 semiautomatic on themselves. After Eric Harris and Dylan Klebold committed the deadliest act of school violence in this country's history at Columbine High School, virtually every federal agent who had been assigned to the Vail case was put on Columbine.

As if to compensate for the lack of investigative firepower, in May the ATF offered a $50,000 reward for information leading to the arrest of the arsonist or arsonists. The feds told VA executives not to offer a larger reward for fear that they'd hear from too many wackos with false leads.

Buck soldiered on, but hit another snag. Doon and two other AFR members who had been granted immunity refused to answer certain questions. Doon told anybody who would listen that he was prepared to tell the grand jury anything about his own activities, but wasn't prepared to name names of others in his group. "The only thing I'm not doing is giving a membership list," he said. Doon wondered why the feds were so interested in having him list the people who were with him at the Two Elk campsite on the morning of the fires; Doon had been present when two Eagle County sheriff's deputies had compiled an exhaustive list that morning.

What Doon and the others didn't know was that the deputies had lost the list. And U.S. Attorney Buck sure as hell wasn't going to tell them.

23

Aspen versus Vail

At the bottom of Vail's back bowls, a little tradition began (as with any good tradition, its origins are fuzzy) when women began taking off their bras and slinging them to a tree that stood close to the chairlift. Soon, dozens of brightly colored panties and bras festooned the tree, which looked like a Victoria's Secret–inspired Christmas tree. When somebody tried the same trick at Beaver Creek, the entire "Panty Tree" discreetly disappeared overnight. Another attempt sprouted at the next closest tree, and it, too, met the chain saw. After a third try met the same fate, the Beaver Creek panty raiders gave up.

When the U.S. Justice Department approved the merger of Vail and Beaver Creek with Keystone and Breckenridge in 1996, you could almost hear teeth gnashing among the executives of Colorado's other resorts. Can anyone say cartel? they wondered. Microsoft of the powder processors? AT&T of the uphill transportation business?

At Winter Park, a ski area owned by the city of Denver, the management was furious. At Loveland, the closest resort to Denver, nobody could believe that Vail was going to get away with it. Steamboat Springs, Copper Mountain, Eldora—even the more southern resorts of Telluride and Crested Butte—all wondered what it would be like to compete with this new yeti of the Rockies named Vail Resorts.

At Aspen, opinion was in character with the attitude concerning the ongoing genteel feud with Vail: "Oh, *them*?"

The lines of demarcation between Vail and Aspen aren't clear cut, but if Vail is predominantly Fortune 500, Gerald Ford, and the Republican White House west, Aspen is Hollywood and Democratic high-rollers. Aspen at least has its Hunter Thompson on the fringe; Vail's counterculture runs to relatively sedate art gallery owners and trust-funder ski bums. Aspen, a town in its own right, dates back to its mining heritage; Vail, a town manufactured solely to be a ski resort, has struggled to create its identity. Aspen is owned by a noblesse oblige private family, the Crowns of Chicago; the family's patriarch, Lester Crown, his net worth nearly $3 billion, is listed by *Forbes* as among the top one hundred richest Americans—yet he has been seen standing in line to have his picture taken for his season pass. (Vail, of course, is MTN on the New York Stock Exchange, and is run by a corporate conglomerator who wouldn't be caught dead standing in line for *anything*.) Vail's merger and new management only heightened the contrasts between Colorado's best-known ski resorts—contrasts perfectly embodied in the respective personalities of their CEOs, Adam Aron and Pat O'Donnell.

The sixty-two-year-old O'Donnell, with his buzz cut, square jaw, and Marine's demeanor, came to the Aspen Ski Company from Patagonia, the ecoconscious outdoor apparel company that has become the choice of the yuppie outdoor set. O'Donnell was appropriately shocked by the fires, but slyly intimated that Vail kinda brought on its own bad karma. "You know," O'Donnell says with a conspiratorial whisper, "Adam just fired somebody because their dog came into his office. Hell, I keep dog biscuits in my office so when dogs wander in I can give them a treat."

O'Donnell had taken a few turns in the ski arena before landing at Aspen. In his early years, he was a rock-climbing bum; during the legendary early Camp IV years he pioneered the sport at Yosemite's granite walls and supported himself by working as a bellboy for the Curry company in Yosemite Valley for ninety cents an hour plus tips. He later worked at Kirkwood ski area in California just as it was opening, then helped start Keystone in Colorado. While he was the chief operating officer at Keystone, he was a team member in the first U.S. ascent of Annapurna in Nepal; his three best friends died in the effort and O'Donnell had to take a sixteen-day solo walk back—with a whole lot to think about.

He thought he had had enough. He resigned as Keystone's COO, dropped out, and sailed to South America. When he resurfaced, he was offered the job of president and CEO of the Yosemite Institute—a nonprofit, environmentally oriented educational organization—despite having no experience either in running nonprofits or in developing environmental education programs. Six years later, he got a call from an old climbing buddy who just happened to be Yvon Chouinard, the French alpinist who had founded Patagonia. How about running my company? Chouinard asked.

Why not? O'Donnell took the helm for six years; he developed an eco-consciousness in the manufacturing process at Patagonia and paved the way for the innovative use of pesticide-free cotton in the company's garments. He became increasingly restless, however, and decided to leave California's coast to return to his beloved mountains. He took a job at Whistler/Blackcomb in Canada, Vail's nemesis and successor as the continent's number one resort.

Then he received a call from Aspen.

When interviewed for the top job, O'Donnell told his potential bosses: "I don't think this is my scene. I'm a granola-type guy. I don't do dinners with martinis. I don't do dinners, period." He was a before-the-crack-of-dawn person, he explained, in the gym at four o'clock every morning. That was okay with the Crowns. O'Donnell had the job.

Adam Aron is the type who sets his alarm early to watch CNBC before the market rings its opening bell; O'Donnell often climbs the mountain in snowshoes before the lifts open, carrying his snowboard and listening to Santana or Bob Dylan ("anything that rocks") on his portable CD player. Then he takes a first-tracks run with some of the ski patrollers before starting his workday.

Nevertheless, when O'Donnell took over from Bob Maynard, his predecessor at the Aspen Skiing Company, the "ski-co," as it's known, was as reviled locally as Vail Resorts has been in Vail. Even without the onus of owning nonskiing businesses that compete with locals, or of being traded on Wall Street, the ski-co had managed to annoy just about everybody with its arrogance and power and its ability to get what it wanted (in O'Donnell's words) "with D-9 bulldozers and lawyers."

O'Donnell set out to change the corporate culture and its relationship to the town; this was admittedly easier to do in a "mature resort," as he calls Aspen, with its mere 3,000 employees and no real estate to speak of, than it was at Vail Resorts, which has more than 10,000 workers scattered over four resorts, golf courses, nonskiing businesses, and a large real estate component. To begin with, O'Donnell instituted an independent environmental foundation run by the employees. He then provided matching funds from the ski-co, and hired a local rabble-rousing environmental engineer to take over its on-mountain greening. Together with the town and a progressive Pitkin County government, Aspen has also made great (though imperfect) strides in creating affordable housing for employees.

O'Donnell thinks the drive to continue expanding ski areas is lunacy, given the payback and the projected skier numbers. "Everybody's caught up in a capital investment shoot-out," he says. "The consumers aren't driving it; we're driving it ourselves. If there were long lift lines, I'd be an advocate [for expansion]," he adds. "But it's not happening." Real estate development, which his company doesn't do, is driving the entire enchilada these days. "We're strip-mining the scenery. There's a developer mentality where the ski area is seen as a commodity, part of a portfolio," he says, careful not to mention Vail by name. "There's no soul to the place."

O'Donnell is also careful not to criticize his good friends at Vail, but he can't restrain himself when the subject of Adventure Ridge comes up. The 11,000-foot divertissement at the top of Vail's gondola, with its laser tag and kiddie snowball rides, has no place in the industry, he says. O'Donnell once witnessed a mother trying to take her child away from a video machine at Vail, the kid begging for another roll of quarters. "Where are the values there?" he queries.

In many ways, the show of money at Vail is slightly more understated than at Aspen. "You can go to Little Nell [a chic restaurant and hotel at the base of Aspen Mountain] after the lifts close and see women decked out in Bogner suits, with their red fingernails, and you know full well those ladies haven't been on the slopes," says Vail's Kaye Ferry. "Who are you kidding, ladies?" Aspen is certainly more status conscious than Vail: Here, Melanie Griffith's bodyguard can close a store so that the starlet can go in and shop in peace; or Saudi Prince Bandar can build a monstrous mansion on Red Mountain, then buy most of the condos at the Inn at Aspen near Buttermilk for his workers and lesser guests. Vail likes to think that because so many people are already Fortune 500, nobody has anything to prove. Ross Perot, for example, often wears a relic of a gray ski parka that looks as though it's at least as old as Vail.

But Vailites become defensive when conversation turns to Aspen. ("The Crown family were just run-of-the-mill billionaires until they bought Aspen," one longtime Vail resident sniffs.) Vail's criticism is like most defensive behavior: It's rooted in something of an inferiority complex. The town feels vaguely threatened by the older and more glamorous Aspen. As another Vail high-society observer puts it, sorrowfully, "They get Barbi Benton, we get Kathie Lee Gifford."

24

Bring On the Batmobile

Welcome to the wonderful world of encryption. You have decided for whatever reason to use encryption to protect your e-mail and other data stored or transmitted electronically. Good decision.

Many people think that people who encrypt their e-mail have "something to hide." Well, they do....

—FROM "A BEGINNER'S GUIDE TO PRETTY GOOD PRIVACY," POSTED ON THE ALF WEB SITE

VA couldn't start its ambitious summer construction and reconstruction projects until after the spring elk calving and migration season officially ended on June 30, 1999; but VA's construction crews were locked and loaded at daybreak on July 1, ready to start a marathon session at the top of the mountain. The big plan was to finish phase one of the Category III expansion by installing two new chairlifts and clear-cutting the old-growth spruce/fir forests into ski trails. Another crew was set to replace Two Elk (adding another 5,000 square feet to the building's pre-fire size), and complete the task in about half the time it took to put the massive structure up in the first place. With the ten-and-a-half-mile dirt road to Two Elk full of axle-sucking mud from some late snows and crews having to run a gauntlet of clever blockades laid in by Cat III opponents, the condensed summer construction season promised to be intense and eventful.

The environmental protestors, led by Berman of Ancient Forest Rescue and Rosmarino of Rocky Mountain Animal Defense, had their own plans ready to go. During the last week of June, environmental protestors from all over the country had been amassing in the Vail area, bent on all manner of havoc-wreaking monkey wrenching. Ancient Forest Rescue, EarthFirst!, the Boulder-based Coalition to Stop Vail Expansion, Colorado Wild, and the Seeds of Peace set up "teach-ins" from a base camp at the same forest service campsite where environmentalists had been camping on the night of the fires. On the mountain, the U.S. Forest Service had closed some of the area to the public, but that wasn't much of a deterrent. "Our mission is pretty clear," said Rosmarino, amped to take the battle from the courtroom to the forest floor. "We're fully aware that it will take more than one action."

Law enforcement was ready, too. The Eagle County Sheriff's Department's SWAT teams had been briefed on the forest activists' likely tricks, and a multiagency Special Operations Group, or SOG, was excited at the prospect of putting those endless training sessions to use. The FBI was hoping that maybe one or more of the arsonists might be stupid enough, or cocky enough, to make an appearance at the protests. Secretly, law enforcement had laid in infrared sensors on Vail Mountain to track the protestors' movements, and were using military night-vision goggles, known as "knives," to conduct surveillance in the area.

The encampments of protestors mingled; Grateful Dead and Phish music wafted through the air, as did the scent of marijuana and pine boughs heated by the summer sun. Guitar players found themselves surrounded by tie-died circles of singers-along; newcomers were greeted with giant hugs and were plied with sun tea. For some, the events were like a class reunion; they had last seen each other at protests in the Willamette National Forest in Oregon, or at the Redwood Summer in northern California. Here they were again, trying to save other conifers from the destructive buzz of the corporate chain saw. It was a righteous cause.

Behind these hippie-esque scenes, serious commando planning had already taken place. Activists had buried four-inch PVC pipe on top of a piece of rebar that had been sunk in the middle of Mill Creek Road, giving the protestors something solid to chain themselves to when the real show-stopping began. The road served as the main access to the top of the mountain, where construction crews would begin amassing truckloads of timbers, metal hangers, nails, units of plywood, and everything else needed to replace Two Elk. Other crews headed up the same road to begin transforming the Category III area into what VA was now calling Blue Sky Basin; the protestors had quickly dubbed it "BS" Basin.

The activists sent word to Aron that they were prepared to negotiate if he would look at their list of complaints. Spokesman Paul Witt told the protestors that the chances of Adam Aron's discussing the tree huggers' demands were "slim to none and slim just left town."

•

On Thursday, July 1, it was "Let the protests begin." One activist planted himself on a twenty-five-foot-high wooden structure that resembled the frame of a teepee and had been strategically placed to block all access up the narrow dirt road. Another activist chained herself to the cherry picker that had been borrowed from the town of Vail to pluck the first activist from the tripod.

At first it was a weird and almost amusing game of musical demonstrators. As soon as one protestor was cut free, another popped up, chained to something else. The demonstrators knew they must not antagonize the cops by shouting epithets at them; instead, they used the "zap-'em-back-with-super-love" techniques borrowed from Ken Kesey's Merry Prankster days. It wasn't a party, but it wasn't the Blue Meanies tear-gassing Berkeley demonstrators at People's Park, either.

The techniques were effective for a few days. But frustration began building at VA, and the cops were not happy about handcuffing one protestor at a time while others looked on, ready to take their comrade's place. Why couldn't they just take the mountain back from these creeps by force?

Then, on Tuesday, July 6, they did. About twenty protestors had been blocking the main access road to Vail Mountain for five days; federal and county officials put together a pre-dawn raid to liberate the area, replete with SWAT teams, camouflage, and a show of force with high-caliber automatic weapons.

Although they had suspected that something like this was coming, the pre-dawn raid scared the hell out of the protestors. Robert Kelly-Goss, the Minturn rabble-rouser, was still covering the events as a reporter for the *Vail Trail*, although his sympathies were no secret at this point. He was up on the mountain with another reporter and a photographer when the cops came swarming. "It was a military-style operation," he recalls with great animation. "Twenty guys in jungle camo came down the mountain in step, screaming 'hup, hup, hup.' Twenty more in uniform jumped up from hiding places." Goss was alarmed by the cops' show of paramilitary force. "They knew these kids wanted to get arrested," he said. "They knew the protestors wouldn't hurt anybody." As the SWAT teams stormed the mountain, Goss screamed for the sheriff while being told to stand still. "I told them, 'I'm press,' and one said, 'I don't care who the fuck you are. You stay right there.'"

∎

VA's point men on the protests, Porter Wharton III and Brian McCartney, had been waiting for the cops to make their move. The pair had made a few preparations themselves. They had consulted with federal law enforcement officers, known as LEOs, and had watched videos about how forest activists had protested elsewhere in the country. They learned that the protestors, though they appeared anarchic at times, were experts at scouting and planning and training. They learned, for example, that protestors pour gas around the areas where they chain themselves so that rescue workers couldn't use acetylene torches to cut them out. "They're creative as hell," says McCartney, over beers one night in town. "You do," adds Wharton, "develop a begrudging respect for them."

While observing the enviros' capacity for planning during these early July protests, McCartney and Wharton became even more convinced that whoever had set the fires had connections to the current environmental protestors on the hill. "They were listening to our radios," says McCartney. "And July wasn't the first time they had done that." He suspects the protestors used infrared sensors, GPS (global positioning system) locators, and other sophisticated electronics, including your basic police scanners and hand-held radios, because the activists always seemed to know what and who were coming and when. McCartney had been told that the underground rabble-rouser network had set up safe houses all over the United States so that protestors could hide out when things got too hot. "The bottom line is, never underestimate these guys," says McCartney.

He and Wharton had become well versed in their adversaries' actions. The pair had watched headlamp-wearing protestors walk up the mountain in the middle of the night, and they noted the many layers of protestor fabric. On the front lines are the so-called expendables. "These are the cannon fodder, the guys who get arrested, sit in tripods, chain themselves to cars," says Wharton. Next, there are what he calls "the talent," or "the planners," who are fairly sophisticated and well organized. The talent trades positions with the expendables when it's time to be arrested and go to the slam. Lurking somewhere in the background, according to Wharton, were some nebulous well-funded bigwigs who could appear in corporate boardrooms as well as on the fringes of the actions themselves.

McCartney, along with many associated with VA, had a conspiracy theory about the entire environmental movement. "The Ted Turners, the Patagonias, the Pew Charitable Trusts that fund these guys, I'm not 100 percent sure they've got a grip on what they're financing." And what exactly is that? "It's a pantheist religion," says McCartney. "I don't think some dirtball who hasn't showered for a month goes into the boardroom at Patagonia asking for a million bucks," says McCartney. "But I think they're still milling around trying to figure out what to do next." McCartney continues that these true-believing greenies are like all zealots: They have the ability to recruit newcomers with their passion alone. He theorizes that in the case of the fires, the main agitators must have enlisted local help from disgruntled employees or ex-employees to carry out the dirty deed.

The morning of the predawn raid, McCartney and Wharton had been alerted that law enforcement was about to move. "We knew it was coming," says McCartney. "I got the call at 3:30, and called Porter." Two words: "It's happening." The two men had moved down to the lower patrol headquarters by 4:00 A.M., and by 5:00 they "could hear shouting and screaming." Wharton and McCartney were convinced that the protestors had the means to detect the raid, and weren't surprised to see the armed, camouflaged cops enter their camp. "It was a mess," says McCartney. "They put themselves in harm's way and challenge you to run over them. Then they'd whine when you tried to remove them." That didn't stop the cops from forcibly removing the protestors, whining and all.

When it was all over, the Cat III protestors arrested and the construction completed, McCartney beamed. "We've built what amounts to one of the largest ski areas in North America in six months," he says, referring to the fact that Blue Sky Basin is bigger than Aspen Mountain. "It's a very fulfilling feeling."

On McCartney's office wall, a plaque commemorates the summer's travails: a pair of bolt cutters spray-painted in gold, with the inscription "The Golden Protestor Removal Award: 7/12/99."

"They kinda picked on the wrong people," McCartney says with his cocky grin.

♦

John Gulick of the Vail Fire Department found himself in a tough spot when he tried to remove some of the protestors. He and his team had been preparing for the July protests as well, and had formed what they called the "ET ET"—the ecoterrorist extrication team. As if he were a member of the International Red Cross, Gulick felt his job was to remain neutral, and to safely, and with as little confrontation as possible, cut loose or pry loose protestors from any device they'd chained themselves to. "Protection for the self-inflicted victim," he says, deadpan.

It was an odd situation for Gulick. As a firefighter, he usually allied himself with law enforcement, and most fire departments subscribe to a paramilitary-type organization and discipline. But this time, Gulick felt a certain amount of sympathy for the protestors' goals, if not their methods. After all, he had been in this valley a long time, and the argument that growth and development was out of hand rang as true to him as the tones that routinely sent him off to chase fires.

Gulick had been raised in California, mostly around the Los Alamitos Naval Air Station. Shortly after finishing high school, he had worked in California as a firefighter for the forest service. In 1973, his girlfriend, whose brother worked for the Vail Ski School, convinced him to move to Colorado. The next year he got a job fighting fires in the White River National Forest, based in Minturn, a few miles from Vail. He started at the Vail Fire Department in 1974 as a volunteer, and was hired full-time in 1976. He worked his way through the ranks, went back to school from time to time by commuting to Denver, and was eventually made chief, less than a year after the Vail Mountain arsons. He proudly shows his photo in *Fire Chief* magazine with the announcement of his promotion.

When he started working in Vail, Gulick bunked in a cramped dorm room at the station to save money. In 1979, he bought a lot in Singletree, about seventeen miles from town, but couldn't afford to build on it until almost ten years later, when he put up a three-bedroom house. When Gulick's second daughter was born, the growing family needed more space and had to move farther down valley to afford it. Gulick was already appalled at the sight of fixer-uppers going for nearly $500,000.

His wife and daughters loved horses, and in 1996 the Gulicks bought a thirty-five-acre parcel fifty miles away from Vail, a ranchette of the sort that has become all the rage in Colorado. Soon, Gulick became aware of a trend that seemed only to be accelerating: It was becoming harder and harder to buy hay. Every fall, when he went to stock up on hay, successive farmers told him they had sold out—to a gravel pit owner or a golf course or a developer. The place where he went to buy hay a month before the arsons was still an empty green pasture. "Now it's just a big quagmire full of belly haulers, dump trucks, and puffs of diesel smoke," he says, with workers laying cables for gas, electricity, cable TV, and other accoutrements for the retirees and modem cowboys who are filling up the area. In the last few years, he's seen a grocery market, a gas station, a Taco Bell, a Holiday Inn, and a Comfort Inn appear where there used to be lonely roads and cattle guards. All summer long, he wakes and goes to sleep to the pounding sound of a pile driver echoing through the valley. He says there are plans for a gravel pit that include digging so deep that the ground level will drop one hundred feet. "They say it's not damaging to the environment, but how can it not be?" he wonders.

Gulick and his team stood on the sidelines until they were called in to dismantle the tripod, which was covered in tar and barbed wire to make it more difficult to chainsaw down. When the firefighters had to use the torches to cut other protestors free, Gulick carefully covered them with the same Nomex suits that his firefighters used to protect themselves from flame, and gave them safety glasses. "They told us we worked for the Evil Empire," he says, shaking his head at the notion of his being allied with the expansion.

•

Later that month, the environmentalists caught a break. VA crews were cutting a new road through a spruce-fir forest that would be used to haul the timber out from the Cat III area, and workers noticed that the area appeared boggy. They put straw down to help sop up the mud, but it didn't help. Officials from the U.S. Army Corps of Engineers and regulators from the Environmental Protection Agency agreed that VA had managed to put an illegal road through the middle of a wetlands—a marshy area that provides critical habitat for animals and acts as a natural filtration system. The EPA declared it would fine VA, and the Corps said it wouldn't have given VA permission to build the road had it known where the company was planning to put it. VA called it an honest mistake, the result of a failure of communication among various contractors over the years.

VA's opponents seized on the issue to continue VA-bashing. "VA keeps saying this is the most studied and environmentally sensitive expansion in ski area history," said Jonathan Staufer. "How could they have missed a wetlands right in the middle of the road?"

∎

Investigators working on the Vail case, on the other hand, couldn't buy a break. The ELF kept hitting other targets, and the FBI hadn't been able to nail a single perp. Soon after the Vail fires, the day after Christmas 1998, somebody claimed credit in the name of the ELF for fires set at the U.S. Forest Industries headquarters in Medford, Oregon, "in retribution for all the wild forests and animals lost to feed the wallets of greedy" corporations. This note was impish, but was also far more specific than the communiqué left after the Vail fires. It read, in part: "On the foggy night after Christmas when everyone was digesting their turkey and pie, Santa's ELF's dropped two five-gallon buckets of diesel/unleaded mix and a one-gallon jug with cigarette delays; which proved to be more than enough to get this party started." Damage was estimated at half a million dollars.

In response, the feds started bearing down harder on Craig Rosebraugh, the vegan baker from Portland who brazenly passed on the ELF's communiqués to the press. Since June 1997, Rosebraugh had publicized more than a half dozen ELF and ALF actions, including seven arsons. Another federal grand jury started looking into the Oregon actions; in February 2000, Rosebraugh's home was raided and his computer files confiscated. The U.S. attorney's office said that there was a "remarkable amount" of evidence on his hard drive that implicated Rosebraugh and others in the various crimes. Rosebraugh was unimpressed. "I think it's ridiculous," he told reporters. "It seems to me if there was really a 'remarkable amount' of evidence on my computer, there would have been an indictment by now."

◆

After the Vail fires, and again after the Oregon Christmas fire, the national media began focusing on the shadowy ELF, only to find that few people knew much about the organization. Even more troubling, the people who "knew" about ELF were almost as shady as the underground organization's members. Self-professed "experts"—Barry Clausen among them—surfaced to talk on television and in the papers about the "rise" of ecoterror. "In 1986, there were about ten terrorist accounts," he told CBS's *This Morning*. "In 1994, '95, and '96 there have been in excess of three hundred a year. And now we're seeing more violence." Clausen, however, had once tried to peddle a story to the press that Unabomber Ted Kaczynski had been linked to Earth First!, in an attempt to discredit the radical environmental group.

Another "expert," Ron Arnold, was identified by the *New York Times* as "a Northern California researcher who studies terrorist acts claimed by environmental extremists," and "the vice president of the Center for the Defense of Free Enterprise, a defender of property rights and a critic of environmentalists who catalogue ecoterrorism." But Arnold, it turned out, had his own agenda.

Arnold is widely credited as the founder of the Wise Use movement, a conservative, corporate-funded 1990s version of the Sagebrush Rebellion of the late 1970s, when loggers and miners and ranchers bridled at new federal environmental regulations that were curtailing their historical plunder of western public lands. The *Seattle Weekly* once branded Arnold "the most dangerous man in America," for his ability to present himself as mainstream when his politics, especially on environmental issues, are as radical in their own way as Earth First!'s are in theirs. According to the *Village Voice*, Arnold has been heard saying such mainstream things about enviros as "We're out to kill the fuckers. We're simply trying to eliminate them. Our goal is to destroy environmentalism once and for all." David Helvarg, author of a book called *War on the Greens,* which assesses the organized, corporate attack on environmentalists, once commented that asking Arnold and Clausen to talk about ecoterror is "like asking David Duke to assess the rise of black militants."

The public presence of Arnold and Clausen gave some of the more radical enviros pause. Even if the COINTELPRO people weren't involved, wouldn't it be possible that some right-wing wacko like Arnold might have organized a few strategic strikes, then blamed it on the greenies? After all, the Wise Use folk regularly defied federal law enforcement by bulldozing roads into the wilderness and driving four-wheelers into areas the forest service had closed. How come the feds didn't harass those people?

●

During this time, a former *Wall Street Journal* reporter who had made his home in Minturn began researching an article about the Vail fires and the ELF that eventually appeared in *Mother Jones.* Alex Markels was intrigued with this shadowy movement, and set out to see how close he could come to a real ELFer. He tried to pass the message through intermediaries that he was willing to do whatever it took to meet somebody involved in the actions. If they wanted to bind and blindfold him, strip him, and drive him through the night in the trunk of a car as if they were off to a meeting with the Hezbollah, or a Burmese drug lord, or Osama bin Laden, so be it. Let me tell your side of the story, he implored.

Markels drove to Boulder and went to what passed for the environmental activism center of the college town, an unimposing building near the University of Colorado campus known as the Environmental Center of the Rockies. Groups such as Zukowski's Land and Water Fund, the National Wildlife Federation, a save-the-wolf organization called Sinapu, and Jeff Berman's Ancient Forest Rescue had offices inside, and Markels sensed their synergy concentrating around fighting the Vail expansion.

Moving further to the fringes of Boulder's environmental warriors, Markels set up a meeting with local Earth First! members, and also looked into the connection between People for the Ethical Treatment of Animals, or PETA, the animal rights group, and the Animal Liberation Front, which had close ties to PETA.

One of his sources told him that he wouldn't have a chance at contacting anybody unless he took some countermeasures against federal eavesdropping. First, he was instructed to download software that would encrypt his e-mail. The program was called PGP, or Pretty Good Privacy, and had been written by a Colorado man named Philip Zimmermann, himself in trouble with the feds for distributing his software overseas. The contact instructed Markels to load a slightly older version of PGP because it was believed that the feds had cracked the more recent versions. To get up and running with PGP, Markels had to register for an electronic "key" that would allow him to communicate with others. He could open another person's mail only if that person had given him a key and vice versa.

Markels scrolled down the list of people who had registered for keys. One name stuck out; it was the name of a woman who worked with the Rocky Mountain Animal Defense group, RMAD—the same group that Nicole Rosmarino belonged to. Markels wondered why somebody from RMAD would need encryption software.

But he never found a satisfactory answer. Even though he was fully encrypted, nobody from the ELF contacted him. Federal investigators, equally stonewalled, disbanded the Colorado grand jury and waited for somebody to make a mistake.

PART 3

THE NEXT LAST BEST PLACE

25

Won't Get Fooled Again?

Why is fame the only ticket to Blue Sky party?

I'd like to express my anger about Vail Resorts' decision to turn the Blue Sky Basin celebration concert into a private fund-raiser.

I have nothing against the Kennedy family except they have no history in the Vail Valley. Most of the stars and assorted rich folks that have tickets to the concert have probably
never been here before.

As a point of contrast, please consider the Ford and Friends concerts of yesteryear.
All the proceeds of that star-studded event went to local charities and the public was
always invited. There was a sense of community. On a nice night you could smell the
flowers from the Betty Ford Gardens.

This event stinks.

Thanks for listening.

Buzz Didier
Longtime local

     —in a letter to the editor of the *Vail Trail,* January 9, 2000

Community support for VA had risen like floodwaters after the fires, but had subsided a bit with the road-through-the-wetlands debacle. For the grand celebration marking the opening of Blue Sky Basin in January 2000, VA officials were casting about for a way to thank the community and mark the symbolic beginning of the new millennium on a good note. They proved themselves remarkably tone deaf.

Somebody got a call from Robert Kennedy Jr.'s environmental group, the Water Keeper Alliance, who said the organization wanted to hold a fund-raiser in Vail. Kennedy's organization had made a big splash nationally for its commitment to cleaning up rivers and lakes, and of course the Kennedy name still meant a lot in Colorado. Maybe they could piggyback the grand opening of Blue Sky Basin with a fund-raising party? Although the Kennedys were primarily Aspen folk, maybe a little Camelot glitz would perk up the staid Vail image.

The idea sounded good, and plans were soon under way. Roger Daltrey of The Who would perform a concert at the Dobsen Ice Rink, the ice covered with a dance floor. They'd bedeck the place with black and white roses and carnations, and the invitations would read "Mountain Formal." There would be a charity raffle: a sailing date with Senator Ted Kennedy; a "Caddyshack" round of golf with Bill Murray, Chevy Chase, and Steve Rockefeller at Rockefeller's private course in Westchester; a Manhattan dinner for four with Dr. Ruth to talk sex. There would be celebrities instead of mere CEOs; Vail would shine in the reflected Kennedy light.

As the night of the event, January 8, drew closer, the Kennedy organizers exercised more and more control over the invitation list, and fewer and fewer Vail locals were invited. By the time the final guest list had been compiled, VA had only a few tickets to dole out. Several of VA's top management smelled a train wreck and refused to attend the event. The last thing VA needed was to irritate the community by excluding locals from the Blue Sky party.

The night of the shindig, Aron was excited; he buzzed from table to table like a bumblebee, telling his people "the A-list is here." Kaye Ferry, who had received one of the rare locals' invitations, was nonplussed. The Hollywood crowd was distinctly second-string, she thought. There was Richard Dean Anderson, the McGuyver character ("you know, the kind of guy who could blow up the world with a bobby pin and a book of matches"), and an aging Cliff Robertson ("he looked as if he had been resurrected"). But Jean-Claude van Damme? Jane Seymour? Jean-Paul Dejouria of Paul Mitchell? Ferry had to admit that there were plenty of representatives from America's eternal first family, which did provide a certain flash: "There were teeth everywhere," notes Ferry.

A fund-raising auction began, and Aron bid $50,000 for a hunting trip for four to Ted Turner's Montana ranch. Even though Aron promised to give the trip to his top lieutenants and it was for a good cause, the gesture rankled. "How come Aron could write a $50,000 check for a hunting trip, and turn around the next day and tell people they can't have a raise?" Ferry wondered, speaking the words that buzzed around Vail for weeks after the event. Aron's sitting on a chair that broke was the evening's perfect metaphor for VA's unchecked and unreconstructed profligacy.

After the auction, Robert Kennedy Jr. assumed the dais and launched into a thirty-five-minute stump speech that was essentially a tirade against big business. He railed against greedy corporate America, always cutting down trees and despoiling the environment. He talked about how big corporations have misled the public, beaten up the little guy, and walked roughshod over greater principles. "It's time to take a stand," Kennedy concluded, his voice rising in a convincing cadence that may have been genetically encoded.

Kennedy may or may not have known how close his words hit home, the day before Blue Sky Basin was to open, but some in the crowd did. "People were elbowing each other knowingly," Ferry says. "Don't you think it was ironic that Bobby Kennedy was here promoting an environmental cause?" says Ferry, incredulously. "Adam was crazy to have that kind of event. But the real irony is that some people just don't get the irony."

The day after the Kennedy fiasco, Blue Sky Basin opened to the public on a gorgeous, blue, and frigid winter's day, with acres of untouched pow-der awaiting an invitation-only crowd. The skiers who had jockeyed for VIP passes to get first tracks at Blue Sky Basin had to shiver for more than an hour while Pete Seibert and Earl Eaton made their way up the moun-tain, late. As the founders emeriti, the two codgers would cut the ceremo-nial cord for the new lift.

Television cameras surrounded the homespun Eaton, who positively beamed to see his dream fulfilled. He started holding forth about his even grander vision: that Vail would be connected all the way to Loveland, though a series of aerial trams, gondolas, and lifts that would haul skiers up one valley and down the other, traversing the state in one unbroken piste. VA's PR team couldn't *believe* that Eaton was talking about building yet more new lifts; they practically yanked him away from the cameras, explaining to the reporters that the old man didn't speak for the company. VA had no plans for more expansion, *no, sirree.*

Robert Kennedy Jr. didn't ski Blue Sky Basin that day.

■

During the summer of 2000, while visiting VA's new faux mining town at Keystone—where construction of tons of condos and new golf courses is in full swing—I ask Aron about the Kennedy event and the community's reac-tion to it. He agrees with Ferry. "Hey, we fucked up," he says.

But he is quick to add that he's convinced things are much better over-all. Aron fervently believes that he, Apollo, the town, and the valley have all learned important lessons since the arson. "The fires were a catalyst and a cathartic event," he says. "It started the process of turning this around." Whoever the arsonists are, he says, "it is the greatest irony that in an attempt to destroy us they helped cause our renaissance. People in this val-ley realized that we had far more in common that united us than compet-ing interests that divided us." Aron says that Apollo's still being around, eight years after buying the resort, should begin to calm locals' nerves. "In this valley, there was and may still be a horribly erroneous conception of what 'Wall Street' and 'Big Business' means," he says. "There's this perception that we would rape and pillage this resort. It's a ludicrous notion of what business is about. We have devoted considerable resources and time to turn it around. We're not driving people here into the Red Sea."

Aron says that although there will always be tension between VA and the rest of the valley, he thinks the message of a "kinder, gentler" company is getting through. "It was clear to me that we were not being perceived as kind and gentle," he says. "I am far from convinced that we actually deserved it. Whether it was fair or not, it was our reputation." He makes his point with an interesting Vail-ish analogy: Gerald Ford. Ford was, according to Aron, "without a doubt one of the most athletic presidents we ever had in this country." Ford, indeed, was a varsity letterman in football at the University of Michigan, and was a fair skier until a knee injury made him hang up the boards and concentrate on golf. Yet his infamous slip on an Air Force One step, coupled with one errant golf shot, made him fodder for years of Chevy Chase jokes. "Well, the local press here is Chevy Chase," proclaims Aron.

Some of the criticism has worsened as a result of Vail's IPO. On the good side, Aron says, the IPO enabled VA to raise a lot of capital and reinvest—"to make things better for our guests." Yet being public means just that—so much of what you do is public. "Every action has to make sense, be explainable, and be in the interest of an array of shareholders," he says. "Every ninety days, we have to announce all our numbers and all our strategies for all to see."

But even with the IPO and early missteps, Aron is bewildered by the way Vail remains a target for such intense criticism, but other ski areas seem to avoid scrutiny altogether. Either the rest of the ski industry is following VA's lead or the VA people are following them, he says. VA and three other companies now control about a quarter of the North American ski market: Intrawest, a Canadian company whose flagship resorts are Whistler/Blackcomb and Copper Mountain in Colorado; American Skiing Company, which owns such East Coast resorts as Sunday River and Sugarloaf, but which recently picked up Heavenly Valley in California; Booth Creek, which is reincarnated Vail owner George Gillett's group, owns the lower-profile resorts of Northstar at Tahoe and Grand Targhee in Wyoming.

Intrawest is primarily a real estate development company, but nobody seems to be burning down their lodges. Alex Cushing, the owner of Squaw Valley in California, was raided in June 2000 by Environmental Protection Agency investigators for alleged violations of environmental laws, and he has repeatedly been accused of flaunting environmental regulations, including clear-cutting ski runs without permits. No ELF activists were sending threatening e-mails to him.

Aron says that "it really ripped me up inside" when he was so personally, and so repetitively, attacked. One local journalist took Aron to task in a two-year anniversary analysis, and among his complaints was Aron's weight. (Aron fired back an editorial that he headlined himself: "Happy Two-Year Anniversary: P.S. You're Fat.") VA-bashing, Aron complains, became something of a civic sport in which the company couldn't compete. "There'd be an allegation: We're lynx killers. We'd deny it. The next day, they'd print another allegation: We steal bicycles from little kids. We'd deny it. We were playing defensive ball. After three years of allegations and denials, the allegations tend to stick.

"Why would I want to screw this place up?" he adds plaintively, opening his arms to encompass the new base village at Keystone, the new golf courses, the new condominiums, the new clubs. "I get paid a lot of money *not* to screw it up."

Why indeed?

26

The Next Eco-War

Each generation has its own rendezvous with the land, for despite our fee titles and claims of ownership, we are all brief tenants on this planet. By choice or by default, we will carve a land legacy for our heirs.

—STEWART L. UDALL, FORMER SECRETARY OF THE INTERIOR
UNDER JOHN F. KENNEDY, *THE QUIET CRISIS*

Just when VA was hoping it had weathered the environmental court challenges, the arson, the protests, the rebuilding, and two successive bad snow years, another ecological Donnybrook broke out in Colorado's high country. This time, the skirmish involved a proposed new forest plan by the White River National Forest, the landlord for both Aspen and Vail. The forest plan, a blueprint for management of the forest for the next fifteen years, mapped where ski areas might expand in the future, what the priorities would be for recreational uses of the forest, where there would be an increased effort to protect wildlife habitat, and where logging might occur. Because the White River National Forest is one of the most heavily used forests for recreation and contains the ski industry's highest-profile resorts, the plan would be heavily scrutinized.

The "preferred alternative" put forth by the forest service, known as Alternative D, was an uncharacteristically forward-thinking proposal for a federal agency that historically never saw a forest they didn't want to clear-cut. Forest service biologists had concluded that, cumulatively, the forest was being carved up and used so much that the critters who lived there needed a breather from more development and so much motorized human recreation. The document also proposed a moratorium on ski area expansions past their current boundaries.

The loudest opponents to the forest service's plan belonged to a well-organized group of snowmobilers and off-road-vehicle enthusiasts; they complained vociferously that they had a right to run their snow machines and ATVs anywhere they damn well wanted to. But the forest service's preferred alternative wasn't preferred by VA, either. They put out an internal memo requesting that employees write to express opposition to the plan. Porter Wharton III engaged in a vitriolic exchange with the local papers; his scary rhetoric suggested that Alternative D would shut down skiing as we know it and bring on the inevitable specter of enormous lift lines and expensive ski tickets. VA also persuaded Republican Senator Ben Nighthorse Campbell and Congressman Scott McGinnis (although Aron entertained Democrats, the company was an equal-opportunity political donor) to support Alternative C, which was much less restrictive to the ski industry. VA's accidental alliance with the motorheads was unfortunate from a public relations standpoint, but they preferred an alternative that would allow them to continue expanding their four resorts and connecting them with more ski-in, ski-out real estate development. "Alternative C is one big contiguous real estate deal," says Minturn's Fire Chief Sean Gallagher. That alternative included an option for VA to drop a gondola down to Minturn to create a new "portal" that Gallagher vehemently opposes.

The forest plan would normally have included a public comment period, to end on May 9, 2000, followed by other bureaucratic steps that would have probably made the plan final before the presidential elections in November 2000. That was risky, however, for those opposed to Alternative D. Because President Clinton had discovered late in his term that he could enjoy great press by being compared to Teddy Roosevelt, Clinton's administration had undertaken a marked greening of its public lands agencies. Elsewhere on the national forest front, the administration had declared a moratorium on building roads on some 50 million acres of so-called roadless areas, and Clinton was using his executive powers to create several national monuments. With Clinton and Mr. Earth-in-the-Balance at the helm, VA figured, the White River forest plan could go against them. Hometown politicians Campbell and McGinnis hurriedly pushed through legislation that would effectively delay the White River decision until after the elections. "If you want to change the decision, change the decisionmakers," sighed one forest-service planner. One VA executive put it even more succinctly: "If Gore wins, we're fucked."

Ted Zukowski thinks the fight over the White River National Forest plan puts the lie to Aron's claim of a "kinder, gentler" Vail. "They sent out 50,000 mailers to Colorado pass owners to get people to comment on the White River Forest plan," he says, sitting in his cramped office in Boulder. In the nonprofit world, that's a lot of mailers; to VA, it's peanuts. "They believe in the brute force theory of public relations," Zukowski says.

"If they ram it [Alternative C] down everybody's throats, there's going to be an eco-war here," vows Kelly-Goss, the Minturn town councilman.

By contrast, Aspen's CEO O'Donnell got together with the forest service and ironed out a few problems the ski-co had with the plan; then they endorsed Preferred Alternative D, making them look as green as the spring-time tips of a fir tree branch with new needles. Vail's president, Andy Daly, telephoned Dave Bellack, Aspen's general counsel. "You're making us look bad, Dave," Daly complained.

"No, Andy," Bellack replied. "*You're* making you look bad."

27

Avenue of the Americas

At Bachelor Gulch, smack in the trophy-home belt, a young architect sat in front of his office phone, quaking at the prospect of telling his client, a Texas businessman, about a $50,000 cost overrun in a new, 9,000-square-foot log home. The lot alone ran $1 million, and the house would cost at least another $3 million to build. The young architect had set the wall heights incorrectly on the foundation, and it was an expensive boo-boo. He steeled himself, made the call. To his surprise, his client laughed.

"Shit, son, I made enough in the market last month to pay for the whole damn house." Not a problem.

On the thirty-eighth floor of the towering steel and glass Credit Lyonnais building in midtown Manhattan, far from the intrigues of the Colorado high country, sits the spacious offices of Apollo Partners. There is no sign on the door outside the elevator. If you don't know what you are looking for, you shouldn't be here. Although the company, and especially its principals, are notoriously press shy, I nonetheless reach an agreement to speak with "an Apollo spokesperson" to see whether he can help explain all that I had seen while investigating the Vail fires.

I am greeted warmly; a full coffee pot, bagels, and a selection of pastries wait in a clean conference room overlooking New York's streets. The "spokesperson" tells me a story about going to Vail with another Apollo partner soon after the acquisition. The two of them went to dinner the first night, and the waitress looked at them and said, "The snow was great today, wasn't it?" They replied that they hadn't had a chance to hit the slopes because they had been in meetings all day.

"You must be those guys from Apollo," she said. The word was out.

The two decided it was important for them to keep low-profile: strangers in a strange land. "There's a lot of scrutiny for who we are and what we do," the spokesman tells me, fully aware of the magnitude of the understatement. When Apollo had begun considering whether it should purchase Vail, he says, "there was a lot of disagreement about whether we should buy a ski resort." The debate was relatively simple: buying a physical infrastructure and building it into a larger, more profitable resort would take time and money. It wasn't the classic modus operandi of the organization, which was geared more toward seizing opportunities, instituting new management, restructuring debt, acquiring compatible companies and merging them, and then moving on to the next. Did Vail, as a company, make sense?

There were definitely possibilities. "George Gillett was a great entrepreneur," he says, with the caveat to follow. "He wasn't a great businessman."

But the cash flow was good. If the company added a little more retail, developed and sold more real estate, and gold-plated the infrastructure, the bottom line looked plenty acceptable. Apollo likes what it calls "franchise assets": a skilled management team, highly respected products or services, strong brand identity, superior operating margins, strong market share, and significant barriers to entry. Vail was a hit on all counts. "We saw a great franchise," he says; and with the Apollo touch, it could be a little more profitable.

The Apollo spokesman is not blind to the culture clash of Wall Street and Bridge Street, but is unapologetic. "For better or for worse, the world doesn't stand still," he says. Vail, he says, "has become a big business in addition to being a good ski mountain." He feels, as Aron does, that the Sturm und Drang over Vail's New York takeover should have diminished by now. "Everybody thought we were going to flip the asset," he says, but points out that eight years later, they still have it. Owning Vail has been a good investment, he says, but it's a better showcase for the kinder, gentler side of Apollo, which, he admits, isn't a side that regularly makes the papers. "It's every perception about us tossed on its head," he says. And, with Aron, he believes the fires were almost a blessing. "We needed an event to show how out-of-hand [Vail's opponents] were," he says.

I ask him to run through the rationale for Blue Sky Basin. If indeed Vail Resorts has no plans to develop Gilman, as it claims, and skier days are so flat, why spend more than $20 million and incur all the bad PR? He walks me through the numbers. Say it cost about $23 million to put in the four new lifts. You can depreciate that capital investment over thirty years. If you want, say, a 15 or 20 percent return on investment, you have to pull in between $4.4 and $5.3 million extra per year to service the debt and put some money in the black ledger. VA makes a profit of about fifty dollars for each incremental new skier it puts on the mountain. So the company needs Blue Sky Basin to encourage between 80,000 and one 110,000 more skiers every year to make it pay for itself—only about a 5 percent to 7 percent increase. The historical precedent of VA's increased skier visits after it put in the China Bowl lift in 1989 was a good benchmark. "It doesn't seem to be a big stretch," he says. They've done the math.

"There had not been a sizzle factor at Vail for a long time," he says, and adds that Apollo has more plans to reinvigorate the "lodging base" at Vail and its other resorts. "What Vail needs is bed base, not another high-speed quad to get a decreasing number of people up the mountain." That's why they've pushed for the new Ritz Carlton in Beaver Creek, the Marriott at Breckenridge, and a big plan to redevelop Lionshead, a particularly unattractive grouping of shops, restaurants, and lodgings near the spot where the gondola starts up the mountain. The "uphill transportation business" is profitable, he says, "but it's even better when you also own a business that profits from the lodging business."

From where the spokesman sits, it's almost comical that Vail has attracted so much attention. "People have lost perspective," he says. "These are small businesses." He is not unaware, though, that deep fault lines run through the country today, and they rumble through Vail as dangerously as they run through Manhattan. "It *is* about balance," he says. "Who gets to decide what's enough? That's the heart of it."

28

On a Mission

My feelings

I never knew the wilderness could be this peaceful. As I look around, I see the true meaning of nature. I see the sun sparkling on the freshly laid snow, and all I can hear is the falling of the snow off the trees. The scenery is astounding, the special blend of greens and beiges takes you by surprise. This is the world I never knew.

As I walk, I come to an open meadow. The snow here has never been touched, leaving the field looking peaceful and fresh. Everything is untouched here, except for a trail of tiny footprints. It leads to a denser part of the forest, places that are unknown to mankind. As I stare across the land, the makings of mother nature, I sigh a deep sigh of satisfaction and fall down in the fluffy snow.

I belong here.

—JOURNAL ENTRY FROM WHITNEY LEFEVRE, A THIRTEEN-YEAR-OLD GIRL
ATTENDING THE GORE RANGE NATURAL SCIENCE SCHOOL'S PROGRAM

For a fund-raising breakfast for the Gore Range Natural Science School at the elegant Sonnenalps Hotel in Vail Village, director Kim Langmaid has invited Jack Shea, founder and president of the Teton Science School near Jackson Hole, Wyoming, to give a pep talk to Vail movers and shakers who are thinking about supporting the school. Jackson Hole has had its share of growing pains, trophy homes, and social unrest—problems just like Vail's; a raid by the U.S. Immigration and Naturalization Service on undocumented Mexican workers almost shut down Jackson's service industry. Unlike Vail, though, Jackson has had to make the transition from a well-formed ranching economy into the brave new world of the New West. "We finally figured out that there was more money ranching tourists," Shea tells the group, his laugh line. Jackson quickly found itself in a bind like Vail's when housing and land prices soared and rich modem cowboys, investment bankers, trust-funders, corporate titans, and Hollywood starlets all wanted a piece of the Marlboro man. In the time it takes to say "Jackson Hole Real Estate," the place went crazy and the impacts accelerated.

Shea ticks off the changes, starting with the workforce demographic and the constant difficulties in finding affordable housing for workers. "There used to be ski bums but they won't do it anymore. They're all selling real estate." The crowd chuckles knowingly; one of Vail's biggest real estate mavens started out as the assistant director of the ski school.

Vail's town manager, Bob McLaurin, the former Jackson Hole town manager, says that "people in Jackson look at Vail in horror. Nobody wants to be like Vail." Indeed, other ski resorts have scrutinized Vail's experience in an attempt to mimic the best and avoid the worst. "What's happened in Vail means it's a canary for the mountain resorts all over North America," says McLaurin. "Whatever is going to happen, good or bad, is gonna happen here first."

As far as McLaurin is concerned, the relationship between Vail and VA in the post-arson era remains an armed truce. "I don't think they've been bad owners," he says about VA's current régime. "I'm not saying they aren't Machiavellian, but they've invested more in this mountain than we have in this town." In the end, he says, "we're like the two convicts running through the swamp handcuffed together."

•

One beautiful day in late winter, Kim Langmaid and I take a walk along the railroad tracks at about 9,000 feet to the spot where she had seen the lynx tracks less than a year before the fires. Along the way, we pass stands of lodgepole pine, aspen, Douglas fir and Engelmann spruce, willows and beaver dams and tracks in the snow from coyotes and marten, black-tailed weasels, and foxes. Suddenly, she stops and points. "The tracks came down from the notch," she says, pointing to a small saddle in a snowy, west-facing slope where she had seen the lynx. "It was on a mission to go somewhere."

A normally quiet woman who hardly fills the role of the wild-eyed radical environmentalist, Langmaid suddenly launches into a tirade against VA. "It's so hard for me to fathom how come they can't be better stewards of this place. Why did they push so hard for that little expansion with so much public sentiment against it? Why?"

Langmaid wonders how to maneuver skillfully among the loud and conflicting voices. "People don't see the big picture and the cumulative impacts of building in every drainage." If people would fly the valley and look down, she muses, "I think people would be surprised at how much development there is." She is frustrated by how few people recognize the importance of maintaining a relationship with the natural environment, whose beauty spawned the development. "Having a sense of place can build a sense of community," Langmaid says, "a lot better than anything that people can build with hammer and nails." We pause over several sets of tracks that resemble the remains of a multispecies dance in the snow. "If you lose that sense of place, the disconnection can be a tragedy. I just want to raise people's awareness and respect for the land and how it works," she says. "Everything," she adds, paraphrasing one of John Muir's most famous insights, "is interconnected."

Langmaid, along with many others, wonders what it will take before people understand that there must be a limit to growth before the natural world collapses. "We're pushing it pretty hard," she says, and worries that by the time the people who run VA and other such companies realize this, it will be too late. She uses the analogy of an elk straining to make it through a particularly harsh winter by conserving its energy. If the elk suddenly has to run from a snowmobile—or even a snowshoer—to get away, that burst of energy may be enough to put the elk over the edge. "I wonder," says Langmaid. "What's that move going to be for us?"

■

On February 3, 1999, the Colorado Division of Wildlife paid trappers from Canada and Alaska to capture dozens of lynx, then had the animals trucked down to Colorado. State wildlife officials, after much internal debate and public criticism, chose to release the lynx in the San Juan Mountains of southern Colorado, about one hundred miles south of Vail and the Category III expansion. The reintroduction program met with mixed results. By following the animals' radio collars, biologists knew that some of the lynx died of starvation; some, in the area near their release, established patterns that looked natural; and others began to seek new home ranges. One of the original lynx had teetered on the edge of starvation before biologists recaptured it, fattened it up, and released it again. The lynx traveled north to the area around Vail, presumably traveling through or near the Cat III expansion before deciding to head even farther north.

When the lynx tried to cross Interstate 70 near Vail, it was crushed by a car.

Epilogue: Who Gets to Decide?

More than two years after the arson that shook Vail and the ski industry's self-image, there have been no indictments, no arrests, and no indication that the case will ever be closed. In September 2000, a grouse hunter discovered a cache of four empty five-gallon plastic gas cans under a fallen spruce tree about a half mile from Two Elk, and investigators hoped to find something useful—a bar code on one of the containers so that they could trace the merchant, perhaps, or possibly a fingerprint they could match. In October, investigators revealed that the fuel residue inside the containers matched the fuel used to set the fires. In all likelihood, the arsonists used the mid-mountain stash to fill up the one- to two-liter incendiary devices used to start the conflagrations at PHQ and Two Elk. Even with the discovery, though, the trail to the arsonists still appeared too cold to track. Law enforcement officials maintain publicly that arson cases often take years to solve, and that the Vail investigation may yet result in arrests. Privately, however, several law enforcement sources close to the case admit that, at this point, only blind luck or a gross act of stupidity on the part of the arsonist(s) will bring this case to a prosecutorial conclusion.

Why, in a case that was so conspicuous, have the culprits remained so perfectly inconspicuous? From the moment I arrived in Vail to cover the fires in October 1998, and through the writing of this book, that question has plagued me. After all, the FBI caught the World Trade Center bombers and the man responsible for the Oklahoma City bombing in relatively short order. The destruction, loss of human life, and law enforcement's response in New York and Oklahoma can't be compared to an arson that resulted only in property damage; but if the Vail fires were an act of domestic terrorism, as has been claimed, then the terrorists, whoever they are, may be poised to do more damage elsewhere. Or, perhaps, to strike again at Vail. If the fires were set by those with a more discrete vendetta against Vail Resorts, not only did they get away with it, but they managed to incite a lot of discussion about "ecoterrorism" and the state of environmental activism in this country.

The easy answer to the question about why the crime remains unsolved is that arsons are notoriously difficult to prosecute. The crime took place on a remote mountaintop, at a time of year when the town and the resort were quiet. Much of the evidence that may have been left was destroyed either in the flames or in the firefighters' efforts to douse them. Whoever planned the arson did it well enough to remain undetected before and after the crime; if more than one person was involved, the perpetrators have maintained their pact of silence exceptionally well.

•

I began my own investigation by trying to figure out who might have lit the match. I have discovered, as many writers have, that some people are afraid to talk to cops, and especially the FBI, but may be willing to talk to a journalist. From the first days after the arson, the limits and fallibility of law enforcement, especially the ego-driven institutional battles among different agencies, certainly contributed to the lack of resolution. I recall that in the first days after the fires, as I sat on a bench inside the municipal building and waited for a press conference, several ATF agents brushed by wearing their trademark windbreakers with the agency's acronym emblazoned in yellow on the back. A local reporter turned to me and jibed, "They sure know how to *set* fires, don't they?" referring to the Waco disaster. I repeated this joke to an ATF agent, who responded, "*We* didn't set them, the FBI did." This kind of institutional rivalry, multiplied over the law enforcement agencies involved in the investigation, did not make solving the crime any easier.

Timing was also a problem. As soon as the Columbine High School massacre took place in April 1999, virtually every FBI agent working Vail was pulled off the case, and the arson investigation became about as active as the fires at Two Elk the day after the blaze was set. Subsequent "actions" claimed by the ELF in various states kept other investigators on those cases. But Vail went on the back burner just six months after the investigation began.

The investigators who were left to sift through the ashes didn't have much to work with; the materials used to set the fires were so common-place that even the most advanced forensic work would lead only to broad-brush clues. The e-mail that claimed credit for the arson "in the name of the lynx" may have been one of the best leads—or one of the most mislead-ing. The e-mail raised as many questions as it answered. In any case, the ELF communiqué was never traced to its original computer server, much less the sender.

The loose-knit and underground cells of self-proclaimed "ecoterrorists" proved an elusive target. My initial reaction to the ELF's claim was, "Who?" —as was that of every journalist I spoke with at the time who covered the environmental beat. In more than a decade of covering national environ-mental politics, I had never heard of the ELF. Certainly they had never claimed an action of a similar scale. Were they coming of age? Was the Vail arson part of a trend toward more violent activism in the name of the earth's critters? "Maybe" appeared to be the only answer.

At first, it seemed likely that somebody affiliated with the increasingly vitriolic Category III protests might have been involved in the arson—if not the leaders, a few of their hot-headed hangers-on. The Colorado-based Ancient Forest Rescue activists vehemently denied any connection to the ELF, however, and after interviews with several AFR activists, I tended to believe them. Although they admitted that they wanted to stop Vail's expansion, admitted to camping on the mountain that night, and admitted to plans the next day to block construction, I thought it unlikely that they had been involved, and equally unlikely that they harbored members who had. The obvious suspects didn't pan out, despite intense efforts by law enforcement to link AFR members with the arson. Later, after offering grants of immunity to several key AFR members in return for their testi-mony, the U.S. attorney's office apparently agreed. Not only did they decline to indict any AFR members, but they even declined to nail them on contempt charges when AFR members refused to answer questions about their membership rolls.

As I continued to dig, I discovered that I was right about one thing: People who weren't talking to law enforcement wanted to talk with me—but not about who lit the match. I was repeatedly sidetracked by people who wanted me to know about the currents of discontent that had been swirling in Vail and down the Eagle Valley at the time of the fires. As I explored the valley and spoke to its most established citizens and its rowdiest newcomers, its Spanish-speaking maids and its jaded ski instructors, I became interested in the possibility that the obvious solution to this whodunit—that a band of ecoterrorists had torched the place—might not be the correct solution. The Richard Jewell debacle, in which the FBI had erroneously leaked that the Olympic security guard had been responsible for setting off a bomb in an Atlanta park during the 1996 games, was still fresh in my mind. And, closer to home, after more than three years of covering the JonBenet Ramsey murder, I had become convinced that the public case built against the parents, John and Patsy Ramsey, through a systematic cascade of law enforcement leaks, was flawed in almost every detail. I had learned, to quote a Gilbert and Sullivan lyric, that "things are seldom what they seem."

■

When I set out to investigate the fires, I began by trying to learn as much about the physical layout of the ski area and the mountain as I could: How would *I* have gone about plotting my approach and escape? Early on, I scouted the mountain with one of the old-time haul-cat drivers, Larry Walker, as we cruised to the various mountaintop restaurants in a VA-owned snow cat. With a handlebar mustache that doesn't pass Vail Associates' dress code—and he could not care less—the forty-seven-year-old Walker carts live lobsters, smoked venison, prime rib, liters of Evian water, cartons of chipotle chilies, and cases of champagne around the mountain in a quarter-million-dollar Canadian machine made by Bombardier. Day after day, he hauls between 20,000 and 30,000 pounds of foodstuffs, alcohol, and other gourmet accoutrements from the top of the gondola to Vail's on-mountain restaurants, each one employing its own executive chef and sous-chef.

Born in Gypsum, about forty-five miles down valley from Vail, Walker's dad homesteaded a place just good enough to support a cattle rig, despite

its being plagued by Colorado's high-desert problems of predators, isolation, and not enough water. "When I was a kid, there wasn't thing in the
Vail Valley except that one old log cabin down by Highway 6," he remi-
nisced. Walker got a job with VA in the early days, but it was a loose enough
arrangement that he could still ply the rodeo circuit as a bull rider around
South Dakota, Kansas, Nebraska, Oklahoma, and his native state.

He recalls with a bit of irony that when VA started, some of the bigwigs
came down the valley to tell the locals what a fine thing having a ski resort
would be. "'This is really gonna benefit you people in the valley,' they told
us. 'You won't have to pay hardly any taxes because the ski resort will generate so much revenue.'"

Walker stops the machine's tank-tracks mid-mountain for emphasis.
"Ha!" he snorts. "Now look at the cost of living and property taxes here."

Working on the mountain, he's seen some changes, too. "Used to be
we'd be the only ones up here on the mountain at night," he says, spitting
some Copenhagen chew juice out the cab window. "No security or nothin'."
Now, with Adventure Ridge carting laser tag players up the mountain at all
hours, and the fires and all that, things aren't as calm. On a full-moon
evening, with snowshoers and hikers and on-mountain activities and what-
not, Walker figures it won't be long before they get the chairlifts running
damned near all night long. Things sure have changed since the days when
the haul-cat drivers used to just dump garbage on the mountain all winter.
They wouldn't even try to pick it up until spring.

Walker didn't have too much of an opinion about who set the fires, but
didn't reckon that the arson set VA back much. "Hell, they rebuilt it bigger
and better and with insurance money to boot," he says. "It might've hurt
'em in the short run, but in the long run they'll come out ahead. A year later
and it'll all be bigger and better."

That, certainly, was an accurate prediction. It took close to two years,
but VA rebuilt everything it wanted to rebuild, bigger and better. Blue Sky
Basin opened on schedule in early January 2000, with two new lifts; Two
Elk was rebuilt 20 percent larger; PHQ and Buffalo's restaurant were both a
lot spiffier; and by opening day of the 2000–2001 season, Blue Sky Basin
would expand by yet another lift. Through an intense public relations cam-

paign and despite two subpar snow years, Vail climbed back to number one on *Ski* magazine's resort rankings in time for the 2000–2001 season. Just as Leon Black and Apollo had sworn it would.

As I got to know the mountain with Walker, I also started getting a better sense of the class warfare that pervades Vail. The recent flood of big money, really big money, into the valley has astounded even such an unflappable ex–bronc rider as Walker. "I never realized there were such terrible rich people," he says. He told me about some "rich guy" who had bought a house for $4 million and bulldozed it. "Who can pay four million bucks for a lot?" he asked incredulously, stopping the snow cat again for emphasis. The boom has driven real estate prices through the roof—even his. Walker built his own fourteen hundred-square-foot house in Gypsum in 1982 for a little more than $100,000—"I built it to live in"—and he's been told it's worth a cool quarter million right now. "It's ridiculous."

His dad's spread, his co-workers rib him, is probably worth a pretty hefty chunk of change, too, which makes Walker a potential multimillionaire. But Walker guffaws at the thought. "Dad doesn't have any hobbies except for work," he says. "Why would he sell it?" Walker spits again, revs the quarter-million-dollar snow cat up a steep section of snow and activates the siren temporarily to warn skiers he's coming.

"Besides," he says thoughtfully, "it's just dirt that costs you money unless you sell it."

◆

If there's one thing that visitors to Vail can't avoid, it's that selling dirt, if that's what you want to call the oversized local real estate industry, is a huge part of the Eagle Valley economy. At the base of Beaver Creek ski area, about fifty feet from the bottom of the Centennial Express chairlift, a sign advertising Slifer, Smith, Frampton/Vail Associates Real Estate brags that they are the exclusive affiliate of Sotheby's, and that they are "the right people" to see about shopping for top-end chalets and ski-in, ski-out properties. This, the largest real estate sales company in the Eagle Valley, is a joint venture with Vail's owners; after the fires, however, Slifer, Smith and

Frampton discreetly dropped "Vail Associates" from most of their literature and signs. But not from the profit sharing.

I was intrigued early on in my project, then, when a friend of a friend put me in contact with one of the local real estate salesmen, who wanted to share some "background" on Vail. The real estate agent, who requested anonymity, was not happy with the way things were going, even though he was doing well financially under the present arrangements. "Have you read *Barbarians at the Gate*?" he asked me. "*Predator's Ball*? *Den of Thieves*? Everybody wanted to know where those eighties guys went. Here they're wolves in sheep's clothing. They're baaaaaaaack."

He didn't care much about who had set the fires. As far as he was concerned, another fire had been raging ever since Apollo Partners had taken over ownership of the resort and gobbled up Keystone and Breckenridge. "This place is run by people in glass and steel towers thousands of miles away," he complained. To those people, he said, "this place is an oil well. They're going to pump it until it goes dry." Unprompted by me, this long-time local spilled over with venom. "They are the worms in the apple, the snake in the garden."

He told me to read the books he recommended, and if I was still interested in learning more about the corporate persona of Vail Resorts, I should get back to him. When I did, I thought he may have been threatened by the Mafia in the meantime. Abruptly, he refused to talk to me, or even to tell me why he wouldn't talk with me. All he would say was that he didn't want to be involved in my book in any way. Click.

My inclination was to dismiss him as an eccentric with some kind of personal axe to grind. But everywhere I went in the county, and whenever I started to talk about the fires, people steered me toward a similar theme: the heavy-handedness of the new régime. At one point, I sat down with one of the county politicians, Eagle County Commissioner (since retired) James Johnson Jr. for breakfast at the Dancing Bear, a locals' favorite in west Vail. Johnson, one of the rare African Americans in Eagle County, moved to the Vail area in 1980, starting as a maid at the Marriot. After holding a succession of jobs, he won a county commissioner's seat in 1992. Johnson participated in all the Category III meetings in the months before the fires, and, with the other commissioners, he felt that because the ski area expansion was on federal land, the county didn't have jurisdiction to block it. Johnson told me after the fires that it was a shame the county commissioners couldn't figure a way to postpone the Category III expansion, at least until after the federal government had ruled on whether to list the lynx as a threatened or endangered species (which the feds eventually did). If the commissioners could have arranged a delay, Johnson conjectures, "Blue Sky Basin probably wouldn't have happened, and the fires probably wouldn't have happened."

•

Slowly, after conversations such as these with Johnson, Walker, and the unnamed real estate agent, my initial idea of conducting an amateur investigation into the likely and unlikely culprits evolved into something much more complex. In a short time, my search for the proximate cause or even the legal culprit for the fires became subordinate to my investigation of the reason Vail was targeted in the first place. I set out on an odyssey of sorts into the new heart of the American West, where a shifting economy and huge demographic changes since 1975 have altered the landscape in as profound a way as homesteading, mining, ranching, and grazing had done in the previous 150 years, ever since whites began arriving in the country's highest and wildest places to settle in the mid-1800s. Federal land managers who now had to referee fights between snowmobilers and backcountry skiers, or mountain bikers and off-road-vehicle users, soon found themselves wishing for the good old days when they were simply haggling over cow pies, mine tailings, and clear-cuts.

Vail and the Eagle Valley, I soon discovered, had become a central repository for almost every troubling trend that had been spreading like knapweed across the West's new lifestyle towns: incredible growth driven largely by wealthy absentee owners, which in turn drives up property values beyond the ability of full-time residents to afford; a thriving, mostly minimum-wage service sector, with full employment but with more and more immigrants forced by economic necessity to live farther and farther from where they worked; environmental stresses from decreasing water quality and quantity, as well as rapid development on traditional wildlife habitat; old-school politics of mostly good-old-boy county commissioners meeting the new-school politics of huge amounts of outside money; federal land management agencies caught in their own transition from their roots as extractive industry facilitators to recreation managers and environmental stewards; population growth in urban centers such as Denver that affect every facet of mountain life; and the pervasive and insidious unintended consequences when people with so much money descend on rural places to play—and no one can muster enough gumption to rein them in when they want another golf course or a 15,000-square-foot vacation house.

As I learned more about Vail's unique origins, I also saw echoes of its current struggles repeated almost everywhere I went in the West. The region is wrestling with mighty environmental and social conflicts born less out of a declining timber industry or played-out mining claims and more out of the newest conquest of the region by hordes of affluent second-home owners and lifestyle refugees. Wherever I traveled for *Newsweek*, whether to research a story on the militia in the Bitteroot Valley in Montana, on a wildlife filmmaker in Sun Valley, Idaho, or on an obstreperous rancher near Silver City, New Mexico, I saw similar strains on the West's self-consciously ingratiating persona. This slow, almost inconspicuous shift of wealth and second-home ownership in the new amenities-based economies of the West was creating deep divisions and enormous conflict almost everywhere. Coupled with a predictable population influx of workers needed to provide the amenities and the service for these wealthy newcomers, the result was nothing less than a powder keg.

Vail is in the vanguard of these changes and tensions. Although the ski area was established at a time when it was still laughable to think that the West could fill up with people, nothing is laughable about growth issues today. It's hard to believe now, but the entire population of the eleven western states has more than tripled since World War II—from 17 million in 1945 to more than 60 million at last count. The West went from being a region without a single professional sports franchise to one where a single town, Denver, has professional baseball, basketball, football, hockey, and soccer. Whether one does or does not subscribe to a Malthusian philosophy of the perils of population growth on a global scale, it is increasingly difficult to ignore the deleterious effects of population growth and consumption on the natural environment of the West. The national parks are seeing record-breaking traffic, recreational use of national forests is at an all-time high, and the problems associated with too many "fun hogs" are being felt throughout the region.

As recently as 1980, the public discourse about growth and development issues in Colorado was nascent at best, although the statewide referendum to kill Colorado's 1976 Olympic bid was a harbinger of concerns to come. Today, growth and development rank as one of the top concerns of Colorado's voters, and the political establishment is uncertain about how to react to those concerns. The U.S. Forest Service and Eagle County's commissioners certainly weren't ready to veto Vail's Category III expansion in the name of slowing the development juggernaut. Concerns about growth, water availability, the declining quality of life, or habitat fragmentation are not slowing the region's growth rates. New arrivals continue to flock to Denver, and to Phoenix, and to Boise, then move to second- and third-tier rural towns such as Driggs, Idaho, or Eagle, Colorado, in search of the next last best place.

■

Many of Vail's residents do have a strong sense of place, and they love their mountains even as they watch them fill with starter castles and absentee owners. The fires were an affront to virtually everybody I spoke to, and for a brief and almost euphoric time after the fires died down, the Vail community did pull together. But the détente didn't last. As I hung out in the bars and on the slopes, in the humble double-wides, and in the sumptuous multimillion-dollar condominiums, I couldn't shake the sense that many people believed the current owners of the ski area somehow *deserved* to be burned. In any company town, it's not unusual for the locals to resent the company; but the depth of antipathy for VA at the time of the fires—which ran through almost every strata of society—was startling. Even discounting

VA as a lightning rod for criticism for forces far beyond its control, like Colorado's burgeoning population, the company was not well liked by many people who lived in the valley. And the company knew it. "It's not good that they call us the Evil Empire," one VA executive said to me, stating the more than obvious.

Every state in the West has at least a half-dozen places similar to Vail; towns that have been "discovered" by the "one hundred best outdoor sport towns"-type articles that flourish in the yuppie lifestyle magazines. People flock to these places, remake them in their own images, then move on in search of the next place when one too many chain stores moves to town. Many longtime Vail residents are already abandoning ship and heading for Telluride or Crested Butte or Bozeman, Montana, in hopes of eking out a few years elsewhere before those places, too, become playgrounds rather than communities. Fires are breaking out all over the West these days. Some are just more conspicuous than others. Or more literal.

As I got to know Vail better, the themes of the conspicuous and the inconspicuous became more pervasive. The obvious currents of conspicuous wealth, conspicuous consumption, and conspicuous power clashed everywhere with inconspicuous poverty, paucity, and powerlessness that were equally rampant in the valley. After a decade of writing about environmental politics, and western environmental politics, I found that Vail symbolized a place where many of these issues came together and roiled in the cauldron of past and present.

The themes for Vail's troubles have antecedents not only in the deceit layered deep in the resort's founding, such as hoodwinking ranchers with the dummy Transmontane Rod and Gun Club, but in the very idea of the doctrine of Manifest Destiny, the philosophical core of white settlement in the American West. Once a land of boundless opportunity, the region absorbed Americans who swept across the country to the Pacific coast, then bounced back and began infilling the more desolate, arid, and isolated stretches of what has come to be known as the Intermountain West: the area between the Sierra Nevada in California and the Rocky Mountains ranging from Montana to New Mexico. The population shifts that made the Rocky Mountain West the fastest growing region of the country during the fifteen years since 1985 have led to enormous cultural dislocation and social disenfranchisement: Westerners have always railed that they were being colonized by the effete classes from the East. Now the New Western-ers have taken, in some ways, to colonizing themselves.

The unique politics of the West have exacerbated the problems of this accelerated population influx. The wide libertarian streak that runs through the western persona has not served the region well during the postwar period when millions of immigrants from California, Texas, New York, and Florida began looking at the Rocky Mountains for what author Gretel Erlich calls "the solace of open spaces." Development went on with-out consideration for how the region's most precious resource, water, would be allocated. Ski areas and developers bought water rights from farmers and miners and put them to use in ways never imagined by the arcane—and archaic—Colorado water laws. Rural people witnessed the suburban problem of sprawl when it arrived at their barn doors. As cap-puccinos conquered the West, the citizen legislators who ran the states were hopelessly outgunned by powerful interest groups. The developers and real estate industry lobbyists were becoming as powerful as the American Min-ing Congress or the American Farm Bureau. Vail Resorts was just one of the new vanguard of power brokers in the New West.

The new power brokers quickly learned that political power and access come cheaper at the state legislature than they do in Washington, D.C. I once attended most of a legislative session in Cheyenne, Wyoming, to chronicle how a citizen-legislature worked at a time when "states rights" was a rallying cry in Washington's conservative political circles. For me, after spending nearly six years in Washington, D.C., covering national politics, this was an intriguing opportunity to see whether local politicians indeed have a better grasp of local issues, and whether they should be more empow-ered to make choices that directly affect them. After all, anybody who stud-ied Washington politics knew that special interest groups, with their powerful lobbying groups and huge campaign contributions, affected the way legislation was crafted and enacted. Perhaps enlightened self-interest worked better closer to the ground.

Not hardly. At one point, I walked into a subcommittee meeting in the state Capitol in Cheyenne, where a stuffed bison graces the lobby. The chairman was calling for a vote on proposed legislation that would monitor and regulate the hog farm industry, a major environmental polluter. One legislator walked in late, then asked the chairman what the vote was about. The tardy representative confessed aloud that he didn't know the issue that well, and called to a man in a suit sitting at the back of the room. "How do I vote on this?" he queried. The man, who I later found out was a lobbyist for the Farm Bureau, a national lobbying group that regularly crosses plow-shares with conservation groups, simply lifted his arm and pointed his thumb at the marble floor. The legislator voted no.

That lobbyists bend the ear of politicians is nothing new, but the unabashed public display still floored me. I wondered: Did we really want to give bigger block grants to these guys?

Colorado's legislature is no different, with the exception that, in Colorado, the traditional logging, mining, and ranching industries have substantially diminished in importance as a percentage of the state's economic output. As a result, real estate developers, as well as the skiing and recreation industries, have become a huge and growing part of the economy, with predictable and commensurate political influence. That trend is repeated in western state after western state, as high-tech companies move into areas where they can offer what University of Oregon economics professor Ed Whitelaw has dubbed the "second paycheck"—an amenity-filled backyard of outdoor activities that gravity and technology can combine to create. The state governments, through a long history of "custom and culture," are still stacked with rural representatives enjoying long-standing seniority, who represent what University of Colorado law professor Charles Wilkinson has very aptly dubbed "the lords of yesterday." The result, if you care much about the natural world and the critters that live in it, is the worst of both worlds. The traditional extractive industries are still disproportionately represented in state politics, and the new, powerful development interests back them up ably. Vail Resorts may very well represent the lords of the future in the West.

Vail Associates' influence didn't begin with Apollo by any means. As I was completing this book, I met a former *Chicago Tribune* reporter named

Len Ackland, who now runs the Center for Environmental Journalism at the University of Colorado, where I had been given a fellowship. When Ackland heard about my book, he went to his files and pulled out a story he had written in 1979 about the Vail gondola accident in 1976. The headline was "U.S. Cover-up in Vail Disaster," and detailed how VA had engaged in a pattern of negligence that may have contributed to the deadly accident—then covered up their complicity by altering documents and firing workers who questioned Vail's safety compliance. What was even more disturbing, Ackland's article described how the U.S. Forest Service, which holds responsibility for monitoring Vail's activities and safety records, routinely worked "cooperatively" with Vail to the extent that they would give VA employees advance warnings of their supposedly spot inspections of the lifts. Another University of Colorado professor told me that Vail had managed to build some of its more profitable real estate developments smack in the middle of an avalanche zone, despite the objections of numerous scientists. VA, in all its incarnations, has been adept at having its way; and just about everybody in Colorado seems to know about it, and frets about it.

Politics in the United States is run by money, and despite the beliefs of Porter Wharton III, Brian McCartney, and Sheriff A. J. Johnson, that money is not concentrated in a few environmental organizations backed by even the most well-meaning environmental philanthropists, such as Ted Turner or Patagonia. Whatever one thinks of professional environmentalists and their groups' hyperbolic fund-raising appeals, they are hopelessly outgunned in the political arena by the contributions of corporations; and the deep-rooted inertia in the courts and the legislature has prevented important issues such as water allocation and land planning from entering the twenty-first century.

In the West, with its apparently limitless landscape, it is still difficult to believe that we could ever run out of space for more growth, more people, more development. Space, though, isn't the problem. The problem is that most of the spaces where humans want to live, along the rivers and streambeds and creeks, are also the places most coveted by the animals and plants that have acted for millions of years as the glue that, literally, holds the place together. It's the impact of "industrial tourism," as the incipient environmental curmudgeon Ed Abbey put it. In Moab, Utah, a favorite weekend getaway for mountain dwellers in Colorado, the impact of mountain bikers over the twenty years since 1980 has torn up significant swaths of the very earth that supports life in that desert region—the rich, lichen-filled cryptobiotic soil that acts as a kind of protective covering that allows plants to grow in the otherwise inhospitable sand. Once the soil has been crushed, whether by grazing cows, marauding jeep drivers, or packs of mountain bikers, the process of desertification accelerates.

Since taking over in 1996, those who run Vail Resorts have sought to hedge their bets against global warming by vastly expanding the company's snowmaking capabilities at each of the four ski areas. Federal regulators have become alarmed by Keystone's taking water for snowmaking from one river that has been historically contaminated by mine tailings, then inadvertently polluting a different, previously uncontaminated drainage when the snow melts in the spring. Colorado ski areas, including those owned by Vail Resorts, have engaged in a perverse snowmaking competition in recent years, with the goal of opening their pistes in the weeks before *Halloween*. The snow must go on.

Any one area, when viewed in isolation, might not present a big problem; but the aggregate effects of all this growth and expansion are becoming clearer, at least to the biologists, ecologists, fisheries experts, and wildlife scientists who study, and advocate for, the natural environment of the West.

VA consistently argued that its Category III expansion had been conceived way back in 1962, and that putting new lifts into the unroaded area had been a foregone conclusion since that time. The company conveniently forgot, however, that the 1962 plan had been put in place before most of the ski areas in Colorado were up and running. A visitor to Vail these days has the choice of visiting a half dozen other ski areas that are closer to Denver— each of them with hundreds of acres of forest that have been clear-cut to make way for skiers. There *is* such a thing as death by a thousand cuts.

Federal land managers speak about "sacrifice areas" when they try to funnel tourists into certain places where their impacts can be controlled, and possibly contained. Vail's Category III expansion, in and of itself, might well represent an appropriate use of public land. But nothing exists in isolation. Blue Sky Basin is just one of numerous western lifestyle meccas, new ski areas, and established-but-burgeoning resort towns—all of which are changing and growing so fast that nobody, it seems, is keeping track of the big picture. From West Yellowstone, Montana, to Sedona, Arizona; and from Crestone, Colorado, to Genoa, Nevada, a never-ending flow of more people, more tourists, and more recreationists using new toys are descending on the region. The gear manufacturers, in turn, happily supply the new-comers with ever more sophisticated ways to explore the region's scenic delights. In the West, a visitor can go llama trekking, mountain biking, heli biking, river surfing, spelunking, canoeing, white-water kayaking, sea kayaking, rafting, backpacking, jet boating, fly fishing, bait fishing, spear fishing. There are off-road vehicles, all-terrain vehicles, dirt bikes, horse-back riders, sleigh rides, rock hunters, bighorn sheep hunters, elk bow-hunters, backcountry skiers, backcountry snowboarders, snowshoers, ice climbers. And you can always play laser tag if you get bored.

In 2000, two years after the arson, the trail to the cause of the fires appears to be as cold as the coming winter, but the legacy of the fires is still up in the air. From all appearances, the only wake-up call for VA was the installation of more surveillance cameras and security teams on Vail Mountain. The company has plans for more construction at Breckenridge, more snowmaking at all its resorts, and more golf courses and condomini-ums up and down the valleys of two Colorado counties.

As I was finishing *Powder Burn*, Adam Aron called me to inquire about its conclusion. "When will you end it?" he asked, obviously concerned. "Things have really turned around here since the fires."

Maybe, but maybe not. There is hope that the lessons may be learned. The U.S. Forest Service's fifteen-year plan for the White River National For-est represents an opening for a new way of defining our relationship with the natural world: as co-inhabitants of a landscape rather than as a con-quering army. With the presidential election of 2000, the size of that open-ing will possibly become clearer.

During the 1990s, conservation biologist E. O. Wilson noted accelerated rates of extinction among plant, bird, amphibian, reptile, and mammal species. From the Brazilian rainforest to the Canadian boreal forest, from the rapid desertification of North Africa to the near-extinction of the Siberian tiger, humans continue to alter their environment in an uncontrolled experiment that an increasing number of scientists from virtually every discipline of earth sciences agree is heading the wrong way on the trend line.

Why pick on Vail, then, with all this going on? On the scale of things, clear-cutting another 885 acres of Rocky Mountain forest, even if it was to feed another building frenzy of high-end homes, pastry shops, and interior designers' offices, is hardly a world crisis. Perhaps because it is so symptomatic of the conspicuous consumption that has become our national creed in these times of unparalleled economic expansion, Vail's tale has attracted so much attention. Even owners of other ski areas recognize that there must be limits. I thought again of what the Apollo spokesman had told me: "Who gets to decide what's enough? That's the heart of it."

The heart of it indeed. Those who set the fires obviously decided for themselves that enough was already enough. Whether the radical fringe of the environmental spectrum was involved or not involved, many people believe the system is so skewed in favor of people like those who run VA that the only sensible reaction is to act outside the system. The existence of the ELF, or organizations like it, shouldn't surprise us.

Right now, the answer to the Apollo spokesman's disingenuous question is simple: He and his partners decide what's enough in Vail; and so do his counterparts elsewhere, whether they're developing ranchettes on the northern border of Yellowstone National Park or paying lobbyists in Washington to oppose further wilderness designation in Montana or Colorado or anywhere else.

The United States in the first year of the twenty-first century is as tortured by contradictory impulses as it has been since Congress created Yellowstone, the world's first national park, in 1872. In that same year, Congress passed the 1872 Mining Law, which essentially gave unfettered access to mineral rights to any prospector who staked a claim, no matter where that claim might lie or what the environmental consequences of that mining might be. Those contrary impulses of crass commercialism and noble conservationism clash constantly: in public debates, in politics, and in acts of frustration on both ends of the political spectrum. In Nevada, vigilantes who opposed the federal government's closing of a road on public land for environmental reasons bulldozed it open again. The ELF have claimed credit for various acts of property destruction in the name of their cause.

The modern American West's history has been marked by a series of discoveries that pulled hundreds, then thousands, then millions of people into the region. First, it was the lure and opportunity of gold, silver, copper, lead; later it was molybdenum, uranium, silica. There were trees to be logged, cows to be driven across knee-high grama grass, fields to be cleared to grow alfalfa, lettuce, and, much later, even grapes. From the Homestead Act to the Reclamation Act, the federal government encouraged development in a land that required incentives to draw settlers. Towns grew haphazardly around each discovery: Some flourished and some were abandoned; some are flourishing again.

Since Vail's inception in 1962, the West has drawn hordes of new prospectors, people who are looking for an escape from the multicultural stews of the big cities, who want a place with clean air and water to raise their children. Vail, and places like Vail, have for some become a Magic Mountain, a sanatorium for modern lifestyle refugees.

But this time 'round, the resettlement of the West comes with an even bigger price to pay than the Superfund sites, extinct animals, invasive species, and catastrophic fires that followed in the wake of the West's early miners, ranchers, and loggers. The sheer scale of the influx—and its accompanying wealth—has altered the landscape of the West in ways that we do not fully understand. Nor, perhaps, do the lynx or the bobcat or the wolf or the grizzly bear. But they are faltering as humans are proliferating. When they are gone, something vital and irreplaceable will have disappeared as well.

It is an intriguing thought to suggest that the arson hasn't been solved because nobody has yet to learn the lessons that the arson was meant to teach. Whoever set the fires was trying to send a message, it seems to me, however awkwardly and, ultimately, unsuccessfully. Whether or not it eventually turns out that a ragged band of anarchic "ecoterrorists" lit the gasoline-soaked sponges that caused so much damage at this glitzy ski resort, I've come to the conclusion that the worst ecoterrorism in the Vail area is far more insidious: It's apathy.

Index

PublicAffairs is a new nonfiction publishing house and a tribute to the standards, values, and flair of three persons who have served as mentors to countless reporters, writers, editors, and book people of all kinds, including me.

I.F. STONE, proprietor of *I. F. Stone's Weekly,* combined a commitment to the First Amendment with entrepreneurial zeal and reporting skill and became one of the great independent journalists in American history. At the age of eighty, Izzy published *The Trial of Socrates,* which was a national bestseller. He wrote the book after he taught himself ancient Greek.

BENJAMIN C. BRADLEE was for nearly thirty years the charismatic editorial leader of *The Washington Post.* It was Ben who gave the *Post* the range and courage to pursue such historic issues as Watergate. He supported his reporters with a tenacity that made them fearless and it is no accident that so many became authors of influential, best-selling books.

ROBERT L. BERNSTEIN, the chief executive of Random House for more than a quarter century, guided one of the nation's premier publishing houses. Bob was personally responsible for many books of political dissent and argument that challenged tyranny around the globe. He is also the founder and longtime chair of Human Rights Watch, one of the most respected human rights organizations in the world.

———

For fifty years, the banner of Public Affairs Press was carried by its owner, Morris B. Schnapper, who published Gandhi, Nasser, Toynbee, Truman, and about 1,500 other authors. In 1983, Schnapper was described by *The Washington Post* as "a redoubtable gadfly." His legacy will endure in the books to come.

Peter Osnos, *Publisher*